CONTROL
Unleashed
The Puppy Program

Leslie McDevitt, MLA, CDBC, CPDT

Editing: Pam Green, Monica Percival, Anna Jonsson
Book design and typesetting: Robin Nuttall
Cover design: Marcy Rauch
Cover photos: Lynne Brubaker Photography, Inc. and Clean Run

First printing 2012

ISBN 978-1-892694-31-7

To purchase multiple copies of this book, contact:

Clean Run Productions, LLC
17 Industrial Dr.
South Hadley, MA 01075
800-311-6503
Email: info@cleanrun.com
Website: www.cleanrun.com

To contact Leslie McDevitt, visit her website: http://controlunleashed.net/

CONTENTS

ACKNOWLEDGMENTS

Thank you to Clean Run Productions, especially my editor Pam Green, who is a superhero and a rock star combined.

Thanks to my friends at Y2K9s Dog Sports Club, particularly Alexa Karaoulis and Jacky Judd, and to Dr. Karen Overall, for their enthusiasm, emotional support, friendship and good humor.

Thanks yet again to Quicksilver Border Collies, for the years of friendship and for my blue boy.

Thanks to my students, both human and canine, and to my own dogs, for co-creating this Control Unleashed® experience with me and giving me an endless supply of problems to solve, successes to enjoy, and stories to share.

And thanks to my husband Bill, I could not do it without you.

PREFACE

Sometimes things don't go as planned. I had wanted to finish the writing and editing process for *Control Unleashed®: Creating a Focused and Confident Dog* before it was time for puppy Easy to come home so that I could put all my focus on raising him. As it turned out, I was still finishing up the book throughout Easy's puppyhood and into his adolescence. The accidental timing was perfect. Raising Easy while finishing the book allowed me to further break down and clarify my explanations as I thought about how they might be applied to this new personality in my pack. And Easy became the first puppy that I raised with the Control Unleashed® (CU) program laid out as an organized system to follow, rather than just my instinctive way of doing things. So, it was good for the book, and good for the puppy.

One of the major messages of *Control Unleashed®*, that of getting to know your dog as an individual and always being ready to adjust the training structure to suit him best, was reinforced heavily for me as I experienced the joy of watching Easy's personality unfold. Like the McDevitt dogs before him, Easy was a complex individual that was going to teach me a lot. I looked at Easy with "Easy-focus," not agility-trainer-focus—not wanting to fall into the trap I have seen many fall into of trying to fit their dog into a training or handling system to the point where they stop seeing their dog and only see the system.

Raising a puppy, giving him the space to grow, and watching his emergent personality, is one of the most joyful experiences I have had in my life. I sometimes see people raising their future performance dogs in an unbalanced way, thinking only of what a performance dog should know and when the dog should know it; paying more attention to these whats and whens than to what the puppy is telling them about his little personality, through his interactions with them and the world. The puppies tell us all the time with their behavior what the best training structure and the best timeline is in terms of our expectations for what they should be able to do. All we have to do is listen.

There isn't a recipe for raising your performance puppy. Every pup is different, and that's where the joy of getting to know the puppy, and the art of adjusting your training style for the puppy, comes into the picture.

So if you have a new pup that you intend to raise with a certain sport (or type of work) in mind, and you are feeling pressured about raising a "sport puppy," do yourself and your pup a favor—relax! Take a breath, look over at your puppy and see how adorable he is, temporarily put your training diary away, and enjoy a walk in the woods. Watch him chase a butterfly. They don't stay puppies for long.

The goal of this book is to get you started raising and training your pup that you hope will grow into a working partner, be it as a performance dog, service dog, or other type of working dog. This process should happen in a balanced way that lets your pup be a pup and helps you stay focused on building the bond and the trust that comes with being able to listen to what your teammate is telling you about his needs rather than trying to push him into a training methodology that may need some adaptation on your part before it's a good fit for him (yes, even if it worked great for your last puppy, or your classmate's puppy!) That information does not come from a book, but from your puppy himself! But through the use of stories, examples, and training exercises here, you will get some ideas and encouragement as you start this exciting journey with your pup.

The concepts and suggestions in this book can also be used for rescue dogs that, like puppies, are starting out as "blank slates" as far as your training is concerned (obviously not in terms of previous life experience). I think of rescue dogs as getting a second chance, to start over again, so it's like they get to be puppies again in their forever home.

Enjoy your puppy. I enjoyed raising Easy so much. I look back at those days often, with a smile and gratitude. All the training we did set the stage for our working relationship, without unnecessary pressure on either of us, and we had fun every single minute. Agility foundation training didn't feel different from any of our everyday interactions—all of our interactions were about creating a dialogue where we could communicate about our needs and how they could best be met for both of us—and about how much fun we could have together learning this new language. We were great partners from the get-go, so much so that in our first puppy agility lesson, our instructor told us to "get a room" because we were so into each other.

Whenever I felt myself getting too serious with my expectations, or feeling competitive with his littermates and where they were in their training process, I took three steps back, gave formal training a break for a few days, and took Easy to the woods instead of class. I made a promise not to let my own intense personality or my natural competitiveness affect my puppy's growing process or put any pressure on our blossoming relationship. I let Easy lead the way. I watched with delight as his personality emerged and I chose what type of work and how it would be presented, based on what he seemed to be asking for.

This is the spirit of co-creative puppy raising; you enter into a contract where you both agree to listen to each other, enjoy each other for who you are—quirks and all—and get your needs met mutually (rather than having a relationship where the human is always telling the puppy what to do without the natural flow and exchange of information that happens when the puppy is also telling the human how best to "talk" to him). Enjoying a co-creative relationship with your pup is how you let the magic in.

Leslie McDevitt

INTRODUCTION

Control Unleashed®: Creating a Focused and Confident Dog was written as a problem-solving book to help handlers with mature dogs that were having problems during canine-sport training or in the competition ring. It set out my basic Control Unleashed® (CU) attention training program and provided the concepts behind the program.

This book is different. Control Unleashed®: The Puppy Program is meant as "preventive medicine" for puppy raisers. Most of the behavior problems people typically consult with me about "after the fact" can be either prevented or minimized by starting a puppy with good foundation training from the beginning. In addition, this book is intended to provide a program that will help you create a puppy that is ready for sport-specific training at the appropriate age—a puppy with the ability to focus on whatever you want, for as long as you want, whenever you want.

When you teach your puppy a new skill, not only is he learning that skill, he is *learning how to learn* that skill. Part of learning how to learn successfully is, of course, learning how to pay attention. It's absolutely true that puppies can learn how to pay attention during the process of training any behavior, if the training is done skillfully. However, I find that many of the adult dogs brought into my CU classes have somehow missed that attention piece of their training, so that the specific behaviors they learned, such as heeling or weaving, fall apart in the face of any distraction. Adding to the difficulty is that it's much harder for a distracted dog to generalize a behavior.

There are lots of wonderful resources available for people raising their puppy with agility or other sports in mind. *Control Unleashed®: The Puppy Program* is meant to be one part of a multi-tiered approach to raising a puppy for a performance sport. What I have presented here is the *attention* part of your puppy-raising program.

"Paying attention" is its own skill set and teaching it should be separate from teaching more complex behaviors. Without attention, you won't get as far as you want with all those other behaviors you're going to teach. So it is wise to teach the attention skill set as your "base of operations."

The attention skill set includes:

- Discrimination skills

- Self-control skills (also referred to as "leave-it" skills)

- Arousal regulation skills

Discrimination tells your puppy what he should focus on in an environment filled with tons of options. It also tells him when he should focus on "it" and what "it" is. You can also think of this as teaching handler focus vs. obstacle focus, with "obstacles" being not just agility equipment, but anything in the environment that isn't you.

The other side of the coin is "leave-it" or self-control skills. While we are telling our puppy what he "should" be focused on, we are also teaching him what he needs to ignore or "leave."

Your puppy also needs to learn arousal regulation skills; that is, to calm down enough to think clearly when he's excited. He needs to be calm enough to work with you while ignoring other things of interest. This is the intersection of relaxation and attention. Conversely, for sports training he may need to learn to get excited about something that has no intrinsic value for him. This is the intersection of motivation and attention.

SECTION I

OVERVIEW

Chapter 1

WHAT IS PUPPY CONTROL UNLEASHED®?

People tend to rush their pups through training so they can get to "the fun stuff"… the agility classes and trials. But when you have a puppy, it's all "the fun stuff!"

Attention training should be started immediately, because without good focus, your agility dog, obedience dog, or service dog won't get very far. As you are doing your age-appropriate foundation work such as body awareness games, playing on wobble boards, walking backward, etc., you can be doing all your attention work so that by the time your puppy's growth plates have closed and he is ready for obstacle training, he will be completely reliable off leash, even if other dogs are running around him. Once attention training is accomplished, you will be able to put all your energy into sport-specific work instead of trying to do everything at once.

Many people try to teach their dog to pay attention and work off leash when they're already in an agility or sport-specific class. At the same time, they are trying to teach their dog how to do the sport, as well as maybe learning it themselves for the first time.

Agility Training and Attention Training Are Two Separate Skill Sets

Dogs will not learn either as well when you lump them together. Since puppies as young as eight weeks can start their attention and off-leash training, there is no excuse not to get them reliable around any level of distraction *before* starting agility class. If everyone followed that suggestion, I would stop hearing so many stories about dogs getting loose in agility class or at trials and chasing after other dogs.

This book will encourage you to look at the concept of "attention" as two sides of a coin: it is both a function of a good working relationship and it is a set of orienting behaviors that can be trained and reinforced regardless of the dog's breed or personality. A skilled trainer can teach a puppy to pay attention to her quickly without having a pre-existing relationship. This is why your puppy kindergarten teacher can take Dennis the Menace from you and turn him into Shirley Temple as if by magic.

The basic attention behaviors all fall under the category of "leave-it training." They could also fall under the category of "self-control training." I tell my students that leave-it training is about teaching dogs the concept of availability. This starts with a simple message such as, "This treat on the floor is not available, but if you attend to me and ignore the treat, the one in my pocket will become available."

This builds up to a much broader message such as, "The kid standing ringside waving a hot dog around is not available (neither the kid nor the hot dog), but, after you run your course, the treats in our tent will become available." Without any concept as to what resource in the environment is available and what isn't— based on social cues from you—your dog is not going to achieve the level of self-control for which everybody strives.

KEY CONCEPTS OF THE CU PUPPY PROGRAM

The foundation of the CU puppy program is made up of a series of key concepts. These concepts will be discussed in detail in subsequent chapters:

- Default behavior
- Availability
- Biofeedback
- Premack
- Shaping

- Integrative training
- Economy of energy
- Bite-threshold model
- Transitioning

THESE KEY CONCEPTS ARE SUPPORTED BY THE FOLLOWING GAMES/EXERCISES:

- **Whiplash Turn/Reorienting:** This exercise relies on repetition to achieve a conditioned muscle memory, which will cause your puppy to disengage from whatever he is attending to and whip his head around to orient to you at the sound of his name. I also use the term "reorienting" in this book to describe the movement of the head turning back to you, away from something else. The difference with the Whiplash Turn is that it must be cued (since it is a conditioned response to the dog's name) and the dog must give a crazy, fast response—fast enough to give your puppy whiplash!

- **Look at That! game:** This game will take the conflict out of attention training. Rather than saying to your puppy, "Don't look at that thing, look at me," you will be creating a behavior chain where the puppy looks at a distraction on your cue and immediately orients to you. "Finding" the distracting thing for you will change the puppy's motivation from really wanting to look at the thing, to wanting to point out the thing to *you* and collect his "finder's fee."

- **Leave it (conditioned avoidance of unavailable resource):** This is my old stand-by and I consider it essential for *any* dog, even if his only job is going to be to sit on the couch watching the Lifetime channel. This exercise will teach your puppy to avoid an unavailable resource, by looking away or backing up, and to orient to you instead. Some trainers think that if you have a good recall on your dog, the dog is ready for off-leash work. Yet, without a good leave it, your dog can't have a reliable recall, because one day you will call him away from something that he will not be able to leave alone! Very organic recalls grow out of the foundation leave-it training, because the source of the available resource will be you. And, if you aren't on top of the puppy, he will learn to come find you to collect his resource.

- **Mat work:** Mat work serves a variety of functions. It reinforces a relaxed response to exciting or worrisome things in the environment; it gives the puppy somewhere specific to be and something specific to do in a distracting or overwhelming environment; and it provides a "safe space" for the puppy while he is learning how to ignore people and dogs coming into his space and doing exciting things around him. Mat work is also used as a "reset button," giving your puppy somewhere to return to and "start over" if he had a reactive response to something; if he got confused, frustrated or overexcited; or if he just needed a break to get his head together. It's also a great "reset button" for *you*. If you find your puppy is not getting an exercise correct and you need to rethink your game plan, call a mat break to give yourself the time to think things through without the pressure of needing to figure everything out on the spot.

- **Off-switch game:** This game is designed to stimulate your puppy to a certain level and then reward him for finding his way back down to "settled" state. The puppy learns he can earn the desired resource (in this case, continuation of the stimulating activity) by calming himself down. The basic leave-it rules of availability apply because access to the stimulating activity is not available until the puppy has calmed down.

- **Box work:** We use box work to set up an environment (a square defined by ring gates or other barriers) where we can expose the puppy to temptations and challenges in baby steps, making sure he is able to happily focus on us at every step before raising criteria.

- **Parallel games:** Once your puppy has the box work basics down, you can set up situations involving other dogs running, doing agility equipment, or anything else you want, and teach your puppy to focus on his task off leash, no matter what is going on next to him.

- **Give Me a Break game:** One of my favorites, this game can be used to build handler focus or to build drive to do a specific activity. The most unusual application for which I used this game was for Dugan, a certified cadaver detection Rottweiler brought to me by his canine handler because he got stressed on the job and shut down. I used the Give Me a Break game to inspire Dugan to grow more enthusiastic about finding body parts concealed in a plastic lunch box hidden in my backyard… yup, you read that correctly!

- **Ping-pong Puppy game:** This game teaches a puppy that is uncertain or worried about something in his environment to incorporate that thing (called a "trigger") into a structure that builds confidence and encourages bravery. In this case, the release from the social pressure of being near the trigger is reinforcing for the puppy. It can also be used to teach handler focus to a puppy that is excited or distracted by something, such as a dog doing agility or a person running.

- **Watch the Distracted Handler game:** This is a game my Border Collie created while we were waiting our turn to go into the agility ring. It will teach your puppy that he can get paid for paying attention to you, even if *you* are totally distracted by the trial environment.

What Do We Do When?

When I bring a puppy home around eight weeks of age I start teaching the puppy the following pieces of his CU program right away, spending just a few minutes here and there:

- **Default behavior:** Puppies enthusiastically learn about default behaviors and this becomes the foundation of their understanding that they can use their behavior to influence your behavior.

- **Release word:** I take advantage of a puppy's default behavior to teach him a release word. I start by rewarding the puppy in his default position, then saying "O.K." as I invite the puppy to come out of position. My release in this context means, treats are no longer available so you are free to move if you want to.

- **Sit/stay/down training**

- **Whiplash Turn:** This is a great one for name recognition and recalls.

Hand targets can be taught as early as eight weeks of age.

- **Targeting:** I start with simple hand targeting, then move onto a freestanding target or cone so the puppy can practice being shaped to move away from me and interact with an object. I then shape the puppy to go to a mat: very fun!

- **Beginning leave-it steps:** I start teaching the concept of availability with "Doggie Zen" (see Chapter 24) and then after a couple weeks I move on to the "treat on the floor" protocol. From there I quickly start generalizing to toys.

- **Drop a tug toy:** I either trade for treats or simply stand there holding the toy at groin level and wait for the puppy to let go; as soon as he does, I invite him to take the toy.

- **Settling for massage, TTouch, and petting**

- **Problem solving:** During the first few months I am very concerned with providing environmental enrichment, encouraging the puppy to play with interactive toys like Kongs and honing his problem-solving abilities with puzzle toys like Nina Ottosson's Brick. I also play clicker-shaping games and provide props such as boxes to shape "get in" and "get on."

- **Leash walking:** I'm also working on loose-leash walking; of course, coupled with the Leash Game that is also one of the preliminary steps of box work. And, in conjunction with leash walking, my puppy will learn to take potty breaks while on leash.

Start teaching the puppy to drop a tug toy by trading the toy for a treat.

I am not big on teaching cues at first, but focus instead on giving feedback about offered behaviors: what we call "capturing" in clickerspeak. In other words, when my puppy sits or lies down on his own, I praise and/or treat him so he starts doing it more and more to see if it "works" to get me to pay up. I don't add cues to these behaviors until the puppy confidently offers them a lot and then it's just a simple matter of saying the word "sit" or "down" just before I know the puppy is going to do the behavior anyway.

Every puppy has his own pace and his own stamina for learning so I don't get that concerned with following a schedule that goes with developmental periods. I am very much a "do what feels right" trainer. Since I am always telling people to adjust what they are asking for and what their expectations are to the mental and emotional state of the puppy, my goal is to help people learn to read their puppies well enough to cover the appropriate material at the appropriate time.

Some puppies will soak up all the stuff I just mentioned right away and be ready for more while they still resemble a fluffy, chubby guinea pig. Other puppies need a lot more time to process each thing, and might need the Give Me a Break game introduced right away so that they can have breaks structured into their training sessions. This will prevent those puppies from getting overloaded and shutting down. These puppies also will need to have at least one of the three "natural behaviors" (Chapter 7) incorporated into their training time.

When determining your training plan, you will be taking your puppy's breed tendencies, as well as the tendencies of his parents and other relatives, if known, into consideration, along with his personality. Don't let expectations about certain breed traits color how you see your puppy; treat him as an individual first. Don't fall into the trap of "My last *such and such breed* did it like this so he should do it like this, too." You wouldn't have liked it in elementary school if your new teacher kept comparing you to your big sister.

By the time your puppy hits adolescence he should be well on his way with the training described in this book. You may have to revisit or tweak his attention training when he hits adolescence. But with your attention foundation in place early, you will tear out a lot less hair when you take your teenager to basic agility skills class! I'm sure by that point he will have started age-appropriate foundation training for your sport of choice as well.

My last couple of puppies earned Canine Good Citizen certificates between six and seven months of age and I started letting them have the run of the house while I was out during that age as well (I'm not saying you should do that too, unless your puppy is really ready for freedom). Social maturity occurs somewhere between two and three years, though for others it never seems to happen.

As your puppy goes from puppy to teenager to sorta grown up to grown up, you may find yourself revisiting some of the attention training in this book. You might think your puppy has mastered it all, and then discover when he meets his first bitch in season as a teenager that he will look at you as if to say, "Control Unleashed®? Never heard of it." You might think your puppy is an old pro in paying attention to you in class but he might take a trip to puppy La La Land at his first trial exposure. Hormones, life experience, and environment are all going to shape his behavior.

With the program in this book as a foundation you will have a much easier time moving through transitional stages in his learning and growing, and you will have a clearer idea as to how to "remind" him of his training if he seems to forget it in certain circumstances. People who miss the opportunity to instill these behaviors from the start usually pay for it later, but you're way too smart for that!

Chapter 2

GETTING TO KNOW YOUR PUPPY

T here are a lot of good resources out there for people who need to learn about evaluating a prospective performance litter for temperament, aptitude, and structure.

Once you have chosen your puppy, if you are able to, spend as much time as possible getting to know him before bringing him home. Often you will observe little tendencies from the get-go that will predict personality and behavior later. Of course you can do this as soon as your puppy is home, too. The important thing here is your awareness of your puppy's quirks and tendencies so that you can shape your training plans to best fit him every step of the way.

PERFORMANCE PUPPY VS. "REGULAR OLD" PUPPY

I got my first purebred puppy, my Belgian Tervuren Rumor, with competition in mind. He was the first puppy I got after becoming a professional trainer and I was out to prove something through him. I wrote about Ru's story in *Con-*

trol Unleashed®, but the very short version is that my expectations and goals for him unfairly colored my experience with him as a puppy. I learned that he was suffering from a degenerative spinal condition when he was one and a half, and simply could not do some of what I asked him. I wasted too much time feeling frustrated and not enjoying him for who he was. Seeing your puppy as a "performance puppy" instead of a regular old puppy can put too much pressure on both you and your puppy, and it knocks your perspective off balance as well.

People can get obsessive about all the things their performance puppies are supposed to learn on a certain timetable. Plus, because they have been told by instructors that their puppy should only have fun with them, they worry about their puppy having too much fun doing normal puppy activities like playing with another puppy. People start creating smaller and smaller boxes for their puppy to live in so that he can be a good sport dog someday. Sometimes this causes behavior problems later. And, it's not necessary.

ALL GOOD PERFORMANCE PUPPIES HAVE TO LEARN HOW TO BE GOOD PUPPIES FIRST

Good puppies get their paws dirty! They chase things, they play, and they find cool stuff to sniff in the woods. If they barked at the neighbor's cat and thought

it was fun, it doesn't mean they won't be able to work for you later!

That said, as with all things, there is a balance. We can strike a balance between training our puppies with their future jobs in mind, while allowing them to have a joyful, normal puppyhood. It is within this balance that we grow as a team, where the needs of both members are met and both members are honored as individuals.

It is normal behavior for puppies to chase things, play, and find cool stuff to sniff.

Don't Try to Fit a Square Peg Into a Round Hole!

It is a thin line we walk as people who have a passion for a particular activity that involves animals. We love the animals, as well as the activity. Sometimes we get a puppy that isn't suited for our passion.

I came from the rescue community where you get a dog for life, period. However, I have met many dogs whose people have spent years training and showing them even though they were just not appropriate for a sport. These dogs would have breathed a huge sigh of relief to go live with someone who just wanted to take them for a walk in the woods. I know dogs that are taken to agility classes and lessons two or three times a week and trials most weekends, but that are stressed the entire time. These dogs are asked to go through the motions and they do it because they are told to. These dogs belong to people who aren't in a position to get another, better suited dog, and who aren't ready to let their dreams go for the good of the dog they do have. These people are passionate about their sport, and spend an incredible amount of time and money working on motivating their dog.

Sometimes the dog has clinical-level anxiety; motivation is not the problem or the answer here. Sometimes people bring dogs like this to me, hoping for a "fix" so their dog suddenly becomes a good performance dog. It is inhumane to keep asking a dog with emotional troubles to do an activity that is so hard on his nervous system. That is the hardest thing about my job right now, communicating to people that their dogs' emotional needs aren't being met, when the owners are so invested in an altogether different kind of fix.

I knew somebody through mutual friends who adopted a Border Collie from her local shelter. She was committed to adopting only adult dogs, but she was also committed to competing in agility and flyball with all her dogs. The Border Collie she chose turned out to be a poor candidate for these sports; the dog stressed easily and needed a lot of training to learn how to cope with the environments in which the sports take place without being reactive to people or other dogs. She shut down easily and needed a lot of motivational training to learn to like the sports. She needed to learn to regulate her arousal in potentially scary social situations instead of flying at people and screaming her head off, and she needed tons of attention training because she got easily distracted.

Not every Border Collie is going to be a good performance dog just because he happens to be a Border Collie; my bet is her original owners didn't know how to deal with her reactivity and this is how she ended up in the shelter. She was a dog that needed behavior modification rather than to be thrown into sports training with the expectation that she would take to it quickly because of her breed.

As I write this, I have several other Border Collies in mind that share almost the exact story. This particular owner dedicated herself to training the dog; she went to big name competitors for lessons, attended all the agility camps, and put an incredible effort into making this work. Her Border Collie improved, but she was never going to be the kind of "wash 'n wear" or "point 'n shoot" dog that her owner wanted her to be, and it would require lifelong training to keep her from sliding backward into reactivity and arousal problems.

How much time should a person put into training a dog for a sport before recognizing that the dog would rather do something else? This person accidentally discovered that her dog loved herding. The dog was a totally different dog when she was working sheep. I was happy that the owner got to experience her dog as this joyful, grounded, totally focused being, quite different from the reactive dog to which she was accustomed.

Sometimes people let their dog choose the sport; they aren't married to one particular sport, they just like doing some kind of structured activity with their dog. This person continued to do tons of training with various people so that she could trial her dog in agility, and she didn't pursue herding. Some of us, me included, do get hooked on a particular sport. But that doesn't mean that our dogs are contractually obligated to get hooked on the same sport. At some point we have to find the balance between asking our dogs to perform and letting them be who they are. I love the people who tell me they let their dogs choose the sport.

Above all, the most important thing is to be fair and humane in what we ask of our performance dogs. We cannot expect dogs that aren't suited to our sport to change their nature just because it's convenient for us. I had to leave behind my old ideals of always keeping a dog when I bought my Border Collie puppy, Chill. I quickly realized he would not work as a partner for me (not just as a trial and demo dog, but also as a suburban pet), because of his temperament. I returned him to his breeder and he was placed in a more rural environment with a hobby herder; exactly the type of home I wanted for him. However, returning him after spending months bonding and working with him broke my heart even though it was the right decision for both of us.

The experience with Chill was so horrible for me that I decided when I adopted my mix Snap, the next dog to join the family after Chill, that I needed to keep him forever even if he was going to end up sitting on the couch all day long instead of being the performance partner that I had been desperately looking for. You need to be ready to adjust your expectations and goals if you are making a lifelong commitment to a potential performance dog.

The best-case scenario is that we get dogs that are well suited to our sport and that love it just as much as we do. May all of us experience the happiness of finding that perfect partner.

Chapter 3

A Different Way to Think About Focus

© DIANE LEWIS PHOTOGRAPHY

Your puppy already knows how to focus. You may be laughing right now, but it's true. Does your puppy eat from his food bowl until his breakfast is gone? Does he orient to you from a distance and race up to you for a greeting? Does he watch a squirrel running, a toy flying through the air, or being snaked on the ground? Any activity your puppy does that doesn't look like "multi-tasking" to you requires him to focus on the specific activity. By watching puppies play with each other, you can see how well they focus on their play.

Our task as teachers is to create environmental conditions that allow for the puppy's natural focusing ability to come out.

Thinking of focus in these terms, we are more in tune to the training situation we are creating and more in tune with our puppies. If our puppy isn't focusing on training as well as he focuses when watching kids playing on the lawn out the window, why? Watch your puppy when he is attentive to something. If he's playing with another dog, do they do the same movement repetitively or do they change it up? Does their behavior seem fluid or stagnant? Do they give each other "breaks" by looking away, backing off temporarily, disengaging and then returning to play? Do they read each other well in terms of honoring each other's communication to play less or more rough or to break? They won't play well together if they aren't communicating well.

Get in tune with your puppy and learn to read him. Watch him play with other dogs and see how they communicate with each other.

If we don't learn to read our puppies well, we will not hear what they are telling us about how effective the training structure we impose on them is. In fact, rather than imposing a training structure at all (for example, I have twenty minutes before work so we are going to work on weave entries for twenty minutes), we should let them tell us how they would process the information best (for example: he seems to check out after ten minutes of weave entries, so next time I am going to do five minutes of training, take him for a walk, and then do another five minutes.)

Many attention problems that people bring their dogs to me to fix are about the handler putting too much pressure on the dog to learn things according to an arbitrary training agenda.

If your puppy is having a "focus problem" maybe you could take a step back, look at the environment and the training situation, and think about what changes to make. If your puppy can successfully give two minutes of direct attention and then needs to play ball, take a sniffing walk, or just rest with a bone for five minutes, before you ask for another two minutes of direct attention, fine. I can't tell you how often I see a dog that is just plain burnt out from being

Taking a "sniffing walk" is a great way to provide a break for a dog during training. You need to relieve pressure after asking for sustained focus.

trained. Especially if the dog is sensitive, or young, the kind of work we ask for can feel like too much pressure without incorporating breaks.

Start thinking of focus as an ability your puppy has, rather than something you have to teach. Think of your job as being the person who creates a learning environment conducive to allowing the puppy's focusing ability to come out. If the puppy isn't being attentive or isn't being attentive for as long as you'd like, take that as information you need to reframe the training picture. When people drill their puppy in "watch me" and focus training without letting the puppy sniff or run around to relieve pressure, they are not doing themselves or their puppy any favors. These people are setting themselves up for a lifetime of hearing that they are not interesting enough or not in charge enough because their puppy is distracted.

When you learn to listen to your puppy you can offer him a training structure that will work for him. If your puppy needs to take breaks or zoom around to relieve arousal or stress, or if he needs to visit or play, that is okay, because you can create a training structure that uses access to those activities as part of the reinforcement for the puppy's paying attention.

Ruby: The Sniffing Schnauzer

I am currently working with a Miniature Schnauzer, Ruby, who is about 18 months old. She was in weekly competition obedience and agility classes. Ruby happens to be very reactive to her environment and has a lot of social anxiety about her interactions with people. She was frequently disengaging to give herself a break in her classes; the instructors told her handler to give a collar correction every time Ruby sniffed the floor. When she was taken off leash, Ruby would run away and sniff at a distance. The handler was working from the theory that Schnauzers are "willful" and they like sniffing, so Ruby was "blowing her off" when she stopped focusing on obedience drills.

Watching Ruby, I saw that her level of anxiety at a number of triggers was through the roof; that her sniffing was about relieving stress. Any time an unexpected thing happened (a person entering or leaving the space, a sound in the training facility, me standing up when I had been sitting down or vice versa), Ruby's response was to bark reactively and then sniff the floor. The handler wanted to correct the barking and sniffing. But the barking and sniffing were not the problem. The problem was anxiety, and rather than telling her she was not allowed to do her natural stress-relieving activities, I ignored the barking and sniffing and taught her some desensitization games to decrease her anxiety.

The barking and sniffing stopped without directly addressing them at all, and Ruby became very focused on me. She followed me off lead around the facility while I kept throwing treats on the floor to get her away from me. She would get the treat and race back to where I was walking. Using the Give Me a Break game structure to take the pressure off her, I was creating a pattern that encouraged her to choose to interact with me and put that social pressure back on herself.

She also would run away when being trained by her handler to the "safe zone" of the handler's husband, who had been banished from class because he was a distraction. The puppy felt best when she was in daddy's lap. Daddy had been forbidden to give her treats because she was supposed to see mom as "the leader" and only mom should have good things for her.

I demonstrated how access to daddy could increase her attention on mom. Ruby's problem was not about some fantasy pack-ranking theory, it was about anxiety that was not being recognized or addressed. I taught her a pattern where if she responded to her name with the Whiplash Turn (Chapter 25), I ran with her to daddy and he would pet her. After three repetitions when we ran to daddy, Ruby turned away from him with no interaction and stared at me ready for more. Then I could not *get* her to pay attention to him. I saw that she had a real separation anxiety about not being able to get to daddy when he was in the room but "not available" because she was working. Using him as part of the reinforcement process was all she needed to be able to focus on her work.

Taking daddy out of the picture was a disservice to her because he provided anxiety relief. Ruby felt better sitting on his lap than anywhere else in the facility; so when I took training breaks and talked to her handler, I had Ruby go back to daddy's lap. Prior to that, the handler had not wanted her on daddy's lap at all because she perceived it was taking away from her leadership. She also had been told by an instructor not to pick up the dog because she was coddling her. Picking up this particular dog was actually a really good idea. It calmed her down and helped her stop her panic-barking at changes in the environment.

Ruby had been going to classes every week where she barked reactively when she felt anxious, was not taught any coping skills or allowed to self-soothe because when she tried to do that with sniffing she was corrected. (I am using the word "corrected" in a traditional obedience training sense, meaning she was reprimanded either verbally, physically, or both.) She would have felt better sitting in a lap or being picked up between exercises, but she was supposed to stay on the floor. She had been attacked by a Jack Russell Terrier in one of the classes and was afraid of the other dogs in the class. Her handler had been given the "you're not being interesting enough so she is blowing you off to sniff" speech and the "you're not being a pack leader, so she is disrespecting you" speech many times. In the meantime Ruby had a significant amount of anxiety throughout these classes, and I think it's a miracle she managed to learn any of her obedience behaviors at all. The calming signals she gave such as lip licking and "shaking off" while she was obeying her commands could have been a clue to her handler, but nobody had recognized that these behaviors were calming signals.

I asked Ruby's handler to drop the obedience classes and to switch to private agility lessons until we felt she was ready to return to a group class. People never want to be told to drop classes, but sometimes it is really necessary.

By recognizing Ruby's anxiety and creating a training structure that would take the pressure off, thereby letting her natural ability to focus shine through, this puppy quickly became attentive to her handler. Her barking and sniffing were just side effects of the problem, not the actual problem. After our first lesson I got an email from the handler saying Ruby was happily doing agility sequencing in private lessons using the Give Me a Break game that I'd showed her, and had paid complete attention off leash (even with the husband in the room!). The agility instructor said she'd improved a lot already.

Ruby is very lucky to have a handler that was open to learning to think about things in a new way. I gave them a difficult paradigm shift challenge, and they took it, which gave the handler tremendous relief, and Ruby, too.

SECTION II

PRE-REQUISITES

Chapter 4

AN OUNCE OF PREVENTION: REACTIVITY

A s you get to know your puppy's personality and quirks, you can adjust your training plan to meet his needs. I have met many puppies that were very shy about meeting people or worried about noises or sudden movements, but their training was focused on performance foundations. Ironically, of course, as adults these dogs tend to have problems working in class and at trials because they are concerned about the environment, which could have been addressed in the beginning.

I have had plenty of students who felt frustrated that their adult dogs were reactive because they felt they had socialized them when they were babies. First of all, some dogs have the misfortune to suffer a trauma or to have a predisposition for anxiety regardless of your good intentions. Second of all, don't just assume your puppy is "well socialized" because you have taken him to lots of shows and made sure he met people and dogs. What was his experience really like at those shows? What was his body language telling you? Is he saying he is having a great time and you don't have to give it a second thought? Is he saying he needs a little time to warm up before being taken around? Is he saying he wants to meet the kid sitting on the chair but not the kid running around? Does he seem a little repressed because he's overwhelmed and needs a stimulus break? Does he wants to meet certain dogs but not others (and what is their body language like)?

To me, socialization is about quality over quantity. It is about teaching the puppy that appropriate social behaviors are self rewarding, and that it's fun to meet nice people and play with nice dogs and go to nice new places. I am super protective of my puppies to make sure they get the *best* experiences possible regarding people, dogs, places, and things, especially during that all-important first three months of life. Part of that is reading my puppy's body language and adjusting the social situation so that it works best for him to have a great experience.

Listen to your puppy about the amount of social pressure he is comfortable with; some puppies, like this rough Collie, will enjoy direct interactions with strangers, while others would find the same interaction scary.

When Easy was little he was very afraid of people who stared at him or walked up to touch him on the hiking trail. Forcing him to meet these people in the name of socialization could have been traumatic. Instead he learned that if strangers suddenly came at him, he could play a game with me instead of worrying about them. At the same time, he learned a "go say hi" cue and I sent him to meet people that I knew would have the right "vibe" for him. Later, if I chose, I could use this cue to help him generalize social behavior onto people whose "vibe" wasn't as attractive.

I have worked with people who accidentally sensitized their puppies during the socialization period by putting too much pressure on the puppy. We've all heard stories about puppies being jumped by older dogs at the dog park and then becoming afraid of dogs. Taking a puppy to an environment that overwhelms him, or introducing him to the wrong person (like the well-meaning neighbor who wants to knee your puppy hard in the chest if he jumps up), can cause similar baggage.

As teenagers, dogs' responses intensify and some become reactive to things that they just seemed timid about when they were younger. I have asked enough handlers of reactive dogs about their dogs' behaviors as a puppy, and watched enough students and friends' puppies mature, to know that most people miss signs from their puppy about what his behavior will be like in adolescence and when he hits social maturity.

I am reminded of a new student of mine who recently got a young dog from Aussie rescue. He has been very reactive to other dogs, to the point that it's become a nightmare for her to take him for a walk (a very typical student for me!) She told me how frustrated and confused she was because the foster mom told her that he had coexisted with her pack of Aussies without reacting to them, and had assured her there would be no problems with other dogs. Of course, just because a dog is okay with, or even likes, other dogs in the household, he can still be horribly reactive to strange dogs. But I didn't think that was the whole story here. From past experience, I suspected the Aussie had given off predictive signals in the foster home.

Upon investigating I learned that the rescue Aussie had avoided interacting with the other dogs and had been described as "timid" and "shy" around them. This was not a dog that was playing happily and suddenly changed his personality upon changing homes. This was a dog that was manifesting his discomfort with other dogs in the foster home, with the strategy that worked best for him in that environment, and now he was manifesting that same discomfort with a different strategy in a different environment. The common thread was his underlying anxiety.

What Do I Mean by Reactivity?

In *Control Unleashed*® I wrote, "Reactivity is an information-seeking strategy. A reactive dog will rush toward something or someone that he is uncertain about, barking, lunging, growling, and making a big display. People sometimes perceive reactive behavior as aggression, but the reactive dog is not rushing in to do damage; he is attempting to assess the threat level of a given situation. His assessment strategy is intensified because he is panicking as the adrenaline flows through his body. If a reactive dog learns to feel confident about something, he is less worried about that thing and therefore reacts less to it."

Three major things make a reactive dog feel better:

- "Escape" from the perceived threat

- Information that the perceived threat is not that threatening after all

- An understanding that the dog can use his own (calm) behavior as a tool to make the situation more tolerable. Puppies raised with CU will be armed with the know-how they need to make this happen.

Again, reactivity is borne of uncertainty and so is some social avoidance (like if you have a puppy that jumps backward, or walks behind you, or just ducks, when a well-meaning stranger bends down with her hand out to pet the puppy). If your puppy is feeling uncertain about a social interaction, let's help him feel safe and confident. If he needs information about the world, let's learn how to give it to him.

~~~~~~

THE NEUTRAL BRIARD

I remember a Briard puppy that an acquaintance, not a student of mine, got. As I was meeting her for the first time at four months, the puppy allowed me to pet her; she did not try to move away from me or do anything dramatic. But the puppy was very "neutral" about our meeting and felt disengaged to me, as though she wasn't there in the moment. Eye contact didn't overly pressure her, and she didn't have the kind of reactions that people walking by could easily point out and say the puppy is stressed or scared. But she was non-interactive.

I watched her meet a few more people that day. It felt like she had very low sociability, which always concerns me.

I would have spent time teaching this puppy that she could play targeting games with people, and increasing the value of interacting with people. But the puppy went to a lot of classes and learned a lot of pre-sport stuff, but nobody ever seemed to notice this lack of response to people. Around the same time the puppy started getting more intense about watching the environment, especially other dogs moving. This is another thing I would have wanted to address with the CU program as soon as I saw any hint of the behavior, especially in a powerful herding breed.

Fast forward to the Briard as a teenager that had started behaving fearfully toward people, backing away, and even growling. She was vigilant about her surroundings, and her obsession with watching other dogs was so strong that she could not listen at all if other dogs were moving. This dog was placed in a pet home because she wasn't a good performance prospect; it may have been a good move for the dog, but I always wondered if the people who adopted her knew what they were getting into. By the time she was placed she was a real handful; I hope her new people got a trainer who could help with at least the social anxiety.

It was frustrating to me to watch this progression of behaviors that I would have been addressing so much earlier if I were involved. I remember hearing this puppy's handler bemoaning that she stopped tugging while being walked around shows. Again, this was an indicator of this puppy's feeling uncomfortable. This "lack of drive" was addressed by putting a head collar on the puppy for better control, asking for constant attention, and taking her all over the place trying to get her to tug. Her increasing anxiety level was never addressed, and the intense hopes and expectations of her handler put a whole lot of pressure on her.

RED FLAGS

Now, I am absolutely *not* suggesting you go overboard trying to find problems with your puppy and fix them. In this book, there is a strong message of finding a healthy balance between training and letting things be, and honoring your puppy as an individual. I don't want *you* to become reactive, looking for red flags. Simply enjoy your puppy and notice his expression and manner when he is engaging with the world around him.

If you see red flags telling you your puppy is feeling anxious, simply use them as information for formulating a training plan. Here is an "off the top of my head" list of red flags:

- **Hypersensitivity to environmental noises:** If your puppy has been worried about noise from the get-go, this may be a predictor that he will experience anxiety about other stimuli as he matures. Hypersensitivity to noises has been linked to other anxieties.

- **Low sociability/low desire to interact with people or dogs:** The more natural attraction your puppy has toward others, the more tolerance he has of behavior or circumstances that could trigger a reaction in a less socially motivated puppy.

- **Constant arousal displacement behavior:** In other words, the puppy that is triggered by motion, sound, social interaction, and changes in the environment, and displaces his arousal onto the nearest dog, person, or toy. For example, I recently worked with an eight-month-old dog that grabbed his leash and tugged whenever anything happened around him: people or dogs moving around, a new sound, etc. He wasn't playing; he was displacing. This behavior isn't "bad," it's just information. If your puppy runs and grabs his toy when you come home instead of jumping on you, good for him. *But, as with most things, it's the frequency and intensity that could potentially foreshadow a problem.* This teenager was already reactive to strangers approaching him and was also freezing and shutting down under pressure. The frequent, intense leash displacement was just another symptom of his anxiety.

- **Lots of avoidance behaviors:** Hiding behind mom, looking away, turning away, walking away when somebody is trying to engage.

- **Information-seeking and appeasement behaviors:** Licking you all over, vocalizing (which could include whining, barking, or growling), rushing toward and climbing up people, defaulting to jumping on or climbing up the handler, or licking in response to social pressure such as a teacher or the handler's friend coming up to interact or asking the puppy to do something.

- **Freezing when things feel too intense:** We tend to not think about the freeze option of the fight/flight/freeze survival strategies. We all know what fight and flight look like, but often I see puppies and adult dogs freezing in response to something (particularly when being walked on the street) and their handler just drags them around thinking they are being stubborn or just not paying attention.

- **Slow to recover:** If something does trigger fight/flight/freeze, or just unsettles the puppy a little bit, how long does it take for him to seemingly go back to "normal?"

- **Over-generalizing because of anxiety:** If a dog barks at the puppy and he reacts, does the puppy continue reacting in that same way every time he sees a dog, regardless of whether that dog is barking? I'm not talking about a puppy that was scared by a big black dog and then was afraid to meet the next big black dog. I'm talking about something much more intense.

- **Intense responses to change in the environment:** What is the puppy's response to sudden changes in his environment, such as a new person walking in the room, or everybody standing up at once? If the puppy gets used to the room one way and you put a novel object in the room, how does he react when he comes in and sees it?

- **Setting up "offices:"** A lot of worriers will lie in corners of the house, sometimes under tables or even in doorways, where they can see all the comings and goings of the house. From these vantage points the puppies will either pretend nothing is happening around them (I like to call that "taking a unicorn ride") because they feel overwhelmed, or they will take notes on every little thing that happens in case there is a problem.

- **The "noticer:"** Related to that, is your puppy just a noticer? Or an over-noticer?

- **Tons of body language that suggests the puppy feels tension or conflict when interacting with the environment or being told to do something:** Behaviors such as yawning, lip licking, scratching, or shaking as if to dry off, scent marking every inch of a new place (not talking about intact socially mature males), sometimes bowing/stretching, looking off into space, displacement grabbing or biting of objects, a hard eye or a "whale eye" (showing a lot of white) in response to being handled or interacted with.

- **Resource-guarding behaviors such as getting stiff and lowering the head over the resource:** This is tricky because sometimes resource guarding is just resource guarding and other times it is a symptom of a general anxiety or feeling of tension. I am remembering a friend's Malinois who as a teeny puppy could not eat when her other dogs were eating (on the other side of a large room) but would stand posturing over his own food bowl—totally ignored by the others—until they were finished, at which point he would frantically gulp his own food. He also guarded me when I would come to visit by slinking slowly around the couch whenever one of the others thought about coming to say hello. He would collect toys or food dishes when company came or when there was a lot of commotion in the house, and lie next to these items or slink around them. I really wanted my friend to address the problem and desensitize when he was younger, but she didn't come to see these things as a problem until he really started aggressing at the others. He guarded space and spots on the carpet where a treat had been dropped hours earlier. He matured to be a very anxious dog and the resource guarding was just one manifestation of that, an early manifestation that warned me of the road ahead.

If any of these behaviors sound familiar to you, using the system in this book will give you and your puppy the tools to navigate these potential issues with a lot less stress and a lot more confidence.

A Note About Resource Guarding

Some young Border Collies get away with a lot of resource guarding of other dogs in the house because their eye can drive other dogs away, and their handler might not even realize it is happening. Easy started keeping my older mix Maggie out of the kitchen when it was time to fix their meals. He would begin creeping in the space between the kitchen and the living room whenever Maggie walked toward the kitchen. Maggie would then run upstairs and I would wonder, "Why did Maggie stop coming into the kitchen when I make her food?" My other dogs ignored this behavior so it all became focused on Maggie, a dog that was more sensitive to that kind of subtle pressure.

After I addressed this and Easy learned to stay near me in the kitchen instead of stalking the threshold, I saw that Easy found another context for this behavior: he started slinking back and forth in front of the front room closet where the leashes are kept. When I would go toward the closet—signaling that the dogs were going to be taken somewhere—everybody would run toward the closet and attempt to present their necks so that I would put their collar on first. Suddenly Maggie was going back up the stairs while everybody else was sticking their necks out at me. I saw that as soon as I even thought about going toward the closet, Easy was starting to get creepy in the direction of the closet and that would send Maggie running. And it was very much about guarding from Maggie; if she ventured toward us, he would keep himself between her and the kitchen or closet and herd her away.

If I had allowed this to continue when Easy was a puppy, there is probably nowhere in the house that Maggie would be able to hang out now. Since I saw what Easy was doing I have brought this up with all my students who get young Border Collies in multi-dog households and asked them to watch for it. Many of them have noticed some level of it happening right under their nose.

Some of us are more sensitive than others and some are faster to react than others. We are all individuals, and so are our puppies. If you think your puppy is on the softer side, or is a more careful or serious type and faster to worry than somebody else's puppy, that is not a problem, it is part of what makes your puppy tick. The problem is when you aren't aware. Then you can accidentally make things worse.

I cannot reach in and rearrange your puppy's neurons, and I can't control the world so that traumatic events never happen to him. What I can do is share these tools with you so that if you do have a puppy that seems more prone to growing up to be a reactor or a worrier, you can build a foundation of coping skills, relaxation, confidence, elasticity, and trust. Your puppy can rest knowing that the structures he lives by are safe and reliable and that you "get it" so that he will never get the chance to spend lots of time practicing to grow up to be a full-blown reactive dog.

SPEAKING OF SUB–THRESHOLD…

Everything I suggest in here is meant to be done sub-threshold (below the point at which the pup will have an adverse reaction) so that your puppy can be desensitized and have a successful learning experience. Keep that in mind when you're reading this book!

DASH: THE DOG IN THE BUBBLE

Dash is an English Springer Spaniel whose owner came to me because Dash's dog reactivity was making it very difficult to keep him in agility classes. His story underscored for me the importance of raising your performance puppy in a balanced way.

Dash had been purchased to show in conformation, obedience, and agility. When Dash was a puppy his owner, Liz, brought him to classes with an extremely well-respected competition obedience trainer. Liz was given an extreme regimen on which to raise Dash. She was told to imagine there was a bubble around her, and that Dash should only move within the bubble—so he should either be in front or in heel position, or moving into one of those positions, all the time. He was not to move outside the bubble—a few feet away from Liz's body. If dogs encroached on the bubble, Dash was not to notice them, much less react. He was corrected with a collar pop for noticing the environment and not paying attention to Liz. Ironically, because he learned so early that dogs coming up were associated with corrections, dogs became a huge source of anxiety for him and this, of course, took away greatly from his ability to work.

When he was an adolescent in competition obedience classes, Dash's anxiety started escalating. It is common for anxious and reactive behaviors to escalate during that turbulent teenage period. It is important during that time to give the teenage performance dog coping skills, and some space to find himself rather than the constant pressure with which a dog like Dash is raised. Dash started growling, not just at dogs in class, but at the practice judges when they came to perform the stand for exam and bent over Dash.

In agility classes, Dash started lunging, barking, growling, and snapping at other dogs that moved near the bubble. A few times in agility class, a loose dog ran up to Dash, who was always facing Liz, and he was startled when the dog suddenly materialized just behind him. This elicited a big reaction, understandably. He was not allowed to look; dogs coming into his space meant he was going to get corrected and he was in conflict between needing to assess the threat level of a "surprise attack" and needing to be obedient to Liz. The anxiety generated by this conflict adrenalized Dash and sent him into a big reaction.

By the time Liz found me, she knew that correcting Dash for reacting wasn't going to fix the problem. She also knew that the methods she'd been using, though they were popular methods within her social circle, weren't the right ones for Dash. She was at a point where she didn't know if this dog that she had invested so much time into training would ever be able to compete, and she was very open to trying a different way.

What struck me the most when they came for their first appointment was the control aspect of their relationship. I always have people come into my yard and tell them they can let their dogs loose. This is actually an important part of my initial assessment period, watching the dog loose in my yard. Liz marched Dash into my yard, put him on a down-stay, and we talked for 45 minutes without Dash moving a hair. He was on high alert the entire time, listening to every sound, and constantly scanning my yard with his eyes. When I brought up Dash's level of anxiety and suggested he be allowed to move freely to release some of the pressure he was under, Liz pointed out that he was lying down and said he was relaxed. My response was, "He may be lying down, but inside his head he is writing the next great American novel about every single thing he sees, smells, and hears in my yard."

Once Liz realized Dash's level of vigilance about a world he had not been allowed to interact with as a youngster, she felt terrible about the strict way she had parented Dash.

Over the next few months we taught Dash how to relax, how to accept dogs moving into his space, and how to cope better. This caused his anxiety to decrease and his reactivity lessened so much that people came up to Liz at shows to say how different Dash was. Without all that worry about the bubble taking up so much emotional energy, Dash had newfound energy to put into focusing on his work. Suddenly he was able to do good heads-up heeling instead of swiveling around scanning, and he finished his CD. He was also doing better in agility class, even if dogs ran up to him, because he'd learned a modification of the Dog In Your Face game I created just for him; dogs behind him meant he could turn around and "point them out" for Liz, to earn a click and treat. No longer was he in conflict between avoiding a correction and making sure he was safe. Interacting with the environment, and noticing where other dogs were, had been "reframed" for him as a game he could play with Liz.

Dash is now a MACH dog! He is so happy to see me at trials that if I don't say hello and make a big fuss, he is very offended. I just love watching their teamwork in the ring and also seeing how much more relaxed they are in general. Finally, they are able to have fun with each other.

I think of Dash's story often because it's a good example of the extremes we can go to when raising our performance puppies. Often we get focused on the future goal and don't even realize the kind of pressure we put on the puppy. There is always a mix of nature and nurture affecting all of us. If Dash had been a naturally bombproof Golden Retriever from obedience lines raised with the bubble mentality, perhaps he would not have become dog reactive. To me that is not an excuse for raising a puppy under such harsh conditions. That hypothetical Golden Retriever would have been a good obedience dog without such extreme limitations on his life.

Dash was a sensitive, careful dog to begin with, so whatever anxiety he may have had about interacting with the world was exacerbated by the way he was raised. Another reminder for all of us who show our dogs to get to know each puppy for what he is and adjust our parenting style and our training to fit the puppy's personality, rather than getting stuck being a formula thinker.

Chapter 5

BEFORE YOU BEGIN

© DIANE LEWIS PHOTOGRAPHY

As we discussed briefly in Chapter 2, "Getting to Know Your Puppy," sometimes when we look at our puppy from the "performance puppy" perspective we allow our goals for that puppy to influence how we see him. We can get "stage mom" syndrome and be so focused on what we want this puppy to grow up to do that we get, pardon an agility pun, tunnel vision. We don't want our puppies to burn out early or turn to a life of crime like a lot of the child actors we read about in the tabloids! The immense pressure they were under to perform before they were socially mature took a huge toll on them, and I see this happen to dogs too.

DON'T PUT YOUR PUPPY IN A PRESSURE COOKER!

Stage mom syndrome takes away from our ability to really get to know the personality of the puppy. And, it's the personality of the puppy that should be dictating how we present training to him, not any formula in any book. Many of us get so formula-focused that we have lists of sport foundation behaviors we think every puppy should know. We are told how to teach our puppy as if all puppies learn the same way instead of being focused on getting to know our pup and creating a training structure that will work best for him. We become focused on the training exercises, not the puppy.

When I taught pet obedience classes, I met a lot of instructors who had this "cookie cutter" vision. They had been taught that "these are the beginner level exercises all dogs should know and you teach them like this." They didn't look at the ability of the handler to carry out the exercise correctly or the personality of the dog. Some dogs can handle lots more pressure than others. Some dogs think that a teacher looking directly at them is too much social pressure and they will shut down in class just from that.

If that teacher has learned that "all dogs need to learn a down behavior on the first night of class, and the way we teach down is the *x-y-z* way" without thinking about how best to present it to your dog, no matter what he does, what is your dog going to learn? Your sensitive dog, that didn't even want the teacher to look at him directly, will learn that class is scary, the teacher is scary, and his owner allows bad things to happen to him in class and can't be looked to for help. He is also going to connect fear emotions to that classroom so that the next time he comes into the room he will already be worried. Each time the teacher pushes him to do an exercise, he will get increasingly uncomfortable until his nervous system puts him into a "freeze" state where he is shut down and can't perform.

I see dogs like this all the time. They freeze when you ask them to do anything. And I know from their behavioral history that this happened because their initial experiences in class taught them to respond to the pressure of training by shutting down.

I met a Smooth Collie that didn't want to come near me at a seminar I gave. Using a version of the Give Me a Break game (Chapter 29), I shaped him to *choose* to interact with me. His owner said he was used to being taken from her by instructors and made to do something. His default became shutting down because it was the only way he could deal with the pressure of being taken away from his mom and being told he *has* to do something, now. That style of interaction was too much for him and took away his confidence. Please note that the majority of dogs in classes are O.K. with their teacher taking them away to demo something. But some dogs aren't.

As a puppy, Easy wasn't—he only wanted to be with me, which made access to me the Premack reward (Chapter 6), of course. We addressed that separately, during private lessons, where he learned that if he went away with his teacher, it meant he would get to come back to me and tell me what a good job he did (this ritual involved his jumping into my arms squeaking). The higher his level of arousal upon returning, the more uncomfortable I could tell he was working without me. He would work for his teacher well as he knew that was his job for the moment—focused on her, doing his sequence—but for him, uncertainty often turns into arousal, the level of which would be revealed during his return ritual. I would never have made him leave me to go with a strange teacher in a group class to learn something new when he was stressed—he wouldn't have learned it very well that way!

OF TEACHERS AND STUDENTS

As a teacher myself, I have taken students' dogs to demo or teach something many times, and I know that the Smooth Collie's teacher had the best intentions. It's hard to let go of being result-oriented when you're teaching a class. You feel the pressure of students watching you, expecting you to fix their dog or get their dog to do something that they were having trouble with. You have a full class of dogs to work with and time constraints. It's not easy to step back from the class structure, breathe, and ask yourself if your normal way of handling things is going to work for an individual dog.

Most club teachers are not trained to do this in the first place. So when I tell stories about my private students' experiences in classes, understand I have as much empathy for the teacher as I have for the student. After all, I am both a teacher and perpetual student myself, and see both sides quite clearly. My job here is to look at the situation, see what went wrong, and suggest an alternative that could work better for the individual puppy.

I worked with an Airedale that shuts down the second her owner takes a treat out of his pocket because she associates treats with being trained, and she associates being trained with having too much pressure put on her. She is a highly sensitive dog. If puppies show signs of being sensitive, it's not a problem. I *like* training sensitive dogs. It's just a message that you need to acknowledge this and adjust their training accordingly, and you obviously need an instructor who gets that. But many of us in the sport training world have become very exercise-oriented and expect all puppies to do things the same way.

One example I see often is agility instructors who want puppies to tug on the wobble board as part of their preparation for teeter training. This helps some puppies learn they can control the board and builds their confidence. However, there are also puppies that are so uncertain about their footing on the wobble board they feel distress on the board and will not learn well without some kind of adjustment to meet their needs. And, when that type of puppy is tugging, he can't put as much concentration on where his body is.

Other puppies are plain scared of the movement and need to be desensitized to it. We could be talking about any board here, not just the one that wobbles. Teachers tried to make a friend's puppy tug on the middle plank of a low dogwalk because he was scared of the dogwalk. He was having a growth spurt and had very long gangly legs and wasn't sure what to do with them; tugging was knocking him off balance. As a result he worried more, not less, about the dogwalk.

Play behaviors are often the first behaviors to leave the building in times of stress. Many people try to make the puppy play on the wobble board rather than separating these two behaviors and desensitizing the puppy to the wobble board without the added pressure to tug right then and there. This often backfires and, like the dog that shuts down when she sees a treat, puppies can learn to shut down when their owner produces a toy because it means they will be put on the wobble board.

I took a puppy agility seminar when Easy was just turning five months old. The instructor wanted Easy to tug on the wobble board and I refused. I could see that his body was getting used to the board moving and he wasn't fully confident; although he could tug on moving boards at home, he was in a strange place with strange puppies. I knew if I asked him to tug while he was still learning about that particular board, he would not have wanted to. Then I would have gotten a lecture about how he should want to tug anywhere, at any time, because apparently Easy came from the Border Collie factory.

Instead I used my method for teaching confidence on equipment, (outlined in Chapter 10) and I tugged with him during the times in the seminar that my instinct told me were the right times to reward with toy play. I gave treats during the times that my instinct told me were the right times to reward with food. I was yelled at for giving out many treats just as I was tugging. I was told to tug with him as he came out of the crate, all the way to equipment, tug on the equipment, and tug him back into the crate. He was already aroused being in this strange situation and I didn't think that was appropriate for him. Arousal, even if it's "happy arousal" can easily turn to stress, and there was plenty of pressure on him just being a puppy at his first seminar. Also, I wanted him thinking about what he was doing and deliberately offering me behavior, not just tugging while he happened to be standing on different pieces of equipment. When he learned jumping, my private instructor told me not to tug because she wanted him slow and thoughtful at first about how his body should be moving. Once he learned how to jump comfortably and well, we added speed and toy play.

Easy's litter sister was at that same seminar and she tugged with the instructor until she got so aroused that she leapt up in the instructor's face and snapped at her nose, which was a behavior all the litter had that I had been trying to modify in Easy. The instructor grabbed her collar and corrected her for losing self-control, which she didn't have yet in the first place. Easy's sister cried as she was put back in her crate for a time-out.

Later I was again spoken to harshly for "making Easy too calm" by using an equal amount of treats and tugging at the seminar. If I had handled him like the instructor handled his sister, I would have been told off for the opposite problem, as his sister's owner was. I felt like I just couldn't win with the instructor no matter what I did. So, I just used the reinforcement that I knew would be the more appropriate and more potent one at the time, because I knew my own puppy. I also knew where his arousal level was and where I wanted it to be, and that his comfort and happiness at his first seminar was more important than following directions that weren't necessarily the best ones for him as an individual.

It's hard when we're under pressure to do things "just so," especially if all the other puppies in a class are doing it that way. But if we want to get the best performance out of our puppies and give them the best learning experience, we need to be able to stand up to even the most well meaning of instructors who think all puppies should learn the same or be motivated by the same things, regardless of breed or temperament. We need to know our puppy well enough to know how to approach his training in a group environment. We absolutely owe it to our puppies to set them up for success. If that means using the Give Me a Break game (Chapter 29) to help a pressure-sensitive puppy come out of his shell rather than doing what the rest of class is doing; in the long run, it will be worth it.

Chapter 6

PREMACK PRINCIPLE

© DIANE LEWIS PHOTOGRAPHY

If you read my first book, you already know about my love affair with the Premack principle, and the huge role it plays in CU.

Named after its originator, Dr. David Premack, the principle states: *You can use access to the performance of a high-probability behavior to reinforce performance of a low-probability behavior.*

What does that mean? You may hear trainers calling it "grandmother's law" and saying it means you have to eat your vegetables before I give you dessert. And it does mean that, but to me it means so much more.

First of all, the more you pair a high-probability behavior (chasing squirrels) with a low-probability behavior (recalling away from squirrels), the more you build passion for performing the low-probability behavior. Why? *Because the emotions the puppy feels while chasing the squirrel can become linked with recalling back to you.* That is the magic of the principle.

To use the grandmother metaphor, the child who sees broccoli on his plate feels overjoyed because he knows the act of eating broccoli is linked to dessert access. Since he feels happy every time he eats broccoli, his body starts generating happy feelings at the sight, smell, or taste of broccoli. After a while, eating broccoli becomes self-reinforcing. The child has actually learned to like broccoli! Just like your puppy can learn to recall to you with enthusiasm and drive, away from a distraction.

In order to use this principle effectively, you will need to teach a release cue (discussed in Chapter 29) so that you can send your puppy to enjoy her environmental reward. For me, Premack took the conflict out of dog training: no longer should people look at it as a "me vs. the environment" paradigm, where they have to ask their dog to pay attention to them at the exclusion of anything else. Now we can present training as a "me *and* the environment" paradigm. That is a *huge* shift in perspective. There is no more fight. Sniffing, chasing, running, marking trees, seeing other dogs, eating dessert: it all goes on cue. Performance of those high-probability behaviors is made possible through handler focus, which is the key that unlocks the doors to puppy Disney. You turned away from that other puppy, great job; now go play with that puppy!

Of course there will be some times when you simply can't use the environment to reward your puppy; it might not be safe or it might not be appropriate. But using the Premack principle when you can creates such a relationship of trust that when you can't use it, your puppy will be okay with that.

Here's an example from a lesson I gave today: A Poodle puppy was bouncing away from her handler when she went to put the leash on. I asked the puppy to hand target, since she had a different emotional association with that cue than she had with her horribly poisoned recall cue. She touched my hand and, as she did so, my other hand sneakily grabbed her collar and I leashed her. I gave her a treat, then unclipped the collar and told her to go play. I did this a bunch of times, walking up to her with my target hand out rather than giving her recall cue, leashing then unleashing, and releasing her. Then I just stood there while she was released, talking to her handler, and she actually came up to me asking to be leashed. I leashed her, unleashed her, and released her, but she didn't have a need to go anywhere; she wasn't interested in playing a run-away game any more. She was interested in her new leash game.

Her person was truly shocked that she would come up to be leashed as she'd spent her entire puppyhood bouncing away and zooming whenever she was approached by somebody holding a leash. That is the power of Premack. Having the leash clipped on, nine times out of ten means having the leash removed and a verbal release to take off. One time out of ten, it means the leash stays on and we have to leave Leslie's backyard of puppy fun. But there will be treats—it might not be as good as an environmental release, but it'll be something.

Another Premack story: Easy was obsessed with water from a very early age. I knew we were going to have trouble when, at ten weeks, he was stalking in circles around the perimeter of the wading pool, creating splashing in front of him and giving Border Collie eye to the splashes. He could do this for an hour, if you didn't stop him. I wanted to let him swim but I needed to know I would be leaving the creek every time with a puppy. He learned that he got to swim when he paid attention to me. He learned it away from the water, where I asked for attention then sent him to the water, and he learned it in the water, because every time he happened to look at me I said, "Go swim!" and he kept swimming. I also asked for the Whiplash Turn while he was swimming, giving his "go swim" cue as soon as he turned toward me.

I had to do this over and over so that I could break the water spell. It still takes him much longer to sit near water than to sit anywhere else, because his body gets stuck in a crouch position; asking him to sit near water is a good way for him to practice switching from instinct to "thinking brain." His recall out of water, however, is lightning fast; it is as fast as his flying into the water after I give his "go swim" cue. When I call him out of water, it's pretty dramatic how he flies out of it. Occasionally I still send him back in for one last swim. I used to send him back nine out of ten times and sometimes clip his leash, then take it off and send him back. At this point I don't need maintenance; we have our swimming contract. Water recall behavior causes access to swimming behavior; mommy always leaves the creek with her puppy.

PREMACK'S ROLE IN CU GAMES

Here is how Premack plays a role in the CU games:

- **Default behavior:** Performance of the default behavior causes us to cue a high-probability behavior.

- **Leave it:** The puppy learns that if he leaves something alone and orients to us, we will most likely send him back to it.

- **Whiplash Turn:** Again, the puppy learns that if he disengages from the environment and orients to us, we will most likely cue him to re-engage.

- **Look at That! game:** The puppy gets to look at something he wanted to check out, on cue, as a reward for looking at us instead of that thing.

- **Off-switch game:** The puppy gets to do the fun activity that he finds super stimulating as a reward for calming down.

- **Give Me a Break game:** The puppy is released to do his own thing after performing whatever behavior we ask of him—the more we take the pressure off the puppy by releasing him from work, the more he will choose to put the pressure back on himself by asking for more work instead of taking his break. Why is that? Because of the reverse psychology component of the Premack principle. Some people call this "transfer of value." It means, the more they do the low-probability behavior, the more they like it.

My training perspective is always about cooperation rather than control, and Premack fits in perfectly with that. It's okay for the puppy to sniff, visit, zone out, chase, and use his instinct brain. I can get the reliability of attention that I want by creating a feedback loop that connects those activities to working with me. A puppy wants/needs to zone out; training is too much pressure. Fine! *Use that.*

People tend to assume treats are the most reinforcing thing when sometimes they aren't. Sometimes the biggest reinforcement for a puppy is to be left alone. If you have an independent sort of puppy, or a puppy that is very soft in training, then a break from pressure is a great Premack reward. Pay attention to me; click/treat; O.K., go away.

You can stand there or even turn away and go sit in a chair for a Give Me a Break game. Puppy turns back to you, with or without your cue; click/treat; O.K., go away. Maybe the puppy isn't even interested in the treat; fine, you don't actually need it if you are working with a puppy that just wants to do his own thing. The release to do his own thing is all you really need. You will find the more you engage your puppy in this ping-pong pattern of come-and-go, the less interest he will have in doing his thing and the more he will offer orienting to you. It's the power of Premack.

This principle also gives you permission to stop stressing over whether you will ever be "more interesting" than the environment to your puppy. So many sports students have come to my place for a lesson and burst into tears because their instructors or fellow club members judged them for not being interesting enough because their puppy got distracted in class. People exhaust themselves jumping up and down, talking in a high voice, and throwing toys around, when all they really need to do to get and keep their puppy's attention is to learn how to tell him to go away and sniff something.

If you keep trying to war with the environment, either you or your puppy is going to lose. There will always be something novel in the environment that will engage your puppy's natural curiosity or appeal to his animal nature; that is when you will lose the war. Sometimes people control everything and put their puppy under severe restrictions so that he never gets a chance to experience anything but interaction with his handler as being rewarding. That, in my opinion, is when the puppy loses.

Or, you could look at this situation as not a war at all, but a wonderful opportunity to use the world to reward your puppy. That's a lot less pressure on you the handler, isn't it?

Chapter 7

THE POWER OF THE RELEASE WORD

© DIANE LEWIS PHOTOGRAPHY

Attention training is mentally taxing on a puppy, so to balance this out, there are three natural behaviors which I like to use as part of the learning process. Remember that well-timed break periods during training are just as important as teaching the puppy a behavior.

Breaks should be seen as part of the training process not separate from it.

There is a phenomenon called "latent learning" where a puppy that learned something new and was then given a break integrated the new information faster than a puppy that learned it without a break. The brain needs rest periods during which it processes new information. Without that rest the brain just keeps getting more and more data; at some point the brain can go, enough! And zone out. People take their dogs to that zone-out point in training too often, when there is a much better alternative!

So, what should the puppy be doing during break periods? He could just rest, or you could give him access to what I am calling "the three natural behaviors." Your puppy already enjoys doing these behaviors and we can use them to help him process training information. The three natural behaviors are:

- Sniffing

- Chewing

- Foraging

These are behaviors the puppy can engage in as alternatives to just being crated. During these behaviors the puppy will have the chance to process the new training information while he does a stress-releasing, relaxing activity that doesn't take much brain power and doesn't involve the direct pressure of handler interaction.

Sniffing is one of the three natural behaviors that can help your puppy process training information and release stress.

To utilize these correctly your puppy needs to know his release word and the "go" cue. Then when it's break time you say, "O.K. puppy! Go sniff/chew/forage!" When break time is over, remember to give the release word again to let the puppy know he's done with his break activity and about to start something else.

STAY AND RELEASE, COME AND GO

It's not a big deal to teach a release word. The way I do it, the puppy learns a stay and the release word in the same session. I reward a stationary behavior, such as sit or down, and I keep rewarding until I say, "O.K."

O.K. is not the greatest release word, but it is the one I end up saying so it's the one my dogs understand. It's best to pick a word that they don't hear in other contexts, such as "done," "free," or "break."

Once I've said "O.K." I invite the puppy to get up, coming out of his stationary position. Then I wait increasingly longer in between treats. The puppy learns that if he keeps his position, he will get intermittent reinforcement until he hears the release word, which means there's no more chance for reinforcement, and he can get up.

When the puppy can sit still for about 15 seconds, I raise criteria by moving around. I will take just one step at a time away from the puppy and then return to feed the puppy in position.

I split up stay training into duration and distance. I work on duration first by increasing the amount of time between treats. Then I add distance by increasing the distance between myself and the staying puppy, but, when doing so, I take the duration aspect out of it and return every second, every step I take, to reward. Gradually, I blend the two so the puppy is staying for longer periods of time while I am moving around.

I teach the stay and the release in the same session by rewarding a stationary behavior, such as sit, and continuing to reward until I say, "O.K."

Now that the puppy is committed to his stationary position while I am moving around, I start saying, "stay" as I move, a couple seconds before I return to reward the puppy. "Stay" means keep doing what you're doing; I'm coming back soon to reward you. At some point I start saying "stay" earlier. By then the puppy is very committed and completely understands the concept, so "stay" is just an extra piece of information about how well he is doing. But the duration of the behavior was really cued by the sit or down cue, and the puppy learns to hold that behavior until he hears the release word.

I can call my dogs off any activity they are doing with their release word. I did not train for this, it just happened. My dogs were running the fence line because the five little kids next door were out playing ball. Instead of saying, "come," I said, "O.K.!" And four dogs whipped round and flew back to me. Now, for any charged situation, I just release them from it when I want them to stop. What I realized is that my dogs understand that the release word ends a behavior. And, if my dogs are told to stop doing something, but they don't have instructions for what happens next, they naturally come back to me to see what's going on. For my dogs, the release is actually more potent than their recall cue. They are equally reliable with both but have more intensity when responding to their release word. The reason why is because of how I used the Premack principle (Chapter 6) in their training.

Because the majority of the time that I asked my dogs to "leave it" or in some way orient to me away from something they wanted, I said, "O.K." and then sent them back to it, the word O.K. became charged with the power of the thing they wanted. This is why Easy literally flies out of the water when I say O.K. even in his glazed-over, herdy trance; because that word has been charged with so much intensity since he was a puppy. When he was younger, I used to call him out of the water just so I could reward his recall by sending him back in to the water—simple Premack pattern. And what did I say every time I sent him back? "O.K. go swim!"

So, even though I started calling him out of the water by asking him to come, I was always releasing him back to the water by saying O.K. At some point I said "O.K." when he was in the water instead of "come," and was surprised that instead of swimming back toward me he shot out of the water like a cannon.

Release words can release a dog from *any* behavior whether you asked the dog to do that behavior or not. Using release words a lot as part of a Premack pattern will supercharge them.

USING THE NATURAL BREAK BEHAVIORS

Now that I have my stay/release, come/go behaviors in place, I can begin to use my three natural behaviors.

I use *chewing* as much as possible. Chewing hay releases endorphins in horses and some horse trainers give hay for this very reason after a training session. I have always told people to give their dogs a bone or Kong toy after a training session, and hearing about the horse trainers reinforced my instinct. Puppies always need to chew anyway and a perfect time to chew is during and after a training session.

This puppy gets a bone to chew on so he can have a mental rest while the instructor addresses the humans in the class.

It should go without saying that any time a puppy is crated in class or at home they should be given something to chew on. But people don't think about giving puppies something to chew on during training. This is an easy and flawless way to give a puppy a mental rest so that you can return to training without burning him out, as well as an awesome way to end a session.

Sniffing is another great one—you can send your puppy off to sniff or you can take him on a sniff-walk, either leashed or unleashed. Which option you choose would be dependent on what's most appropriate for your situation at the time.

Foraging is a behavior that I never see get used; I started using it just on intuition without giving it any thought. Then I overheard a zoo trainer talking about using access to foraging as a stress reliever in exotic animals. Think about a wild baby animal nosing through grass for fallen berries, or for bits of flesh from the pack's recent kill, or whatever. During and after training sessions, especially during, I just sprinkle tiny pieces of treats all over the grass and let the puppy "hunt" for them. This is a great stress reliever. I also use foraging for dogs or puppies that worry about people or dogs approaching, noises, or other stuff—the triggering stimulus becomes a predictor of the treasure hunt. That way the puppy isn't "stuck" there next to you, getting one treat at a time, which gives him a lot of time to start reacting badly to the stimulus. Instead the puppy is getting a bunch of treats that take some time to find, a puzzle that engages his mind, and a much longer visual break from the stimulus. If the puppy is too stressed to forage, then obviously you would change

This puppy is given a break during a training session for a sniff-walk.

Sprinkle small treats in the grass and let your puppy forage for them.

Allowing your dog to play is another way to use a natural behavior to give him a training break.

your criteria and change the situation drastically until he was under his threshold.

Another natural behavior is *play*. If play with humans, which comes with rules and a need for some self-control, is too much direct pressure or too much for the puppy to think about, don't use it as a break behavior. Use one of the more restful natural behaviors instead. If you are a sport trainer, you have likely been using toy play as reinforcement throughout your training session anyway and your puppy probably gets very amped up by it and knows the rules. Toy play always has its place during a training session, but do provide more restful breaks where the puppy can settle for a minute and chew or sniff. You may find that access to play with another dog doesn't mentally tax your puppy in the same way that playing with humans does. If so, experiment and see which break behaviors suit your puppy best. For many dogs I have worked with, fetching a ball or Frisbee is a good break behavior, but for other dogs, this type of arousing activity really wouldn't be appropriate for their break. As always, it depends on the individual puppy.

A MADE-UP TRAINING SESSION: PUPPY SPEEDY IS LEARNING TO STAY!

As puppy Speedy stays in position he gets treats. Of course he never moves out of position until he hears his release word! Intermittently, so that he doesn't get tired when working on duration of staying still, he is called out of position to play with his favorite toy or chase a treat as it rolls on the ground. Simply calling Speedy out of position can be used to reinforce the stay, per the Premack principle, if Speedy prefers motion to staying still. It may actually be more rewarding to just get up than to get the treat!

Let's say Speedy does three minutes where he is mostly rewarded in position, but gets rewarded out of position a couple times to mix it up. Then his handler says, "O.K., go get it!" and throws a bunch of tiny treat pieces into the grass. Speedy noses around finding his treat pieces. When it looks like he's found them all, his handler says, "Come!" and rewards the recall with a treat, then asks for a sit and stay again. A couple more minutes of that is followed by, "O.K., go sniff," and Speedy's handler points toward a bunch of pine cones, grass, pine needles, and sticks strategically put together for puppy enrichment in the backyard. Speedy likes to climb in the pile and sniff. Then his handler say, "Come!" She rewards the recall, sit, and stay. After a few more minutes, it's, "O.K., go get your bone." Speedy is done with staying for the day and now gets to work on a marrow bone at his leisure. Speedy thinks stay training is pretty cool and he is ready for more.

Let's contrast this with puppy Orbit. This puppy is being told to stay and hearing a lot of "uh-uh!" because he keeps moving before he hears his release word (which means his person needs to adjust her criteria and set him up to succeed). Maybe his person works on this for ten minutes nonstop. When she finishes the session, Orbit is relieved to go do his own thing, whereas Speedy stayed fresh enough to keep going indefinitely. Speedy wasn't relieved to finish practicing staying still because that was connected to running around and doing the natural behaviors puppies enjoy, and because he had enough breaks that his attention span was not taxed.

Chapter 8

Give Your Puppy a Break

What about time-outs? Time-outs are punishments that get overused with our performance puppies. We need to look at when and why our puppies receive this punishment so that we can readjust their training and prevent creating the situation that causes us to use time-outs in the first place.

Time-Outs vs. Time Offs

I don't give time-outs, I give "time offs." I give dogs lots of breaks from training, either in their crate or free to sniff in the yard or chew on a bone. If you feel you have to give a time-out, it means you need to take a step back and look at the big picture. Which criteria can you change; which environmental variables can you adjust? The more time-outs you give, the more it tells you that something in your training needs adjusting.

Two major reasons sport trainers use time-outs are for the dog disengaging during training and not showing good self-control. If you are giving a time-out because your puppy disengaged during a training session and started sniffing around or doing something else, maybe you needed to have a shorter training session; maybe you could have spent the same amount of time training but broken it up with little breaks to sniff or chew. You should always be aiming to set up a situation where the puppy is asking for more work, rather than you asking the puppy to work more.

If you are giving a time-out because your puppy resorted to an arousal behavior such as leaping at your face while tugging, wildly barking at you, or even grabbing at you during training, you need to balance out the overly stimulating training with some calming exercises. I see a lot of people trying to teach self-control by letting the puppy get as high as a kite and then when he does, punishing him by giving him a time-out. How is the puppy supposed to learn how to regulate his own arousal level if he doesn't get the chance to learn how it feels to get excited and then calm down (like we teach in the CU Off-switch game)? Just crating is often not enough. Many puppies do not calm down in their crates on a time-out. They could be spinning in there excited about coming out. Or they could be on a down- or sit-stay in there but still mentally "vibrating," not actually settling at all.

I always say to my students, learning to come out of a state of arousal is a physiological learning. It's not a mental thing. The puppy's body is flowing with adrenaline. Of course the puppy can learn operant self-control behaviors such as sitting when excited, but he also needs to learn how it *feels* in his body to truly calm down from a high-arousal state. This simple thing that all puppies should learn prevents so many arousal-related problems later on, such as barking/grabbing in the ring and the dog not being able to think straight when excited or under pressure.

Another reason people give time-outs is because the puppy made a mistake. But whose mistake was it really?

Puppies I train learn a strong default behavior early on. If something goes wrong in their training, I stop what I'm doing and sit down, as if it were the Give Me a Break game (Chapter 29), and the puppy offers his default behavior. This resets the situation and I can re-cue the behavior the puppy didn't do. For example, when Easy was a puppy, if he didn't do something as I wanted during a training session, I sat on the couch. He then gave a default sit; I got up and asked for the behavior again, with adjustments to what and how I was asking, if needed.

Responding like this to a puppy that hasn't been raised with a solid understanding of a default behavior would not be fair to the puppy.

Another way to reset the situation is to give the "go to mat" cue as discussed in Chapter 27 (which should be totally reliable if you're going to use it for resetting) or simply take the puppy to his mat, and ask for the sit/take a breath. This keeps you from repeating the cue the puppy isn't getting and gives both of you a chance to relieve the pressure that comes with learning something new so that you can start fresh.

I'm not saying time-outs are a horrible punishment (unless your puppy has separation anxiety). I'd much rather have people use time-outs than use a physical "correction" or scream at their puppy. But if you find yourself giving one or more per session, you really need to step back and look at how to readjust the way you present training to your puppy. I gave Easy exactly one time-out in his entire puppyhood/adolescence and it wasn't during a training session. It was for resource guarding the hall closet where the leashes are kept from my other dogs. An open crate happened to be near the closet, and when he started creeping around the closet and giving eye to my other dogs, to his absolute horror I sent him right into the crate and put the other dogs' leashes on first.

Sometimes a well-intentioned time-out can be used inappropriately and can make things worse instead of better, as in the case of Bragger, the field-bred Golden Retriever.

Bragger had his first agility lesson at the age of nine weeks. He was highly aroused by the playing and running around and, at some point, he needed a break from all this rushing so he wandered off to sniff around in the grass. His owner, Jane was told by her instructor to grab him and put him in his crate and immediately do a lot of high intensity work with her adult dog in order to make the puppy jealous.

While in a state of arousal and anxiety, Bragger watched his new mom tugging, running, and revving up the other dog. He screamed and bit at the crate bars. This was seen as a good thing—the puppy was very distressed so the time-out must have gotten the message across. After several minutes of screaming and bar biting, Bragger was let out for more arousing play. The fact that nine-week-old Bragger probably needed the little break he took (a failure on the part of the trainer, not of his) escaped them as they concentrated on this anthropomorphic concept that the puppy was "blowing off" his handler and needed to learn it wasn't acceptable.

What Bragger was really learning was that agility lessons are frustrating, and, in that moment, a six-year-long history of losing his mind during agility training, yelling, and being unable to think or settle, was born. I met him at six years of age and he had not started trialing yet because agility still sent him into this state of arousal/anxiety that began during that very first lesson.

I taught Bragger how to take a breath, how to relax, how to think through arousal, and got him sequencing agility obstacles without getting his trademark zoomies that could go on for an hour if nobody could catch him. He learned to do a few obstacles, then relax on his mat, a few more obstacles, take a breath—agility became an Off-switch game for him. Suddenly he was thinking and no more zooming. His mom cried as she watched her dog doing obstacle work with me while staying completely engaged, even in his excitement. Talk about creating a conditioned emotional response—from lesson one Bragger's nervous system was being primed for this arousal behavior that prevented him from doing agility successfully… and how had the behavior been dealt with? More time-outs!

Chapter 9

LESLIE'S PROTOCOL FOR FOOD AROUSAL

Some people save every piece of kibble as a training treat and don't give their puppy the chance to eat a meal in peace. There are variations of this—many people use one meal for training and let the puppy eat the second meal on his own, while others just put less food in the bowl so that they can use some of the puppy's daily ration for training, but still give their puppies the chance to have a "normal" meal twice a day.

I think it's important to take this last option, for two reasons:

- For their digestive health
- For their mental health

Puppies need and deserve to have mealtime in peace without the pressure to perform or the anxiety that their food will be withheld if they don't get something right.

USING FOOD AS REINFORCEMENT WITH THE PERFORMANCE PUPPY

I have worked with hundreds of sport dogs who flat out lose their mind around any type of food because it means training. These are the dogs that don't have their behaviors under stimulus control, and see their owner's clicker, bait bag, or taking out of a toy or food as a signal to go into a frenzy of offering every behavior they can think of. Before we can do whatever behavior modification a particular dog with that level of food arousal needs, we have to teach the dog how to be still, reasonably calm, and focused in the presence of their reinforcement.

Teaching these dogs how to relax by using food rewards is a long, hard road; before you can use food to reward them for relaxing, they first have to learn they can relax around food. So they have to go through a protocol for food arousal before we can even start with foundation relaxation work.

If you already have this problem, here is my solution. If you don't have this problem yet, please don't create it by associating all food with your puppy having to do something to earn it. How would you feel if you had to take a test in order to earn every single meal you ate?

GOOD THINGS COME TO THOSE WHO WAIT

Your criteria are first that the dog learns he is capable of sitting or lying still in the presence of food *without offering behaviors*. So many dogs I work with have absolutely no idea this is possible, and it makes me sad to see how frantic they get. Their owners inadvertently make it worse by reinforcing the frantic behavior, reading it as enthusiasm to work and missing the arousal and stress aspect of it—

and missing how this kind of arousal will have an impact on training for performance later on.

Some owners make it worse by giving a reward for every third or fourth or fifth offered trick just because it was cute or funny, which communicates to the dog, "keep trying everything you know over and over and you will get intermittently rewarded for going nuts."

This puppy has learned to wait calmly in his crate in a down even when food is placed on the floor outside his open crate.

From the foundation learning of being still in the presence of food, you can build to the point where you can use treats to reward relaxed behavior without getting the dog all frantic again because food is involved.

Let's focus on the first stage of this process. Before you begin this protocol:

- Make sure the dog knows how to take a breath (see Chapter 17).

- Make sure the dog understands his release word (see Chapters 7 and 29).

- Make sure you have a history of rewarding a stationary default behavior—usually a sit or a down (you probably don't need to do this protocol if you have a strong enough history!)

Now you are ready to build the foundation learning of being still in the presence of food.

Count out five treats in your hand. Ask for a sit or down. You can also ask for a "go to place" (see mat work in Chapter 27), if your puppy already knows this behavior, and then your effort here will have the added benefit of reminding the puppy that the only behavior that works on his mat is being still. Rapid-fire reward the puppy in position before he starts moving or offering other stuff and then give his release word. (Guess what—the food arousal protocol can double as stay training!)

Get another five treats in your hand. Ask for a sit or down. Reward the puppy in position, but start counting off half a second between each treat. Give his release word before he starts moving.

Use this technique to *very gradually* (one-half to one second at a time) build up to at least 20 seconds in between treats. The goal is for the puppy to *commit* to the behavior you asked for and *trust* that the reward will come, rather than decide you have taken too long to reward what you asked for so he needs to show you a bunch of other tricks to see which one will work.

Most helpful here is if the puppy has a strong stationary default behavior. That way he knows he doesn't have to try other stuff but can relax knowing good things come to those who wait.

If the puppy offers a different behavior or starts fidgeting instead of the sit, down, or mat you asked for, act as if you'd ended the session and give the release word.

If he's on his mat, remember to release him off the mat. Remember, the only behavior that works on mats is being still, as discussed in Chapter 27.

A common arousal fidget is the dancing feet. If your puppy starts giving you dancing feet during this protocol, give the release word and follow the instructions above. Dancing feet is a gateway to other arousal behaviors. Many high-drive pups need to learn they must keep all feet on the floor when in a stationary position in order to get their treat.

If you've had to give your release word early because your puppy offered a different behavior or started fidgeting, before restarting the session just work on having your puppy take breaths. Do a couple breaths from whatever position he took after being released, and then if he isn't sitting, ask him to sit and do five more breaths. If he is sitting and taking breaths correctly, you can then start counting your one-half to one second in between treats again, thereby sneaking him back into the protocol structure without the initial excitement of "starting over." Just do it a few times and then release the puppy to do one of the natural behaviors (sniffing, chewing, foraging.) He will really need that at this point.

Chapter 10

Using Reinforcement Wisely: Pressure and Premack

The most appropriate reinforcement depends on the environment and the situation. Sometimes people get stuck on using a particular kind of reinforcement for their puppy and use it blindly without taking the bigger picture, such as the environment or the situation, into account. They can accidentally set up their puppy for failure in this way.

For example, I have a friend who wanted her puppy to tug anywhere, any time, no matter what, so she brought him to different places and asked him to tug. He did love to tug naturally, but as she went to different places she discovered that proximity to unknown dogs shut him down. Tugging then became more of a control issue and less of a reinforcement issue. He *had* to tug because she asked him to, no matter what else was happening. This put a lot of stress on the relationship and turned what should have been enjoyable and interactive play sessions into a mental and emotional tug-of-war.

I have always taught people that you can use willingness to play with toys as a gauge of the dog's emotional state; that is, if he is feeling comfortable and happy, you can get him to play. If he isn't feeling comfortable and happy, it's going to be much harder. For some of these dogs, if you keep trying, you can get them interested in a toy and if their instinct takes over, then the toy play itself can change their emotional state. But, for many other dogs, you would do better to help them relax and take the pressure off, which will allow them to access a more playful frame of mind.

For the puppy who didn't like to tug around dogs he didn't know, my friend first did the mat work steps using strange dogs from the training club, ending with the Look at That game from the mat (Chapter 26). Then she incorporated toy play into the mat work. When she cued the Look at That game by asking, "Where is that strange dog?" the puppy would indicate the dog from his mat. The puppy would get a treat, which he was able to take and enjoy near the other dog, as simultaneously the other dog was walked behind a barrier out of the puppy's view. Once the puppy couldn't see the other dog, we invited him to tug. Then we'd cue the puppy to return to his mat and ask him where the dog was. He'd look around and "find" the dog as he was brought out from behind the barrier. My friend would click and treat, and invite the puppy to tug as the dog was leaving again. Soon the puppy was "pointing out" the barrier to his mom and expectantly waiting to play. Release of pressure was in the form of putting the strange dog behind the barrier.

Creating a structure like this can take the worry out of a situation and toys can easily be incorporated. Another alternative here would have been to use the Give Me a Break game with the tug toy (Chapter 29.) Again, this would be about creating structure that felt safe and comfortable so that the puppy's natural drive could come out.

I had another friend whose puppy had a similar problem. Her puppy did not want to play in all locations all the time. She kept trying to make the tug toy and herself more interesting, running around and slapping the ground and asking him over and over if he was "reeeeady." What her puppy learned was that when her mom produced a toy in a new environment (not at home or at the club, where she was happy to play), it meant *Pressure* with a capital P, and the puppy started shutting down when mom got the tug toy out.

When what we perceive as the reinforcement does not have a value that makes it *relevant* to the situation, we are creating a lose/lose for both ourselves and our puppies. At the club, a tug toy was highly relevant to this second friend's puppy, but at a park she hadn't been to before, it wasn't. At that point, the tug stopped being reinforcement, and since my friend kept trying to make the puppy interact with it, the tug ended up becoming a signal that something unpleasant was happening.

I worked with an American Eskimo dog that sat down with a blank look in his eyes whenever he was offered treats in the vicinity of weave poles. He loved treats but he had learned that treats near weave poles meant *Pressure* and he would just say, "Nobody home." If you walked him away from the poles and offered him treats near a tunnel, he ate the treats with enthusiasm.

If you want your puppy to enjoy eating or tugging anywhere at any time, then introduce him to this concept skillfully. Don't just expect him to like the same things no matter where he is or what he is doing. Just like us, our puppies' preferences depend on their fluctuating moods and on their ever-changing environment. If you want your puppy to tug near stuff he doesn't feel good about tugging near, teach him to get comfortable around that stuff and create a situation where the puppy will start feeling good enough to want to play with you. That way the toy does not become a predictor of "ick," and you can use your "reinforcement" as a real reinforcement.

Often the most valuable reinforcement you can give to your puppy is release from pressure. This is a concept that most people I come across do not use enough. Sometimes a situation—a training situation or just an environmental situation beyond your control—puts too much pressure on your puppy and their performance suffers. To offer a reinforcement that has lost its relevance because of the situation is to set the team up to fail.

The first example that comes to mind is a Cavalier King Charles Spaniel that was taken to a seminar I gave at an agility club. She was scared and did not want to come out of her crate. Her mom had brought her favorite treats but she was huddled in the back of the crate not wanting any part of it. So when it was her turn to start box work, I put her crate in the box of ring gates. I played a little game by myself, rolling treats around the floor, and when she finally came out I clicked and threw a treat into her crate. She ran back to get it, then ventured carefully out again as I did my own thing. When she took a step out, I clicked and threw another treat back in the crate. After a few minutes she was willingly offering coming out, taking several steps toward me before her click. It was then easy to get her doing other stuff within the box before sending her back to her crate.

So what was this Cavalier's most relevant reinforcement? She was eating the treats, but to me it seemed that release from the pressure of a training situation with a stranger in a novel environment was much more rewarding. The treat delivery in the crate was my way of rewarding her for her bravery. My message was, if you come out, you get to go back in. *In other words, the Premack principle strikes again!*

After a while, as her confidence built, she didn't need that immediate security blanket and I could ask her for more.

Any time you ask a dog to do anything, you are putting pressure on the dog. It does not matter if you are the most positive trainer in the universe; any social interaction puts some measure of pressure on the social beings involved. To leash that Cavalier and not give her access to her crate, and give her treats for paying attention or doing obedience, is what many positive trainers would have done in that situation. But I don't see that as "positive." Just because you aren't popping her leash, and are giving food instead of corrections, if you aren't reading the big picture and giving her what she needs to feel good about what is happening, you are not being positive. Even though she wanted her treats, she wanted to escape even more. If that weren't the case there would not have been a problem with her hiding in her crate in the first place.

It's never my intention to use pressure, physical or psychological, in a punishing way. I cultivate a respectful awareness of how I use my body, and the space between my body and the dog's body, during my interactions, trying to approach training with a neutral/open posture. I see people often approaching dogs with this "I'm going to make you do this" aggressive-style energy—that is not a partnership, that is a dictatorship. If I do use my body to block a dog from seeing or going after something—which is a form of pressure—then I will first teach the dog that my standing in front of them is a cue for eye contact/take a breath so that they have a pre-conditioned association with my "body block." If I step toward the dog's haunches because I need to turn him around quickly when he can't respond to a verbal cue, that step is introduced as part of Whiplash Turn training (Chapter 25) and treated as just another way for the dog to earn a reward for responding to a head turn cue.

However much I don't want to pressure a dog, sometimes I work with dogs so sensitive that my very existence is pressure. Because of them I have had to recognize that as a trainer, I am constantly putting some form of pressure on dogs simply because training creates a social situation that involves the dogs being asked to do things, and having certain things expected of them. For many dogs this type of social pressure is stimulating, and environmental cues that tell the dog you are getting ready to train, such as picking up your clicker or putting treats in your pocket, are cause for celebration. But for a dog that shuts down easily, is scared, is independent and not very socially motivated—or is just having a bad fur day—access to leaving this artificial social situation called a "training session" is sometimes the most potent reinforcement we can give them.

This is why I use the Give Me a Break game structure in so much of my training, because it gives the dogs the opportunity to tell me that they want to keep working. It gives them the choice to take on the pressure of social interaction and work, or to take a break. It makes the conversation between us much more dynamic and much less arbitrary. It is the best way I know of letting the dog tell me how much he is ready for and when he is ready for it.

Shaping is another technique I use in conjunction with the Give Me a Break game, again for the purpose of creating an environment where the dog has the ability to choose to keep doing the pressured activity, or take a break from it. This concept is illustrated in Quinn's story; although Quinn is an adult dog, it's a good example of using release of pressure to reward your puppy. Another example is my student's Border Collie Zip; he is extremely sensitive to social pressure caused by judges watching him in the ring at trials.

Quinn is a handsome blue merle Border Collie. When he was a young pup he took a puppy agility class where all the puppies practiced banging the teeter. The more classes he attended, the more sensitive he became to the loud noise and rambunctious play of other puppies flying down their new favorite obstacle. I happened to be taking this class with my own puppy, so I witnessed the beginning of Quinn's teeter problem firsthand.

With every bang of the seesaw, Quinn had a small, but noticeable response. His expressive blue eyes had a, "What the heck is going on" look, and he backed up a little bit, away from the source of the noise. I was concerned that he was becoming sensitized to the teeter. Meanwhile, Quinn's owner, Liz, felt pressure to bring Quinn up to the level of his classmates. The instructor suggested Quinn play near the teeter more, which only served to increase his fear as he heard the banging more and more often.

As Quinn matured and continued agility classes, the teeter remained his nemesis. Liz received some suggestions on how to treat Quinn's teeter phobia. They were all well-intentioned, but none of them convinced Quinn that the teeter was his friend. In fact, these efforts increased rather than alleviated the problem.

Suggestion #1

Play with Quinn near the teeter while other dogs are smacking it down.

This is a popular way to treat teeter fears, and for a less-sensitive dog than Quinn, it might have worked. However, each dog needs to be taken into account as an individual; Quinn was not only anxious about teeter noise, but he was also on his way to developing what was later diagnosed as clinical noise phobia. The phobia originally manifested at home when he hid upstairs in a panic whenever Liz went into the kitchen. He hid because he was terrified of the sound of pots and pans being moved about.

There are three major reasons that attempts to "make" Quinn play with a toy near the teeter did not work.

1. Bigger Picture: There was a much bigger picture to consider here than Quinn's instructors simply observing him in class and saying that tugging when the noise occurred would teach him to like the noise. There

was genetic predisposition, Quinn's age (a common age for sensitivities and "quirks" to escalate), and Quinn's history of being exposed beyond his threshold to the teeter's noise at a young age.

2. Pressure: There was too much pressure being put on Quinn to interact with the teeter. The teeter was being made into a "big deal."

3. Misapplication of Learning Theory: Since Quinn was a very high-drive dog that in almost any context (besides being around a teeter) would turn himself inside out to tug or play ball or Frisbee, everybody remained convinced that his love of toys would trump his teeter fears. Actually the opposite started to happen. By the time I worked with Quinn, the sight of a Frisbee in the same yard as the teeter was a signal that he was going to have to interact with the teeter. Therefore, he lost interest in playing with the Frisbee. The connection, Frisbee = teeter, had successfully been made, and it had backfired. Anything that equaled teeter was the enemy. Quinn was losing motivation to play with his favorite toy!

This is a phenomenon that often happens when people attempt to countercondition a dog without simultaneously desensitizing him. Counterconditioning and desensitizing are learning theories that must be thoroughly understood before applying them.

Counterconditioning is meant to change the dog's feelings about a stimulus he finds distressing by pairing that stimulus with something he enjoys. (Every time you see the UPS man, you get a pig's ear!) Desensitization is a gradual process by which the dog is exposed, sub-threshold (below the point at which he will have an adverse reaction), to the stimulus he finds distressing.

When you work above an individual dog's threshold, you are "flooding" the dog. Depending on a dog's temperament and the circumstances, flooding a dog can work. But, in my opinion, there is too much potential for fallout from this technique; and it is stressful on the dog, so I choose not to use it.

Quinn was accidentally being flooded during the process of teaching him that Frisbee or tug equals teeter. That's why it backfired. He was still kept close enough to the teeter that he was having a reaction to the sound and was being exposed above his threshold. As long as he was reacting, he was not in the optimal state to learn what people wanted him to learn. Anxious dogs do not learn well.

Suggestion #2

Put your hand on Quinn's collar, make him go up and down the teeter, and play with him at the end. If he tries to jump off, gently keep him on the teeter and make him keep going so that he learns he can't jump off—he has to do the teeter.

This is a popular form of flooding that I do not like to see happen to dogs with obstacle fears. It certainly was not helping Quinn to "get over it" or "get used to it." Rather, it was reinforcing his belief that the teeter was the worst thing ever to happen to him. Not only that, he was learning not to trust his handler when a teeter was in the picture.

Suggestion #3

Go back to teeter foundation work, such as playing on the wobble board and putting the teeter on the floor. Shape the dog to smack the bottom of it and make it fun. This is a great suggestion, but it didn't work for Quinn. He was totally fearless on the wobble board ever since he was a puppy. I remember him in classes, jumping up and down on the wobble board and tugging with all his might, while thinking he was hot stuff. Quinn's feelings about the wobble board had not changed. He still associated it with fun and tugging. He also had no problem with the teeter when it was collapsed flat on the ground.

It was the noise and the visual picture of other dogs on the teeter (predictors of the noise) that had started the trouble. Exacerbating this was the pressure he had been under consistently to play near it, and on it, and be walked up and down it by people holding his collar. That pressure was turning the teeter experience into an ordeal to survive rather than a fun game to play.

In addition, some well-meaning helpers felt Liz created the problem by showing her anxiety, a gross oversimplification when you step back and examine the various pieces of Quinn's teeter puzzle. Being human, Liz did start feeling some anxiety about Quinn's teeter training. After she saw there was a problem she tried various suggestions that didn't fix the problem. But she didn't cause the problem.

Quinn was a little over a year old at the time I worked with him. Taking Quinn's history and personality into account, Liz and I were able to formulate a plan to help him embrace, rather than fear, the teeter. Since Quinn reacted to the sound, not the movement, we needed to separate that startling banging sound from the rest of the teeter picture. We started the teeter at a low height, hoping to decrease the sound and fury, though ultimately the height was not a concern. We also worked with an outdoor teeter, which made a much softer sound than the one in the noisy training facility. With a padding of blankets and pillows, the teeter made no thudding sound at all. But the teeter still creaked when pressure was put on its pivot joints, so we held the middle of the teeter and controlled the plank's descent to keep it as quiet as possible.

Everyone had focused on the sound, which was in fact the problem, but by doing so had connected the rest of the teeter experience to the sound. We surmised that once Quinn figured out he could operate the teeter without any sound he would then go back to his "normal" self and be enthusiastic about learning and playing. If necessary, we could record an un-muffled teeter sound and go back to the noise issue later, once Quinn had learned to love the silent teeter.

Before bringing Quinn near the teeter I had my Border Collie, Easy, run up and down it. Quinn noticed immediately that it had no sound and I could see him make a huge mental note of that.

When Liz and I stood near the teeter, Quinn would run to a certain spot at the other end of my backyard where he could hide behind a tunnel. I let him do that while he watched Easy play on the teeter. He was intrigued and came out of hiding to watch. He was starting to relax because he wasn't anticipating the sound. There was no sound! Also, seeing a dog on the teeter did not signal the end of the world, as it had before. Again, sound could be added back to the scenario later.

Before coming to my yard, Quinn had gotten to a point in his teeter training where he would tentatively offer touching the bottom of the teeter with his front paws, but he would panic if he felt any pressure to go any higher on the board. Liz had been guiding him up the rest of the way using his collar. Because he would already touch the bottom of the teeter, I did not have to shape him to do so, which saved tons of time.

I warned Liz ahead of time that I was going to allow Quinn to come off the teeter without doing the entire obstacle. She was very concerned that I would be teaching him that he could jump off the teeter whenever he wanted. I explained that we needed to just work on teaching Quinn it was safe to inter-act even a tiny bit with the teeter. There could be no pressure from humans trying to keep him on the obstacle against his wishes. I also explained that release from the pressure of being on the teeter was a tremendous reward we needed to use. This approach seemed very counterintuitive to Liz, but she decided to give it a try.

The instant Quinn put his paws on the bottom of the teeter plank, I clicked and threw his Frisbee. He would catch it and run back to his safe spot on the other side of my yard, behind the tunnel. My instinct told me to run over to that spot and play Frisbee with him there. Access to his safe zone was part of the reinforcement process. The Frisbee, which is what everybody had been concentrating on as the primary reinforcement, was the least potent part of the reinforcement process for Quinn. In fact, my entire teeter plan for Quinn hinged on my feeling that a cue to get off the teeter was the most potent possible reinforcement. Once he learned to enjoy being on the teeter with-out anxiety, his natural enthusiasm and work ethic would shine through and it would be much easier to desensitize him to the sound component.

To recap, the reinforcements at work here were:

- Getting to run away from the teeter
- Getting to play in the safe zone (no pressure from only being allowed to play next to the teeter)
- The Frisbee

Because so much pressure was taken off Quinn—he was not being physi-cally forced to stay on the teeter, he could control how high he went up on it, he could choose to leave, he could return to his safe zone at will—he very quickly started offering a new behavior. Quinn was going a little bit higher up on the teeter plank before jumping off. Although letting him feel empowered was very important, I wanted to cue him to jump off rather than wait for him to jump off. So I read Quinn very carefully and asked him to jump off just before it looked like he was getting ready to jump off on his own. I did this so that I could take full advantage of my favorite dog training principle—the Premack Principle.

The Premack principle tells us that you can reinforce a low-probability behavior (going up the teeter) with access to a high-probability behavior (jumping off the teeter). This takes the conflict out of training and is a very powerful way to change a dog's mind about giving us the low-probability behavior. The hierarchy of motivations starts to shift and the dog begins to get excited about performing the low-probability behavior, while it becomes a predictor of getting to do the high-probability behavior. In Quinn's case, this meant, "Touch the teeter so you can run away from it and play Frisbee in your safe zone."

Quinn needed a customized teeter protocol. In the meantime he should not have been exposed to other puppies in the training facility smacking down the teeter, because every time he heard it, his nervous system got tweaked and his fear heightened.

It can be hard for instructors to provide sensitive dogs with the opportunities they need to succeed in a group class. Here are some things that might have helped Quinn avoid developing teeter fears:

- Take him out of the classroom during teeter training so that he was not exposed to the noise repeatedly when it was over his threshold.

- Give him a break from teeter training and work on foundation behaviors that are fun, without the mental pressure that "you have to learn the teeter now." Don't let a problem make you think that you need to rush to a solution; complete other goals that will build self-confidence before addressing obstacles that your puppy does not feel comfortable approaching.

- Understand that there is no universal way to teach obstacles. Some instructors subscribe to the notion, "This is when puppies learn the teeter, and this is how they learn it, so you have to do it exactly the same." Allow your puppy to learn in his own time and way.

So, every time Quinn took a couple steps up the teeter, I called him off the obstacle and ran with him to the safe zone where we played Frisbee. Then I released him to go do his own thing, put the Frisbee in my pocket, and returned to the teeter. I did not ask Quinn to accompany me, but every time he chose to follow me back to the teeter and touch it. Each time I waited for him to go a little bit farther up the plank before I called him off. This was a very careful balance of raising criteria and getting the timing right so that I could release him from the teeter before he jumped off.

This process didn't take long at all, and suddenly Quinn was offering running up and down the teeter. We made it higher; that did not matter in the least. Then I stopped holding the pivot joint. The creaking bothered him slightly and we could watch the thought process as Quinn decided not to care about it. At that point I decided to experiment. I called Quinn off the teeter and ran to his safe zone with him to play. This time when I put the Frisbee in my pocket and released him to go about his business, I stayed in the safe zone, ignoring him rather than going back to the teeter. I wondered if Quinn would take any steps toward the teeter without me. Liz's jaw dropped as Quinn ran full speed across my yard, ran up the teeter, stopped just before the tip point, and turned his head backward like an owl to make sure that I was watching. I praised him and ran up to the teeter while he waited for me. When I got there he finished the teeter and then I played Frisbee with him near the teeter rather than running with him back to his safe zone.

Taking the pressure off, knowing how to reward the dog, where to reward him, and what to reward him with, were all Quinn needed to jump-start his teeter rehab.

It turned out that Quinn was so pleased with his newfound friend, the teeter, that Liz did not feel the need to make a recording of the noise. He was not worrying about the thud the teeter was making in her backyard when she removed the pillows after two days of short training sessions. He was also using the teeter at the agility club during private lessons, which was the same teeter he'd panicked about before.

There is one final piece that needs to be added to the teeter puzzle: Quinn still needs to be desensitized to the sound of other dogs smacking the teeter in group classes. This will be Liz's next project, so that Quinn can attend group agility classes without feeling distressed when the teeter is being used.

The various elements of Quinn's story remind us that we need to remember to step back from a problem and see the bigger picture for each dog. We need to read each dog and become familiar with his history and personality so that we can know how to meet his needs as an individual rather than falling back on a one-size-fits-all approach. And we need to be ready to be creative when adjusting the training structure to suit a dog's needs.

Zip: The Wilting Border Collie

Zip is a Border Collie about 14 months old that has just started trialing. He is one of my current CU group class dogs. He loves agility and loves his dad. What he does not love is judges or teachers who come up and look directly at him or lean toward him or move near equipment when he is on it. This scared the daylights out of him.

When Zip first came to class he learned all about mat rules and that became the foundation to help him through his pressure sensitivity. He learned that when people approached him while he was on his mat he could "point them out" to dad and get rewarded. He became an expert in the Look at That game. Then I started putting his mat in sequences so that he would do a jump or two and get sent to his mat. Once Zip was there, myself or a helper would walk past the mat, etc. I experimented to figure out how much was too much. If somebody leaned a little too far toward the mat or was just a little too direct with their intention or energy, he would start wilting into the mat. Obviously, it is very important if you use a mat in your training that the dog always feels it is a safe and happy place, so you must make sure you are not "poisoning" the mat the way the teeter got "poisoned" as it did with Quinn.

When he became very good at staying confident while people walked around the course, I removed his mat to make sure he could deal with us without his security blanket. I then put his mat on the contact zone. I spent many class sessions with him teaching him that he could use mat rules from his two-on/two-off contact position any time the scary teacher came up to look at him. In the beginning, he would rush down the A-frame and hit his contact happily. While he was watching his dad for the next cue, he would start wilting when a person started coming up. By "wilting" I mean Zip's ears would go back and down, and his body would look sort of deflated. The worst would be that he would slowly walk off his contact looking sad. It was my mission never to make Zip sad in class so I did everything I could to keep things sub-threshold for him, which was tough.

I had the thought that we could also use release of pressure as reinforcement while he was on the mat. So I incorporated his dad releasing him from the contact as the next phase of his mat rules understanding. Zip would hit his contact and his dad would wait for me to walk up, Zip would orient to me and right back to dad, "pointing out" the scary judge per step three of mat work, and as soon as he did so his dad would mark and release him from the contact, throwing his toy away from me. I wanted Zip to see that he could end this uncomfortable social situation with his own behavior that he, in fact, was in control here.

Zip improved tremendously and began his trialing career successfully—until a judge ran up behind him while he was weaving. This was traumatic and he looked back to see the monster, popping out of the poles as he did so. So when they came back to class I made some Parallel games for Zip to teach him he could stay happily in the poles no matter what.

First I stood a certain distance from the poles while Zip was sitting in front of them waiting for his cue from dad. I had to figure out at what distance I could stand before Zip's ears started drooping. So Zip practiced doing poles with me standing there. I put his mat near the exit so that he could run to it for his reward after. We did that for several repetitions and then I decided to let dad throw the Frisbee when Zip came out of the poles, feeling he had graduated from mat work in that context. Next I moved up the poles, standing at each one from that distance, and then I started standing closer. Zip occasionally would look wilty, and we would backtrack and set things up so he could be successful. I then started walking slowly while Zip did his poles (we started just with six). Next I had to figure out what distance I needed to be from the poles while I was moving. When Zip was okay with that, I decreased the distance. I saw that it would be easier for Zip if I stood at the last pole and started moving when he was finishing, than for me to go to the middle and start moving when he was half done. I put a tunnel near the poles so that he would pick up speed before weaving, and I continued moving while he was in the poles. I also picked up speed until we were both running. Whenever he was ready, I decreased a little distance until I was running as fast as I could right next to the poles with him.

I also made use of an "intermediate bridging stimulus" here. I taught him a sound (a sort of whooshing sound I like to make to encourage dogs to move faster) that began when he started a behavior and continued until he ended the behavior, at which point he got his click and treat. This sound told him to keep doing what he was doing. I taught it to him by throwing his Frisbee and whooshing while he chased it, marking with "yes!" as he caught it. The whooshing lasted as long as the chase behavior lasted. Then I started whooshing as he was in his poles, with his dad throwing his Frisbee as he exited the poles. The whooshing became a familiar, encouraging stimulus that said, "You are doing great. This is a structure you know, i.e. Frisbee at the end of it, keep going!" It was an extra support to help him stay in the poles. It was also something his dad could use in the ring to help Zip keep his confidence as a judge moved closer.

At the end of that lesson (the entire weave Parallel game training was done in a one-hour private lesson) Zip was totally ignoring me and enthusiastically rocking the weave poles, no matter how close I got, even if I ran up behind him.

We continued practicing in this manner and adding other "judges" into the picture. Zip is now looking happy and comfortable at trials and his dad has learned how to watch for signs of stress and how to cheer him up in the trial environment. One thing Zip *loves* to do while walking around trials is offer looking at people for his dad, because he became a Look at That freak. When people approach, Zip helpfully points them out and then everyone tells him he is a smartie.

A year after his CU class, with many successful runs under his belt, Zip took seventh place in the 20" division at the 2011 NADAC Championships. Even with the additional stressors involved in traveling far from home, Zip sailed through all seven of his courses without any anxiety about the strange judge and ring crew. Go team Zip!

We have almost unlimited ways to reinforce our puppies. To use reinforcement wisely we need both perspective and imagination. We need to step back and see the big picture and then figure out how to either adjust our environment, or our training, to make the most of what we've got.

Chapter 11

CONTROL VS. COOPERATION

NILIF ("nothing in life is free") is a well-intentioned idea that has been taken to an extreme by the sport culture. The basic concept of teaching your puppy that he has to earn stuff he wants by behaving politely is a good one. But people have gotten carried away with it, severely limiting all resources and using a lot of environmental deprivation. The thing about this tired old concept we should keep is just that it's important to teach the puppy that "good behavior earns good stuff." Simple as that!

My favorite example of somebody going crazy with this concept is the agility trainer in my area who actually boarded up her windows because she caught her terrier puppy watching a squirrel out the window and she never wanted him to have that chance to "self reward" by enjoying looking out a window again. That is a far cry from the puppy having to sit before he can have his cookie.

So I don't use this term, as I think it's silly (Nothing is free? The agility puppy is still allowed to breathe air on his own). What I do is establish the default behavior and continue strengthening it at the same time I teach the concept of "good behavior earns good stuff" by picking up a primary resource and waiting for the puppy to offer the default behavior. So I have the food bowl at dinnertime and my puppy goes, "She has something I want. How do I communicate to her that I want it? Let's see, what behavior can I do that causes her to respond to me? Oh, I know! Every time I lie down, that seems to work." He lies down and gets his bowl.

Another great way to practice this concept and Off-switch games at the same time is by asking the puppy to let go of his toy, and waiting for his default behavior before giving the toy back.

Note above that I wrote "primary resource." I have a short list of what I need my dogs to ask for under the "good behavior earns good stuff" umbrella. The highest value things for the McDevitt pack would be food, favorite toys, going out the front door (which means we're probably going adventuring), and access to off-leash hiking or swimming. A quick default behavior—sit, down or eye contact—causes me to say my release word. And since "leave it" is a lifestyle for my dogs, behaviors that cause me to say "The Word" are very well rehearsed and joyously offered. That's it. And to me, my dogs' offering of their default behaviors is part of the conversation we have concerning what works for both of us and how our teamwork is fueled by the spirit of cooperation—not, "I control all things and you must obey if you want this Triscuit." Yes, I have toys and bones laying about the house. Oh, and cats walking freely around the house that my dogs can interact with whenever they want. And they all have windows they can see out of!

As an aside here, people get carried away with making their puppy wait for mealtimes, too. They can put way too much pressure on mealtimes by doing prolonged sit and down stays with the bowl on the floor and the person saying, "Stay! Stay!" to a hungry puppy. The puppy *needs* to have a stress-free mealtime without all this pressure. My dogs see me getting food ready and they automatically lie down. They get their food as soon as they down and everybody is happy. They still "asked" for dinner politely and since it was "their" idea I did not have to put any pressure on them by telling them to do an obedience behavior before they ate.

Your Puppy Can Have His Cake and Eat It, Too!

So many people come to me very frustrated and disappointed because their dogs like "stuff." People in the sport culture have been programmed to think that if their dog likes things in the world, they have failed as a trainer—and possibly as a human! I have good news for you. With creative application of the Premack principle, and the foundation training in this book, you can enjoy a cooperative relationship where you get the focus and control you want and your dog gets to satisfy his dogginess. This is a reduction of frustration for both team members.

Back to those people who come to me so upset that their dog likes the world. First of all, since I work with so many dogs that are reactive, it's *nice* to meet well-adjusted dogs that find things in the world they enjoy rather than thinking everything in the environment is a potential problem. So if your puppy thinks the environment is interesting, good! It's not a cause for feeling like a failure if your, say, terrier that was bred to go to ground, actually enjoyed going to ground in the backyard. That doesn't mean you can't teach your terrier to do agility and pay attention to you when asked. But, as with all things, some people take concepts such as controlling the environment to an extreme, so that some dogs find their lives getting smaller and smaller.

Second of all, when people complain to me that their dog likes stuff, I say to them, "Good! The more stuff they like, the more things we have to reward them with!"

We can use the whole world to help us train our puppies! That is a huge paradigm shift for people. Once they start thinking in terms of how can they create a learning structure that makes the world work *for* us not against us, they relax and suddenly training their puppy is a lot more fun! If a puppy sniffs some grass, instead of my student feeling she has failed because the puppy didn't only want to tug with her, we can practice our CU foundation behaviors of leave it, Whiplash Turn, and the come-and-go game. Once the Premack principle has helped us make the grass less of a big deal we can incorporate tugging and play the Give Me a Break game. Tug, tug—"go sniff." Oh, you weren't done tugging? O.K., I guess a little more…

Then both handler and puppy have had a good experience where both team members' needs were met and that dark cloud people carry over their heads about their puppy's "self rewarding" and how that reflects on them, can dissipate and we can see sunny skies ahead. It is all a matter of perspective. So next time your puppy notices something in the world that he finds interesting, if it safe to do so, incorporate it into your training. Don't fall into the trap of making your puppy's world smaller and smaller ("he liked that thing—okay, never let him have access to it, because he can only like what I decided he would like before he was born!") Let your puppy tell you the best ways to train him that honor his personality and his intrinsic likes and dislikes. The world is a big place, let's play in it!

A REWARD SHOULD BE REWARDING TO YOUR PUPPY!

It disturbs me that there is an attitude among many sports trainers that humans always get to be in charge of choosing the reinforcement. Behind this attitude is a message that "I will pick what you like, and you'd better like it." Because of this I have seen people force their puppies to take treats. There are several reasons why a puppy that is working may not want to take treats:

Maybe he is too stressed to eat! If you have a generally food-motivated puppy and he isn't taking treats during a particular training session, take a deep breath, erase thoughts of "he has to take the food because I said so!" and check him for signs of stress.

- Maybe he is in a mind state not conducive to eating. This happens frequently with young Border Collies, in particular. These are the pups that are happy to do the work, but will refuse to take, or will spit out, a treat if you offer it. They would rather have a toy, or just plain continuation of the work, without a "food interruption."

- Maybe it's been a long session and he is getting tired, or fried, or full.

- Maybe he needs a potty break, or to end the session.

- Maybe he feels out of sorts.

- Maybe he doesn't feel like eating.

If you were in the middle of, say, running a marathon, or performing brain surgery, or singing opera, and somebody said what a fabulous job you were doing and offered you a Twinkie, you might say, "I can't eat that right now, I'm busy." Yet if somebody offered you a cup of Gatorade as you passed them during your marathon, you might just find that to be an appropriate "treat" and accept it gratefully. People can get upset over their puppy having an opinion as to what he does or doesn't want. How would you like it if somebody shoved a Twinkie down your throat while you were running your marathon?

Why do people care if their puppy takes treats or not? The main reasons are totally rational and I agree with them:

- It's convenient to use food to train, plain and simple.

- The more tools you have in the toolbox, the better, and personally, food is usually a major tool in my box.

- There are times in training when you do not want to, or flat out cannot, use toy play or access to the environment—which would be my usual non-food reinforcements—to reward your puppy.

- There are times when it makes better training sense to reward your puppy in position, and times when you need to keep your puppy's arousal level in a certain place and a treat would be more appropriate than tugging or something else.

- I'm sure there's another reason. The main point here is that it's good to use treats to train your puppy.

So while I completely agree that it's wonderful if your puppy likes treats, I hate to see people literally stick treats into their puppy's mouths and make them eat it. I thought the word "treat" suggested some kind of nice thing that the puppy would enjoy, not something we have to stick down his throat when he would rather have something else. To me, the act of forcing a puppy to eat when he doesn't want to is an act of aggression. Imagine doing that to a child instead of a puppy. My grandmother once forced me to swallow a lot of whole sardines, with the eyes and tail. It was traumatic because I associated them with my pet goldfish and I was extremely agitated while having to swallow them. Because of the traumatic nature of the experience I haven't eaten seafood for more than 30 years.

So what are you supposed to do if your puppy doesn't want to take a treat, and your friends or teachers are fussing at you that you have to make him eat it?

I suggest you prevent that peer pressure from happening in the first place. You can do this in two ways:

1. If you have a puppy that prefers toys or environmental rewards, such as access to social activity or exploration, use the Premack principle.

2. Teach your puppy that his treat predicts the toy play or "go" cue that we discussed in Chapter 7. This will raise the value of the treat as it becomes paired with doing an activity that your puppy loves. Get him used to a pattern of treats-toy play-treats-toy play so that he can easily switch from one to the other.

When Easy was a puppy he didn't want to take treats when he was in toy mode. Different parts of the brain are being engaged here and it is not an easy thing for dogs to learn to switch from instinctive to operant states. (I do not have the current neuroscience terminology for this. But suffice to say, it's ridiculous to get upset with your puppy because his normal brain function isn't following your training agenda.) It was hard for him to take a treat from my hand if I was holding his toy in my other hand, so I would put his toy on the table and give him a treat a few steps away from the table. I just had to figure out the right distance between him and the toy to help him get into a mental space where taking a treat seemed like a good idea. Then I would play with him, put the toy back on the table, and start over. We worked up to his taking a treat from my hand while I held the toy, and then worked up to switching between taking a treat and tugging.

This process took a while. That's fine. Training your puppy can take a while. I also wanted to raise the value of tennis balls, since Easy liked tugging best but I sometimes want to roll a ball as a reward instead of tugging to do distance training. So, he learned to switch between a ball and his tug.

This process should also be fun and you should approach it with an attitude of, "there are so many fun things in the world for you to try!" not, "I said you have to like this, so you have to like it."

After I was successful at putting equal value on various toys, I took a step back from training and thought, "I can just as easily throw a tug toy as I can throw a ball, and often I just leave the toy out in the field to direct him to rather than throwing it anyway. So why did I just spend all that time doing this when I could have been doing something else?" The treat/toy switching was important to me, but the toy/toy, in retrospect, started making me question how much control I needed over choice of reinforcement; it's an issue of where you choose to draw your line.

I once had a student whose puppy was too stressed to tug in a class I was teaching. He would accept treats, and he was learning the exercises well. I was happy with his performance and knew that we'd get him to a comfort level where he would enjoy tugging in class, since he liked it at home.

I kept in mind the dictum that play behaviors get dampened by stress, and focused on continuing to decrease that puppy's stress in class so that his natural play behavior would come out, rather than trying to "make" him play when he didn't feel like it. To me, his being able to take treats and learn well in class said that he was on the road to being just where his handler wanted him to be. But, she couldn't enjoy him for where he was in his process because people had told her that her puppy should be able to tug anywhere, anytime. He wasn't ready for that, but he was doing very well.

I don't see the need for these extreme ideas; I am not an extremist except when it comes to using positive reinforcement. My puppy raising and training is about balance and cooperation, so I just don't see the point of these extreme statements of "your puppy has to… no matter what… or he won't be able to do agility later!" I have heard some really ridiculous ones. This particular student's puppy got comfortable enough in class to start playing with his ball. I was thrilled at his continued progress, but the student was still upset he wasn't tugging. They got to a point where the puppy was tugging on his ball. I knew he would be tugging on a tug toy soon enough. I was pleased that he felt comfortable enough to play, because he'd been a little dog-reactive and we had to help him work through that. The fact that his confidence had increased in class to the point where he could play, was a good thing.

This student took a private agility lesson and came back even more upset. The teacher had lectured her that it wasn't "good enough" that the puppy was tugging on a ball, he had to be tugging on a long fleece or it didn't count. The student continued to be frustrated with her puppy, while I kept saying, "But look how well he's doing!" We were looking at two different puppies.

In the end it's all about how you choose to parent your puppy.

You can learn to read your puppy well, so that you don't put him in a situation where he will refuse to take a treat during training. Get to know how many breaks he needs; what displacement behaviors does he display when he's stressed, etc. I can always tell the most appropriate reinforcement for a dog in the moment, because I am hyper-focused on his body language, his energy, and the messages he is sending, as well as the training environment and its limitations. Become hyper-focused on your puppy and you will always know the right thing to do for him in the moment, to meet his needs.

LEARN TO LAUGH IT OFF

If your puppy does something you don't like during training, remind yourself that he's a puppy! And it's just dog training, not world peace! If your friends are judging your puppy because he doesn't live up to their concept of the imaginary perfect sport puppy, laugh that off, too. Remind them as well as yourself that it's just training! It's just behavior! The world isn't ending, and whatever doesn't go exactly how you wanted it to during training, is just more information for you so that you can set up a better experience for both you and your puppy next time. Lighten up!

Chapter 12

ATTENTION IS JUST ANOTHER BEHAVIOR

© DIANE LEWIS PHOTOGRAPHY

When peoples' future performance star has a difficult time paying attention around distractions in class, or in the world, a lot of judgment about their lack of relationship gets handed down.

Of course, relationship is the most important thing here. To me, the whole point of animal training in the first place is to cultivate a relationship with an animal. And yes, the better your relationship with your puppy, the easier they will be to train.

What does relationship actually mean? It has become such an emotionally loaded term in the sport culture and I think it gets overused as a blame Band-Aid to cover a range of training issues. Your dog didn't do x correctly? You have a bad relationship.

To me, "relationship" just means the state of relating between two beings.

If you are relating well to your puppy, you will have empathy for his situation. For example, perhaps he is thinking, "It's hard to pay attention in this loud, smelly place while other puppies are tugging next to me!" You know his personality, what kind of day he's having, what training structure works best for him, how many breaks he needs, his rate of reinforcement, how much balancing of arousal and calm behaviors he needs to be at his optimal state to learn, etc.

If he is relating to you, he understands what you are asking him to do, he is reading you well, and he is getting important information from you about what's working, what's not working, and what the rule structure is here.

Some puppies are going to get distracted. As the environmental criteria get harder, the puppy may have a harder time processing that and staying focused. I don't think always pointing the relationship finger and making a judgment is the most constructive or accurate way of looking at this issue. I don't think if you take your puppy to a new class and he wants to play with another puppy, it automatically means you have a bad relationship with him. Relationships are fluid and they are about knowing the right conversation to have with your puppy, and when. However, I do know a lot of instructors that go straight to "it's a relationship problem" and I get a lot of disheartened students coming to me feeling they have failed.

I remember one student who got her Border Collie puppy for flyball and spent huge portions of her day playing tug games with him. The first night of puppy kindergarten he was so turned on by all the other puppies running and playing during free time that he did not come to her to tug. The instructor, knowing he was being raised for flyball, actually yelled at her in front of the class, saying, "Your puppy wants to run with the other puppies instead of tugging! Haven't you been tugging with him at home?" First of all, playing the tug games at home doesn't necessarily mean that when you raise criteria by asking for the same games outside of home your puppy will get it right the first time, so that response was illogical. Second of all, because this puppy was supposed to play flyball when he grew up, he was being treated vastly differently from the other puppies in that class that were being allowed to socialize and whose owners were not publicly shamed if their puppies got distracted.

Just because that puppy, a naturally ball-crazy and fast Border Collie that would have no problem as an adult running over four jumps, getting his ball and bringing it back quickly, was going to play flyball in the future, an unnecessary double standard was being employed here.

That puppy needed to experience the same puppy kindergarten setting the other puppies were experiencing—some training, some breaks, some free time. He was a bit fearful of other puppies and had already had some very loud reactive behavior to big adult dogs.

Puppy class for him could have been very helpful in terms of learning about interactive play with other puppies and learning to work near them calmly and confidently, but his owner became so anxious about the tugging that she used the class just to work on tugging near other puppies. She was distraught that she had a bad relationship with her puppy because that first night of class he noticed other puppies. In reality, she had a good relationship with her puppy when she wasn't being anxious about what other people in her club might say about her. She had a lot of empathy, knew his personality well, and could read him well enough to be able to easily predict what he was ready to give in class. And he, being a fearful puppy who was very bright and very bonded to her, spent a lot of time reading her and taking his social cues from her (she seems happy that this puppy is running up to us... I guess it's safe).

The lack of tugging wasn't about their relationship: it was a criteria issue. Also, remember that in times of stress, play behavior flies out the window. This was a puppy who was concerned about dogs. Perhaps seeing a bunch of young dogs running around playing in a small, enclosed space for the first time dampened his playfulness. Again, that wouldn't be about how much he respects his human but about a puppy telling us that he needs to learn how to be comfortable in a puppy class environment. Yet both these issues got lumped into the "bad relationship" box.

It's Time to De-emotionalize Attention or Focus

Attention is just another behavior, like a sit or down. You could say that there are certain behaviors associated with paying attention, such as orienting to the handler, which is a behavior that you can reinforce. The puppy learns attention first without distractions, and then you keep raising criteria until he can pay attention anywhere, just like you naturally taught him to sit or lie down and then helped him generalize that to a variety of places.

If you look at attention as just another behavior, like sitting, it will neutralize all the judgment that sport puppy parents sometimes feel when their puppy's behavior tells them that the training structure needs to be adjusted. Then, instead of pointing fingers, our well-meaning fellow club members and teachers could support people as they figured out the various pieces of the puzzle that would allow their puppy to have performance success.

Chapter 13

REASSURANCE-SEEKING BEHAVIOR

©DIANE LEWIS PHOTOGRAPHY

One punishment I sometimes see agility handlers use when dogs or puppies run toward people during training is to have the person they are running to stamp their feet or do something aversive to scare the puppy. This is beyond inappropriate. Other people simply stand still and ignore the puppy; this is a much more reasonable response, but even then I have seen some puppies that are socially sensitive get worried about people because they aren't acting "normal." Some people will stand rigidly and make a point of ignoring, rather than just continuing to do whatever it is they were doing when the puppy approached them. It isn't necessary to freeze up, if you're going to simply not respond to a loose puppy, be neutral not weird.

Easy was shy about certain people when he was little, and he could be reactive, barking at them uncertainly then hopping backwards in fear. Once, at our club, he went up to say hello to somebody—and I was pleased with his initiative. That person assumed I would not want him socializing with anybody at our club, because he should only be interactive with me, so they stood still and ignored him. I watched his body language go from cautious-friendly to fearful. I saw he was going to start his barking and hopping backward sequence so I called him back to me, never wanting him to practice being reactive to people. Easy ran back to me, and I felt he looked relieved at leaving a social situation he was uncertain about. My calling him was less of a recall cue and more of a reminder that he had the power to leave disturbing situations rather than getting "stuck" in them and reacting.

It was that experience that made me start looking more carefully at dogs' body language when they are being ignored. I am not talking about handlers' choosing not to respond to their own dogs in situations where they remove attention to show the puppy that an attention-seeking behavior such as barking at you because he wants something from you does not work. I am talking about strangers behaving in a way that could be perceived as "abnormal" by not responding in the typical socially appropriate manner. So, once again, my point here is to adjust for each puppy. For many puppies, neutral nonresponsive people just standing there talking to other people will not be traumatic! But to get around this potentially stressing out a sensitive puppy, I think a good general rule is just to ask people to calmly return the puppy to his handler.

Of course the puppy shouldn't be given an opportunity to run off during training, but when doing off-leash training it can happen. So you should have a plan of action everyone agrees on just in case.

I have taken agility classes where people asked me to clap, stomp at or yell at their dog if he left the course and wandered near me, or came over to me, and I refuse. I have seen many dogs get stressed and scared, understandably, when people start behaving so inappropriately. Those dogs are just learning that agility is stressful and strangers are potentially threatening. I have even seen people smack jump bars on the ground near the dog the way a shepherd might smack their crook. Do we really want our dogs to think jump bars are punishing? I will happily clip a leash on the dog and return him to his person, if asked to. But I won't abuse somebody else's dog just because that person asks.

I was told once that the point is to teach a dog that the only good thing in class is the handler and that everything else is negative or scary. That way, the dog will only want to be with his handler. For reactive or sensitive dogs, or for puppies still learning about how the social world works, this is an extremely harmful way of thinking. We want our dogs to be behaviorally healthy *and* be good performance dogs. Believe me, unless our dog is totally bombproof, if we subject him to training techniques that teach him to worry about people, other dogs, the environment, anything that isn't "mommy," we are going to have problems with the dog later in his performance career (and why subject a bombproof dog to this just because you may get away with it?) A dog worried about potential trouble with the world cannot give you 100% of his mind and energy to work!

Some puppies or dogs run up to people because they are uncertain about them and need to check them out rather than because they want to say hello. This is a very important distinction most people don't pick up on. Very often when people bring dogs to me that are thought to be too "friendly" because they run away on course to visit ring crew or judges, the dogs are actually going up to those people out of stress, social anxiety, and uncertainty about the situation. This is attention-seeking, or reassurance-seeking, behavior and we put a stop to it by lowering the stress level and giving the dog clear and timely feedback. There are two reasons for this behavior.

Do You Know What's Going On?

Many green dogs, or puppies that aren't exactly sure what their handler is asking of them, will go ask the nearest person for more information. They aren't getting it from their handler, who is either not fast enough with her feedback, or stressed herself, or maybe even annoyed with the dog for not getting something right—so the dog finds somebody else who may be able to explain better what is going on.

There was one time in a handling skills class, when Easy was about a year old, when I couldn't get the handling of a particular sequence of jumps down right. It was a bit over my skill level and I struggled with where and when I was putting my cues. Easy, as always, tried to get it right but we kept repeating the sequence and I kept getting it wrong. As I grew increasingly frustrated, Easy saw my stress and saw that I wasn't going to be able to help him get the information he needed about how to handle this social situation. I wanted to get that sequence right and was concerned with how I looked to the teacher and to the class.

I should have asked if the sequence could be adjusted or broken into smaller pieces so that I could handle it right for once, which in turn would mean Easy could run it right. Or I should have just pretended it was right, had a party for Easy, and asked to be excused—but I was stuck in "good student mode" where I just repeated the exercise as told without thinking about the effect it was having.

I forgot that Easy, as a sensitive dog that always looks to me for information about the world, and that absolutely hates to be wrong or think anything is out of place, would pick up on my stress and have a bad class experience because of my behavior. He reminded me of this by leaving the course and walking over to a person standing observing us. His body language was submissive, he was low and wiggly; the same posture he'd have if he thought he was in trouble. When he greets somebody out of joy he looks quite different—he squeaks and hops and kisses, his tail is up and he looks electrified. Of course, that person, and everyone else, then felt that Easy was misbehaving by leaving me and visiting somebody.

I knew perfectly well, however, that Easy was seeking reassurance from that person because he couldn't get the necessary information from me. He knew something was wrong, and he knew I was upset. I called him and he came back and I played with him and stopped trying that sequence. He never left me in class again, and I never left him either. What I did with my behavior in that class was to leave my dog even though physically I was still beside him. Because of my stress I disconnected and was not present for him when he needed me. How could I blame him for hoping a nearby person would save him from a weird situation that I was causing?

ARE YOU A PROBLEM?

A lot of dogs and puppies that aren't totally certain about people, or may be very confident with people in general but get concerned in novel social contexts, will go up to people to ask if they are a problem. This could be, for instance, on the puppy's first time working loose in group class, a stranger walks into class and stands in the corner to watch. These dogs don't want a fight but need more information because they think there might be a threat.

Reactive behavior—rushing toward, barking at, or growling at something in an adrenalized and panicky way—is information-seeking behavior designed to determine the level of threat from something or someone the dog feels concerned about. Running over to check somebody out because of uncertainty about them is just another point on the same continuum.

This behavior needs to be addressed by teaching the puppy he is safe so that he doesn't have to put his energy into anything but enjoying training.

The Look at That game is a favorite tool with CU students because it creates a rule structure that "normalizes" seeing novel or unknown things for your dog; making the unknown stimulus itself the cue for a reliable, fun game the dog can play with his handler. Think of all your classroom experience as box work (Chapter 31).

So feel confident and don't worry! Be fair and don't overdo it or ask for too much. Let your puppy set the pace on this journey of teaching the behavior of attention.

Chapter 14

TARGETING

I n *Control Unleashed*® I wrote that much of life is about targeting. I've had a few years to re-evaluate this statement and I am happy to report I still think it's true.

Targeting teaches us about how to interact with our environment. For example, driving a car is a series of targeting behaviors; from pushing the gas pedal to putting the car in drive, to turning the wheel, to pushing the controls for the A/C and the radio. Agility is about targeting, too. Dogs are either targeting their handler (handler focus) or targeting an obstacle (obstacle focus).

Targeting demands two things: a certain level of *attention* so that you can connect with the object you are targeting, and the *understanding* of what your target behavior is (push the gas pedal vs. keep back feet on a contact vs. put your entire body on a mat). For our purposes, targeting is going to help our puppies build their handler focus in very distracting environments, such as class, and later, trials. Here are some ways targeting works behind the scenes in CU games:

- **Reorienting (Chapter 23):** The first target behavior a CU puppy learns is "reorienting." The puppy uses her handler as a visual target in a distracting environment. Handler targeting is a traditional way of teaching focus, too (think heel position and eye contact!)

- **Mat work (Chapter 27):** The mat is a just a big old target.

- **Look at That! game (Chapter 26):** An orienting game where the dog is either visually targeting her handler or something in the environment that the handler has cued him to orient to.

- **Leave it (Chapter 24):** You can even think of leave-it games, including Doggie Zen, as a target trick. Leave it asks the dog to disengage from one target and engage with another (drop the squirrel, make eye contact with mommy).

Since becoming a student of Buddhist meditation a couple of years ago, I have been very struck by the similarities between what I teach and meditation. Both are about refining your skills of focus and relaxation so that you can find your optimal mental state. Both are about finding the space to meet any environmental stressor or distraction with equanimity and keep your balance. Both are about making a lifestyle out of cultivating non-reactivity.

And, meditation has everything to do with targeting! For example, if you are focusing on the ins and outs of your breathing instead of on the pain in your neck or the gossip du jour at your dog club, then you are target training yourself using your breath as the target. When you are successful at this, your relaxation skills will improve along with your focusing skills. You will still have passing sensations and thoughts but you will not be reactive to them. You will take them less personally, and give yourself the mind space to let go.

Similarly, your puppy can learn that, yes, stuff is out there but he does not have to react to it by noticing it, worrying about it, getting excited by it, barking at it, sniffing it, playing with it, or hiding from it. Your cue, whether it is "leave it" or "look at that" or whatever, will function for him the way the bell that starts a meditation session functions for me. That bell is my focus cue.

TEACHING A TARGET BEHAVIOR

A simple, quick way of teaching your puppy the concept of targeting is to teach a hand or finger target. I start this by holding up a fist with a treat in it and presenting the flat palm of my other hand next to the fist. And, here is the connection between leave it and targeting: in order to get the fist to open and give up the treat, the puppy has to leave the fist alone and touch the empty hand instead. Not all puppy/handler interaction has to involve the puppy looking at you; the puppy touching you is a powerful connector as well.

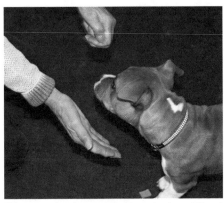 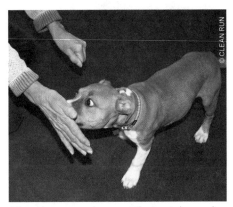

This puppy has learned that in order to get the closed hand to open and present the treat, he needs to target the open hand.

You will need to decide your target behavior criteria: the puppy gently putting his nose on my hand, with mouth closed, is what I click my puppies for. If your puppy is excited about this exercise and you click when his mouth is open touching your hand a number of times, that is how he is going to learn to target.

Once your puppy gets the idea, raise criteria by moving your empty hand around and asking these questions. Can your puppy touch:

- A hand held out to the side?

- A hand over his head?

- A hand under his head?

- A hand that moves, so that the puppy must follow a short distance in order to successfully touch it?

Once the puppy understands he can follow the target hand, you can use this behavior for all kinds of fun stuff: heeling, spinning, and other tricks as well as distance work and leave-it games. You can even teach retrieve to hand and drop it as part of the hand target repertoire, as illustrated in the following story.

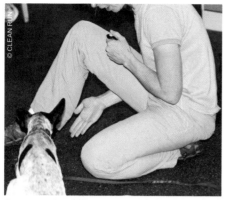

Once your dog understands to target your hand, you can start presenting your hand in different positions and even use it to get other behaviors, such as going under your leg.

A friend's Belgian Sheepdog was having a hard time holding the dumbbell until my friend could take it. When my friend reached her hand out, the dog would drop the dumbbell prematurely. I reframed this exercise to my friend as a variation of a hand target exercise, since that was a behavior her Belgian already knew quite well. My friend asked her dog to "touch" her hand, while he was still holding his dumbbell. Dutifully, he touched her hand and in the process it was very easy to take the dumbbell. I described this exercise as asking the dog to hand target with an intermediate object rather than his mouth.

You can easily shape your puppy to pick up an object using touch as the basic behavior. If you stop clicking just the nose touch, your puppy will start trying other behaviors, including opening his mouth near or on the toy. You can also teach greeting behaviors using hand targeting for puppies that are either shy or overly excited to meet people. Having the visitor stand neutrally with their hand out, while you give your target cue, will put your puppy in a familiar and safe structure of interaction.

If your puppy is hand-shy, then teaching a hand target is important. Well-meaning people will approach your puppy, stick their hands out, and try to touch him. If your puppy learns that a hand reaching toward him is just another target cue, and that he can "work the system" by putting his nose to the hand to make a treat happen, he can view the rude stranger as a fun slot-machine game.

Once your puppy understands this basic behavior, it is very easy to transfer it onto other objects. You can hold an object in your hand and give your touch cue.

It is up to you whether you use a different cue for touching an object than you do for touching your hand; I tend to use the same cue.

After your puppy has put his nose on it several times (with you treating him each time) you can put that object on the floor right under him and wait for him to touch it on the floor. Even if he just lowers his head toward it at first, that is clickable. An alternative is just to put an object on the floor, sit back and shape your puppy to move toward the object and then touch it.

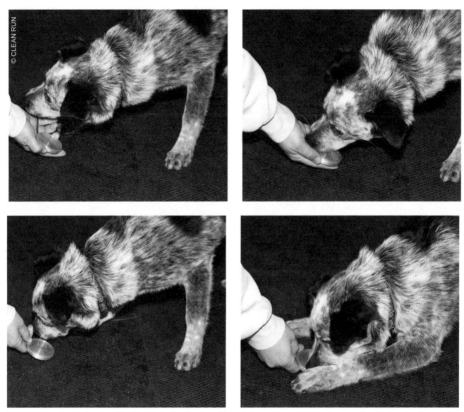

Here we are transferring the touch behavior to a Touch It device. Initially the handler holds the Touch It in her hand. With successful touches to the device, she starts moving it closer and closer to the floor.

SECTION III

KEY CONCEPTS

Chapter 15

DEFAULT BEHAVIORS

© DIANE LEWIS PHOTOGRAPHY

The default behavior is the first behavior your puppy will try in order to make something happen.

Let's say you have a very vocal puppy and he wants you to hand over his toy, so he barks. Building a strong default behavior, such as a sit or down, gives the puppy a tool he can use to communicate that will work for both of you, and it is the very first step toward learning self-control. It also starts teaching him about availability; resources are available to defaulting puppies but not to unruly, delinquent puppies.

When your puppy is excited, or confused, or he needs something, he can learn to trade an instinctive behavior for an operant one. For example, the first time Rumor saw sheep he instantly got very high. His instinct at that time would have been to run like a bat out of hell toward the sheep, dragging me with him if I didn't drop the leash.

However, what he did instead was sit. He did this because from the age of eight weeks, that default behavior was instilled. It was so strong that as a teenager seeing his first flock of sheep he automatically sat even though he was as excited as I'd ever seen him. Sheep are only available to a sitting Tervuren.

How Do We Build a Default Behavior?

Now that we have discussed the why, it's time to discuss the how.

To instill a strong default behavior, I just build up the reinforcement history with that behavior. When you reward a behavior, say sitting, frequently, your puppy will start offering the behavior to you when you haven't asked for it, to see if it still "works" when he doesn't hear the cue. Reward the sitting even when you haven't asked for it. (Remember these are *default* training instructions, not general training instructions). Then, to further get your message across, start waiting to give access to the "big guns" resources until the puppy has offered sitting to you—a favorite toy, a food dish, the door to the backyard, another puppy to play with—your puppy can learn that *he makes access to those things happen with his own behavior.* The default is his way of communicating with you about what he wants, in a manner that works for both of you (as opposed to his barking, or stealing, or chasing, or whatever). This is also the way my own puppies learn to ask to be let outside during their housetraining; it's a no-brainer to them to sit near the door when they want out because they learn immediately that the sitting request works to get my attention and response. My only job is to notice and let them out when they ask. Default behavior is such a convenient form of dialogue!

The default does not need to be a sit; actually I let the dogs pick for themselves which one they want to use. I prefer sits, downs, or eye contact. Many conformation dogs default to stacking (how they are taught to stand for the judge's exam at shows). The default behavior can be anything you would like it to be! Once your puppy is defaulting reliably in contexts where he wants something from you, watch him start generalizing. He may sit in front of another puppy he wants to meet, or sit when he sees sheep or his teacher in puppy class. When he starts trying that out, you will know he is getting it. Praise him for that and give him access to what he wanted as much as possible. Start adding default behavior into off- switch games; when you stop tugging, or running, stand still and wait for the default behavior before you start up again. Just remember that *default behavior is not cued!* It is the first behavior the puppy tries when he wants something—or, when he isn't sure about what to do. He will give his default when he isn't sure about what to do, because he trusts that behavior will work to get your attention and response. So it is his way of asking for information about the situation.

You can add biofeedback (Chapter 17) into default behavior. You can use it when the puppy has defaulted during an Off-switch game, to deepen his level of calm before releasing him to keep playing—you'd just ask him to take a breath, etc., after he gave the default behavior. Or you can make it part of the default, period. My Pit Bull mix used to default to sit/eye contact/take a breath. It was strongly programmed in there, to help him relax.

DEFAULT BEHAVIORS FOR SELF-CONTROL

The stronger the default behavior, the more your puppy will be able to substitute it for a behavior that you really don't appreciate. My favorite example of this is Rumor's butt-nipping proclivities.

Ru had some dogs in his recent bloodline, including his mother, who loved to sneak up behind people and nip them on the butt. Ru showed this tendency early on. Because I raised him with the default behavior concept, Ru was able to substitute sitting for going after me when I turned my back. I incorporated turning and presenting my back as part of an Off-switch game. We would run around together and I would randomly stop and wait for his sit before starting again. I would invite him verbally to start moving again even though I didn't cue the sit. Sometimes I would run away from him after inviting him (probably something like "come on!" or "let's go!" or even just "O.K.") and just as he was catching up to my backside I would turn around and he would automatically sit. I knew the butt nipping was an aroused herding dog thing, and I wanted him to have the tools to think through it.

I remember a friend once showed me how she handled the butt nipping with Ru's half brother. She would be standing talking to me and the half brother would creep up behind and nip her. She would then turn around and make her body language very intimidating; she would tower over him, making eye contact, grab him by the scruff, and tell him "no." He would appease her by getting low and wiggly and slinking off, so she thought he was learning not to nip. But the fact she had to keep repeating this ritual showed that he was really not learning that at all—he was just learning that if he acted submissive while she was being physically threatening, he could leave the situation. He wasn't learning to control his impulse to bite her butt, and he wasn't learning he could do something else that got rewarded instead.

I knew that certain social contexts triggered butt-nipping desires in Ru so I made sure he practiced his default behavior in those contexts. A major one was my walking briskly through the hallway to the back door to let the dogs out—while all the dogs are super excited about going outside. The excitement could put him into overdrive in that situation. I could have managed it by leashing him, but I wanted him to learn to "leash" himself, so to speak. So I just kept that eye in the back of my head open (and I listened for intensified panting, always a giveaway with him since he is a big excitement panter) and, if I sensed Ru was coming up behind me, I stopped moving and turned my head. Ru would sit and then I'd continue walking. Ru learned to do this in the midst of the other dogs rushing to the door. It was his behavior of sitting that caused me to keep going to the door, which is ultimately what he wanted much more than nipping. The nipping was a symptom, not a goal.

Ru also really loved a terry cloth bathrobe I had and wanted to hold on and hang from it. So I would put on the bathrobe and initiate an Off-switch game. I would make the hem of the bathrobe move a short distance from him and he would sit. I would give him a cookie and make the bathrobe move again, building up to running around with him while wearing it. If he started orienting toward the bathrobe, I immediately stopped running and stood still, waiting for him to sit. I don't remember him grabbing it, but if he had I would have either just taken it off and walked away, or held onto it so that he could not tug while I waited for him to settle down. Then I would have lowered my criteria, making the training session easier.

What I *did* do was turn the belt of this bathrobe into a tug toy, cueing him to tug on it during our Off-switch games. He already had learned that when I stop tugging/stand still, he should drop and sit. So I used Premack here and taught him that if he did a default sit instead of going into stalk, chase, grab, bite, and kill my bathrobe mode, I would then give him access to killing a part of my bathrobe. I have done a similar thing with tons of puppies that grab scarves, skirt hems, etc. Puppies seem to prefer doing this when their people are walking down the stairs. I don't let them tug on the clothing like I did with Ru, and it's not something I would tell every student to do—I just start moving the items around as part of an Off-switch game, treating the puppy for sitting. The connections to leave it here are obvious.

In my original book, I wrote about the problem of dogs nipping their handlers on the agility course. Teaching a default behavior and playing Off-switch games early on will give you tools to prevent that from becoming a problem. Your puppy will be desensitized to certain movements, items of clothing, etc., and he will learn to regulate his arousal better. Dogs nipping on course tend to have a low-frustration threshold and a low-arousal threshold—they get excited and frustrated quickly and then they need an outlet for it, like your leg. These dogs may need you to improve your handling skills so that you can give them clearer information faster about where to go and the right path to get there. Giving correct feedback will reduce the frustration; Off-switch games and default behavior will teach the dogs to calm down when aroused and reconnect with you instead of reacting.

Sometimes I put mats down on a course and work a dog with these low thresholds through two or three obstacles, then send the dog to a mat, ask for him to take a breath, and maybe play Doggie Zen (Chapter 24) with a toy. I want to make sure the dog is able to stay on the mat calmly breathing and looking away from his toy (not mauling his handler for it, as many "before" dogs do when they first come to my CU class) before I release the dog to take the next few obstacles. I also want their handlers to start seeing body language that predicts these dogs are going to bark, bite, or get the zoomies so that they can help the dogs settle before they pass that point.

Chapter 16

AVAILABILITY

A ll of the exercises in this book will teach your puppy about the all-important concept of availability, as well as about building a great relationship
with you. And, your puppy won't even realize it's "work" to become reliable
around distractions when he's loose because he'll be having too much fun.
Always keep this concept in mind while reading this book. When your puppy
understands how to read what is and is not available in the environment, dependent on your cues, you will have zero attention problems. Seriously!

What is leave-it training if not a discussion about what the available resources
are? From the dawn of time, dogs have learned to survive by interpreting information from the environment about which resources come with a "help yourself"
sign attached. I used to tell my students that leave-it training and this discussion
of availability was counterintuitive to dogs because in a natural environment, if
they saw a treat on the ground, they would just eat it. By asking them to leave it

alone we were asking them to do the opposite of what was "normal" to them. I told them this as part of my effort to teach my human students to be patient and forgiving when training.

But now I think that leave-it training isn't all that counterintuitive. Wild dogs need to be able to read the environment to know when it's safe to eat what. We are part of the environment, never separate from it. In that sense we are translators, helping our dogs make sense of the rules of our human-oriented world.

I can find a connection to this concept in pretty much every game in this book. Here are some:

- **Leave it:** When you teach leave it (Chapter 24), you are once again driving the point home that some resources are green-lighted and some are red-lighted; and, that red-lighted resources can sometimes become available, depending on your cue. That is where the all-encompassing Premack principle comes into play: if you have asked your puppy to leave his toy alone and he has turned away from it and oriented to you, you may choose to release him and send him to get his toy. Giving access to what is already in the environment strengthens the leave-it training beautifully.

- **Whiplash Turn:** When you teach the Whiplash Turn (Chapter 25), you are teaching your puppy to turn his head away from whatever is drawing him, and to turn toward you instead.

- **Look at That! game:** When you teach the Look at That game! (Chapter 26), you are giving your dog information about what degree of availability a thing has: he can look at something, but he can't interact with it.

- **Mat work:** When you are going through your mat work (Chapter 27) steps, your puppy is learning that, when he is on the mat and people and dogs approach, those people and dogs are just more environmental information and a treat is coming his way. Or, if somebody did jumping jacks with a tug toy near the mat that could mean a treat is available to a puppy on his mat.

- **Off-switch games:** Availability is part of Off-switch games (Chapter 28) as well; once you have stopped the stimulating interaction, your puppy must calm himself in order to make that particular stimulation available to him again.

- **Give Me a Break game:** If you are using the Give Me a Break game (Chapter 29) to build drive to tug or to go to a mat or to do a piece of equipment, when you release your puppy to take her break, you will be bringing the toy, mat or piece of equipment (when possible) back to your chair. Those resources are not available until your puppy "asks" for them by coming up to your chair.

- **Parallel games:** In all the Parallel games (Chapter 30), as well as box work, your puppy will be learning that stuff happening outside his box or on the other side of his gate (dogs running, etc.) is not available for interaction or exploration.

Thinking about this thread of availability will help you understand how all of the exercises in this book are connected. It will help you understand that this book will teach you how to have a discussion with your dog about the environment in a way that will work for both of you.

Once you start thinking about this concept you will see its relevance in other contexts in your dog's life. Three examples that come to mind in the ordinary daily life of your puppy are:

- Greeting houseguests (guests should be available to calm puppies, unavailable to puppies that are jumping or flailing around)

- Taking turns, if you have a multi-dog household ("your brother's treat is not available to you, but this one is!")

- Trading or redirecting, especially if you have kids ("veterinarian Barbie is not available to you, but this lovely fuzzy hedgehog is!")

By thinking along these lines, you will start seeing how important these leave-it skills are for successfully operating in the mundane world.

Chapter 17

BIOFEEDBACK

"Heart rate, attentiveness and respiratory rate are all linked. If we can teach a human or a dog to take slower, deeper breaths, they relax, their heart rate decreases, and they can be more attentive to focusing on the task at hand. These responses are all coupled to changes in hormonal and other chemical signals that shift the brain's and body's reactivity from a system ready to act on a threat to one ready to focus on learning." —Dr. Karen Overall

This is when people start looking at me funny, because it's such a foreign concept to dog training. *But it shouldn't be!* I learned this concept from my mentor, veterinary behaviorist Dr. Karen Overall. Biofeedback training enables us to access a dog's nervous system "from the outside in." I believe in this concept so strongly that I spent several years going to weekly biofeedback sessions myself as part of my personal program to overcome my anxiety. If you ever go see me give a seminar, biofeedback training had a lot to do with my ability to give that seminar, from leaving my dogs to flying on the plane to speaking in public. I was hooked up to a machine that read my brain waves and let me know when I was in the optimal zone—a state described as both relaxed and alert—so that I could basically clicker train my own brain to return to that zone when it started wandering into a more reactive zone. You can't hook your puppy up to a machine and tell him to click himself—yet, anyway—but you can achieve a similar result by putting on cue behaviors classically associated with relaxing and being in a receptive, rather than reactive, state.

This is important to grasp. Your brain can be in a receptive or a reactive state, and so can your puppy's. But it can't be in both states of mind at once—they don't mix. Which state you're in will directly affect how well you absorb information and how well you learn, and how you respond to stuff and how you behave. Would you rather your neurosurgeon operate on you in a receptive or reactive state? Would you rather your dog enter the ring on what could be your MACH run in a receptive or reactive state?

Biofeedback will help your puppy be in a receptive state during training. Like mat work, it can provide an awesome "reset button" when things aren't going how you want them to.

Interestingly, research is finding that when people are told "no" repetitively, it puts them into a reactive mind state, and when they are told "yes" repetitively, it puts them into a receptive mind state. *Chew on that the next time you find yourself telling your puppy she is wrong during a training session!*

So how do you teach this? You can catch, mark, and reward any behavior that your dog does when he is relaxing, but I like to start with the breath.

Take a Breath

Yes, you can teach your puppy to breathe (sort of). If you have a puppy that is panting from stress or excitement, you can teach him to close his mouth for a second and then exhale. If you do it multiple times within one session you will find a calmer and more easily focused puppy in front of you. This is not an exercise to just do once or to do randomly. To get a result you need to make it a natural part of your feedback process during work: your puppy got a little worked up, distracted, worried, reactive, and zoomy, during training… take a breath and start over. This is good advice for you, too. Sometimes I make my students smile *and* take a breath during a training session. I don't want any frowning, hyperventilating students!

How do you get your puppy to close his mouth if it's open? I don't feed puppies that are panting from anything but running around in the sun. I have found the fastest way to teach this is to hold a treat where the puppy can sniff it (if he jumps up for it, he hasn't started learning about availability yet! That is okay; just hold the treat behind your back and then start over, holding the treat a little higher than last time). When puppies air scent, they typically start closing their mouth. So, stare at your puppy's jaw; as soon as it starts lifting, mark and then let him have the treat.

Once the puppy gets the message, as soon as he sees you produce a treat, he will close his mouth for a second and exhale if he is panting. The treat itself can easily become the cue for the puppy to hold his breath/exhale.

© MITCH GRABERT

As soon as the dog stops panting and closes his mouth, deliver the treat. Notice the dog's high head position, which is similar to if he was air scenting.

What if his mouth is always closed? No problem—hold your treat out and stare at his nostrils. Wait for his nostrils to flare even a little bit. Some students find it's easier to see the flaring if they are sitting on the side of their puppy. I typically stand in front. It's easier to see if you have a puppy with a liver-colored nose, or a puppy that tends to hold his head high. You probably have a black-nosed puppy that always looks at the ground. This will take longer!

If you are having trouble catching the flaring, you can hold the treat out so that your puppy air scents it; be ready to catch nose movement, whether it's flaring or just sniffing it's somewhere to start.

When your puppy is an expert at looking up at your face, holding his breath and exhaling, or flaring his cute little nostrils at you, you can get fancy if you like. What expression does your puppy have when he is in a receptive mind state? I tell students all the time, biofeedback is about rewarding expression. Expression is linked to your emotional state. It's why some people try to smile a lot even if they don't really feel like it, in an effort to perk up their attitude. So an easy thing to look at is eyes. I like soft eyes in a puppy. If your puppy is jacked up you may even want soft and sleepy eyes, as your way of communicating, "Take it down a notch please!" So start rewarding your dog for lowering his eyelids while he looks at you with flared nostrils.

Another one is the base of the ears. Regardless of whether your puppy has naturally floppy or prick ears, the tightness of looseness of the base of the ear can indicate their level of relaxation and receptiveness. Your puppy's ears may remain pricked but perhaps you will notice the base relaxing and the ears moving a teeny fraction as a result. If your puppy has helicopter ears that fly around picking up information all around her head when you ask her to sit still, mark and reward when her ears assume a neutral position. Alternatively, mark and reward happy ears (people do this with their horses all the time, since annoyed horses flatten their ears).

Another one is carriage and motion of tail. If the tail is high from arousal, watch the base until it relaxes and the tail lowers; mark and reward that. If the tail is giving a drum solo on the ground, mark and reward a slower, "lazier" style of wag. It's just another way of asking the puppy to take it down a notch. I do this all the time with Snap because he wags his tail so fast when he is aroused I worry that he is going to fly away. He knows to offer slower wagging, and stopping the wagging altogether. It looks really funny when he lies on his mat with his tail thumping, looks at me and, bam! He smacks the tail on the ground perfectly still.

Another one is the "settled" down vs. the "sphinx" down, when the puppy's hips relax and he lies down with his weight to one side; you can use that one, too. If you are clicker happy you will want to click all these behaviors, but with many dogs I just mark these things with a smile or a very soft "yes" or I may just give the treat immediately after the behavior without marking. I don't want the excitement level to undermine what you are doing. I'm very quiet when I do this training, just as I typically am when doing the Relaxation Protocol.

DR. OVERALL'S PROTOCOL FOR RELAXATION

Biofeedback is the driving force behind Dr. Overall's Protocol for Relaxation (*Clinical Behavioral Medicine for Small Animals, 1997*), which can be found online through a Google search. This is a protocol that rewards dogs for remaining relaxed rather than reacting to increasingly challenging situations. It is an aerobic workout for the handler involving jogging, jumping jacks, etc. After each more exciting or distracting task that the handler performs, the dog is rewarded for remaining in a down or a sit. This protocol was developed for dogs suffering from clinical behavioral disorders *but* turns out to be a terrific puppy protocol as well.

The protocol should not be read as simply a stay exercise just because the dog is staying in place (although bombproof stays come out of doing this protocol). What makes this protocol magic is the biofeedback component. The question to your puppy should not be, "Can you stay while I open the doorbell, ring it and invite imaginary guests in?" But rather, "Can you stay with soft eyes and breathe while I open the doorbell, ring it and invite imaginary guests in?" There is a difference. After each task, you would return to the puppy and treat her in position. Simply hold the treat up, or tap your nose if you use the eye contact/breath cue. When the puppy does a little nostril flare or closes her mouth, you give the treat.

You can do this protocol in a variety of places, starting at home and then practicing it in class, or at trials, or at the pet food store; wherever the distractions take you. It should come as no surprise that I have my students teach their dogs this protocol on a mat.

An example: Easy was a teenager, in his first agility class where other dogs actually ran and did agility in the classroom at the same time as he did. When he saw this happening, he found it rather exciting. I saw his body language and flashed back to his mother, a dog that started screaming and flying at dogs as a teenager in agility class (this was remedied quickly by my friend who owns her!). I had taught him to hold his breath and exhale with a nose-tap cue. So I said his name—Whiplash Turn cue—and he turned back to me. I tapped my nose, and he closed his mouth, held his breath and then exhaled. We did this several times and then I incorporated the breath work into the Look at That game—a great combo by the way—asking him to watch the running dogs, turn back to me and breathe. This may be the first time I ever used those two games together. It worked beautifully and he was then able to work off lead just fine. Another great combination is breathing and an Off-switch game.

A funny story: I once had a student who refused to believe that my dogs would blink or hold their breath on cue. I was teaching her Karen Overall's Protocol for Relaxation. I was showing her how you add the breathing and sleepy eyes, ears, etc., into the protocol steps. She thought I was nuts so I brought Rumor out and sent him to his mat. He ran to the mat, slammed down on it, looked straight at her, and very deliberately did one big blink to her, because she had food in her pocket that he smelled and he knew that behavior was supposed to work on the mat. It looked to her like he understood English and was purposely showing her that, yes, in fact he was trained to blink. Okay, it looked like that to me, too.

So, at any point when you are using the exercises in this book and you think your puppy could be helped into a more relaxed or receptive state, or you aren't sure what to do next and you need a reset button, remember to think about the breathing! If you learn to use it skillfully, you will find new and interesting applications for it later. Hint: it's a great thing to add to your start-line stay cue if you have a very high dog that breaks his stay! Now if you go to a trial and see one of my students doing this, you'll know what's really happening. She isn't just scratching her nose.

Chapter 18

SHAPING

I am a clicker trainer; that means I shape behavior. You do not need to be a clicker trainer to use this book, but it will help you better understand where I'm coming from if you understand how shaping works.

In my quest to create a meaningful dialogue between a puppy and his handler, rather than a one way "do it or else" command, I like to use shaping to teach puppies that they are half of the learning team, that they have the power to give feedback, and that, yes, we are in fact engaged in a conversation about the best ways to make rewards happen.

Rather than making a puppy do something, like pushing his butt on the ground to teach sit, for example, *shaping* allows your puppy to figure out for himself what behavior will make a reward happen. With this method you would watch your puppy's body for shifts in weight or balance, any sign that he was moving toward a sitting position.

Another great clicker-friendly option is *capturing*. To use our sit example: since puppies sit on their own naturally, that explains the concept of "capturing" perfectly. When I see the puppy sitting on his own I reward it. After a few times, the puppy tries out sitting to see if it will cause me to produce a reward, and it will. Once the puppy is offering sitting to me reliably, I will name that behavior "sit."

That is how clicker training works: we will shape or capture the behavior, mark and reinforce it, then name that behavior—rather than command it. When you cue a puppy, you are using the name of a specific behavior to let the puppy know that reinforcement is available if he gives you the behavior that goes with that name (a little clicker tie-in to my whole CU concept of availability). If you are a clever trainer, you will always ask for what your puppy can give and adjust depending on the situation, so that your puppy will always make the right choice once he hears her cue. It is always a challenge for me to give a private lesson, or advice at a seminar, to somebody who is still using traditional training, because the way I see everything is just so different. Clicker training is not about using a clicker, it is about the kind of conversation you choose to have with your puppy; it is about how you perceive what "training" is really about.

Shaping your puppy to get into objects or to climb on them is a fun and easy way to practice your shaping skills.

Now back to shaping. Shaping is about breaking a behavior into small pieces and rewarding each piece, letting your puppy figure out for herself which behaviors are earning clicks. An easy way to introduce shaping is to put a target object on the floor. Let your puppy in the room and go sit on the couch. Whenever your puppy moves toward the object, click and either toss a treat to your puppy or feed from your hand. Other alternatives are to toss the treat away from the object so that the puppy gets to turn back and move toward it again after getting her treat, or toss the treat near the object to help the puppy stay near the object.

As you practice you will develop a sense of how and when to adjust so that you can be a flexible trainer. So in shaping we do not wait for the puppy to go all the way across the room and touch the object before clicking, even if that is the end result. *It is not the goal, but the process, that is important here! I encourage you to think like a process-oriented trainer while reading this book.* We click the very first step in the direction of the object and all the rest of the steps in the right direction. If the puppy isn't moving, but sitting and staring at you and she even looks away from you—not even toward the object, but just away from you—we would even click that because we can turn that behavior into the start of her moving away from you and orienting to something else. We can always find something to click, and we always want to set the puppy up for success.

This same shaping technique can be used to teach a puppy that she makes good things happen when she goes into her crate: a much friendlier technique for a puppy that doesn't love going into her crate. And you can use Premack here, too, of course: as soon as the puppy goes into her crate, click and call her out of the crate! A treat can be given in the crate or you can throw it away from the crate—keeping in mind that leaving the crate may be a more powerful reinforcement than the treat. Pretty soon you'll have a puppy that rushes into her crate because you've made a ping-pong game out of it rather than pressuring her to go in and stay in.

There is tons of information about shaping and clicker training out there; please go to clickertraining.com and learn about the available resources. If, at all possible, attend a ClickerExpo. If you are not already a convert, ClickerExpo will do it.

Chapter 19

INTEGRATIVE TRAINING

© DIANE LEWIS PHOTOGRAPHY

Integrative training is the name I'm giving to the concept of the balance of body, mind, and spirit in animal training. We will discuss how to cultivate awareness of each of these aspects of our puppies so that we can further tailor their education to bring out their highest potential.

When we clicker train or do any type of operant conditioning, many of us focus on the mental aspect of learning. We shape or lure or capture a behavior, we reinforce the behavior, we associate the behavior with a cue, we generalize the behavior to different locations, etc.

Most of us are staying at a somewhat superficial level of judging success. For example, you teach your puppy to sit. Your puppy learns to sit at home, in class, at the park, in the store. Your puppy can sit even when he sees another dog coming, or sit instead of jumping on somebody. That sounds like you have been successful in teaching your puppy what sit means, doesn't it? That was the mind component of body/mind/spirit. What happened to body and spirit? Is your puppy comfortable and relaxed? Does he *like* what you're asking him to do?

Let's say that your puppy is uncomfortable sitting in a "straight" obedience sit and wants to let both his back legs go in the same direction instead of putting weight evenly on his haunches. When my Tervuren, Rumor, was a puppy he always wanted to sit like that. I spent a lot of time teaching him to sit perfectly straight because I wanted to show him in obedience. I never thought about the possibility that he was telling me something about his body when he sat "sloppy." I just trained him to sit straight and felt frustrated when he didn't and asked him to fix it. The sitting was a hint I didn't process at the time that something was wrong.

Sometimes puppies are going through a growth spurt that makes it uncomfortable to move a certain way. Sometimes they actually have a condition that makes it uncomfortable, such as Rumor's lumbosacral condition or my current client's English Mastiff puppy, Captain. Eight-month-old Captain was also having problems sitting and would keep getting up. So I let sitting go for a while and did his stay and leave-it training while he was in a down instead. It turned out the vet diagnosed him with a neuromuscular condition. I am willing to bet that is why he had so much trouble with the sit.

I remember visiting Captain in a group puppy kindergarten class and all the puppies were doing "puppy push-ups" where they went from a sit to a down to a sit to a down, over and over again. Captain looked uncomfortable to me. I saw he was having trouble moving from a down to a sit and I pointed out to his owner that when he lay down he was not in a "sphinx" down but in a "sloppy" down, with his back legs spread out to the side. Therefore, when he was asked to sit, he was not in the right balance to be able to sit as quickly as the other puppies.

The choices seemed to be, teach him a sphinx down or ask him to stand from his down, get his feet back under him, and then sit, which was the easier way to handle it in class. There was another choice, which was not to do the exercise, but in the heat of the moment that one did not cross my mind.

What do I mean by spirit here? I really mean your puppy's emotions, particularly joy. *When teaching puppies the CU way it is essential to understand that whatever emotion any animal (including you) is feeling at the time he is learning something, will affect the learning process.* I cannot tell you how important this concept is to me. I am certain this concept is behind my lifelong hatred of all things math.

When I was in first grade my family moved, and I started mid-semester in a new school that taught math in a completely different way. At my old school, we were told to take our time and we had a supportive learning atmosphere. According to my mother I was fine with math there. At my new school, the big thing was "timed testing." Our teacher would give us a page of math problems, set a timer, and we had to finish as many as we could before the timer buzzed. As a child with a then-undiagnosed anxiety disorder who was having a lot of emotional trouble adjusting to a new school, a new state to live in, a new home, and a new life, I panicked. I went into my typical fuzzy-headed state where anxiety overrode all my attempts to function and I felt like I was dreaming. The teacher was always very negative with me, saying I did not do enough problems before the timer rang and I made too many mistakes. I was sent to remedial math class and I got the idea that I was bad in math. That belief colored all my math classes through college and stays with me to this day, even though I can look back with more perspective now.

The problem was not actually with my ability to learn math. *It was with how my already overloaded nervous system reacted to the way math was presented.* As a teacher myself I always strive to find the best way to provide information to fit the nervous system of the individual; both dog and human. You have to know your student and know how to talk to him. One thing I always do is ask my human students questions about what they do for a living because it helps me figure out how their minds work. On a given day you might see me explain the same thing totally differently to two people. You might see me explain the same thing differently to two puppies, too.

Joy and confidence happen in training when the material is presented in a way that honors the individual. I am not interested in a puppy that will sit anywhere, any time, but looks stressed every time he is told to sit, and I do see that type of thing. That's like asking first-grade Leslie what 2+2 is. If you were coloring a picture with her and asked casually, she would have told you the answer with confidence, but once you set the timer she would have told you the answer with her heart racing, unable to think clearly.

Who wants their student to feel like that about learning, regardless of the species? Learning is fun. It is how we understand how the world works, and what our place in it is. *No student feels motivated to learn when he thinks he is "bad" in a subject, and I see that hold true for dogs all the time.*

So, when honoring your puppy's spirit as you begin a training session, ask him the following question in your head: How am I going to help you learn with joy? Here are some ways you could do just that:

- Reinforce his behavior with exactly what he wants. Does he want to see your friend, does he want to swim, or does he want to be left alone? Then use that as reinforcement for your puppy at that time. Use the Premack principle to keep your training fair and motivating.

- Determine how he learns best. Does he like watching other dogs do it first? (Yes, really!) Does he like a lot of physical contact during training, or none at all? Does he need lots of play breaks or rest breaks? What tone, expression, and energy level does he respond to best? Some puppies are all-business and some are no-business. How you present the material to them is going to be a bit different, I hope.

Let's go back to sit. In my career of training literally thousands of dogs, I have never found a harder one than Easy to teach to stay in a sit position. He was physically capable of doing exactly what I wanted. He was mentally capable of doing exactly what I wanted, *as long as he was under his "instinct threshold."*

I am making up that term, because I don't have a better way to describe it. When I would move away from Easy while he was in a sit position, his head would lower and he would assume the Border Collie posture my friends and I call "vulturing." You have seen them do this at a start line, anticipating their release over the first obstacle. Usually I take vulturing as a good sign that the dog is into his work and I don't think of it as a problem… unless the dog always gets up after lowering his head. That is what happened with Easy. His head would go down, and with it his balance would shift, his body would assume that low, stalky look, and he would stand up and stalk.

I knew Easy understood the concept of stay/maintain a position until released. I knew he knew how to sit, too. What I decided he didn't know was that he could hold his head in a neutral position while he was sitting. So I started shaping him to hold his head in a neutral position. I then added duration and distance to it. Reframing our stay training, which had started driving me insane, to "hold your head up" and adding duration and distance criteria, provided relief for both of us. He didn't have to be wrong anymore. Previously, whenever he got up from his sit, I asked him to sit again. He knew that meant he'd done something wrong, and he doesn't like to be wrong, ever. He couldn't help switching over to instinct mode. The way I was walking away from him when he was in a sit, seemed to create this space where pressure was being taken away, the pressure I had put on him simply by standing near him while he was sitting, and he was compelled to move into that space.

Thinking of it as teaching him to read a verbal cue over a pressure cue was another way I reframed our stay training. Within a couple of sessions, from this new perspective, Easy was sitting with a neutral head and not moving a hair while I ran around raising criteria all over the place.

I think this example illustrates integrative training very well. Yes, Easy was physically capable of maintaining a sit. *But*, his body wanted to assume a creepy, crouchy position in response to my moving away. So, physically the sit-stay actually was demanding since it went against his instincts. Yes, Easy was mentally capable of learning a sit-stay, but to set him up for success I needed to find the best way of explaining to him what I wanted; I needed to be a good clicker trainer, splitting the behavior of sitting into components so that I could hone in on the key behavior, which was his head moving. And, to address the spirit part, to help him learn with joy, I had to first laugh about what I'd been thinking of as a training problem rather than a training *process* and lighten up. Then, I had to step back and appreciate how amazing a dog's instincts are and how well refined and beautiful the predatory motor patterns imprinted in the Border Collie's DNA are. What an amazing thing!

And, with that appreciation, I could also appreciate how to use pressure differently to help him learn to stay in position. So, in addition to training him to sit with his head in a neutral position so he did not start vulturing, I started walking away from him slightly differently: taking a small step to the side before walking away. That was my intuition for keeping him stationary rather than pulling him toward me with my motion, and it worked. I was quickly able to fade it and leave him with any motion in any direction.

When you train, you are training the whole being! It really is an amazing gift we are being given.

Chapter 20

ECONOMY OF ENERGY

The idea of what I call economy of energy is important to the CU puppy program mindset. All of us have a certain amount of energy to spend in a day. If you have a long day at work, and a stressful commute home, you will not have as much energy to do your kid's homework after making dinner, as you would have if you had been sitting poolside with a strawberry daiquiri all afternoon.

Dogs are the same. And, like many humans, they are not always great at economizing their energy, (that is, saving some for later when they're really going to need it.) Anxious dogs spend a lot of their daily allotment of energy worrying about the world, and that energy could have been spent learning coping skills and alternative behaviors (this is where medication sometimes comes into play).

Anxiety takes a *huge* amount of energy and leaves you without much left over to get your work done or learn something new, like standing with your back feet on a board and your front feet on the floor to learn the two-on/two-off contact position. Processing information about a highly distracting or overwhelming environment also takes a huge amount of energy, which brings us back to our puppies. So, imagine a puppy that walks into a horse barn where his puppy agility class is being held!

He is hit with all the sights, smells, and sounds of the barn and has to walk past an advanced class, where a dog is sequencing at high speed while barking, in order to get to his class. From his class, he can still see and hear the dogs in the advanced class on the other side of some ring gates. In his class there are seven other puppies, some tugging, some barking, others pulling toward him trying to check him out while their handlers try to re-engage them. Perhaps on top of this there is a teacher who takes him away from his home-base handler and tries to engage him in high-intensity play or teach him a brand-new behavior and he feels unsure about working with a stranger.

All of this is information he has to process in the moment, and all of this processing takes up a huge amount of his energy. There isn't much left to put into his class performance (and we're not even counting all the stuff that happened throughout the day that he had to process, before coming to class). When this puppy is halfway through his class and has nothing left to give and checks out, are we going to say he blew off his handler and therefore needs more restrictions in his daily life? Or, are we going to say he needs a time-out to learn that disengaging is unacceptable or that his handler wasn't interesting enough and needs to re-engage him in more vigorous toy play?

Based on what I have just said about economy of energy and all the stuff this puppy had to integrate into his experience just to get into his classroom, that would be ridiculous, but these are the typical things a sport puppy's handler would hear.

We really need to be aware of how much energy goes into processing the environment. Many dogs I work with that shut down in the ring are what I call over-processors. The trial environment is a big energy suck for them; they are constantly taking it all in at once with no filter and no break. There is just not much energy left to give the performance for which their handler was hoping. Think about how much energy it takes to do a complex task with full concentration—for a dog! A dog that has been walking around a trial going, "Holy heck, there is a lot going on here." It's not surprising, somewhere after the adrenaline rush of the first few obstacles (the last burst of energy before the burn out), the dog has nothing left to give. Once you are aware of this issue, there are steps you can take to minimize its effect.

CU creates a dialogue with our dogs about the environment. It allows them to process information without spending too much energy being worried about it, excited about it, or distracted by it.

This is energy left in the bank that your dog can spend later in the ring. So, addressing problem behaviors in the ring isn't just a performance problem. It's an economy of energy problem, and it starts with teaching the dog how to integrate the information about his environment in an economical way.

For some dogs this is a nonissue; they will work all day and ask for more. But for many others, this is a problem that doesn't get recognized or dealt with as such. We don't think about how much we are asking of our puppies just walking them into class, much less how much concentrated energy it takes for them to learn something new in the middle of the environmental smackdown of smells, sounds, and sights that is puppy class.

Chapter 21

BITE THRESHOLD MODEL

© DIANE LEWIS PHOTOGRAPHY

Tied into the idea of economy of energy is the learning theory concept calledthe Bite Threshold Model. "Surely I don't need to know this," you are saying. My puppy is not a biter. The Bite Threshold Model is not just for aggressive dogs anymore.

This concept plays an important role for CU trainers because it reminds us to be aware of everything affecting our training situation: the environment, how our puppy is feeling, what his day has been like so far. It helps us learn to make skillful adjustments in criteria so that we can make the most of our training sessions.

It is vital to be aware of how this model works when training our performance puppies in order to get the best out of them. The Bite Threshold Model teaches us that a given number of variables must be present in order to push an animal past its bite threshold—or, for our purposes—the threshold beyond which it is able to learn well and behave well.

Some puppies will "stress up," while others will "stress down." Some puppies will respond to overtraining, too much pressure, or a challenging environment by getting really aroused, others will respond to the same things by shutting down. Rather than looking at just the arousal or shut-down behaviors, start training yourself to see the big picture.

Before you asked your puppy to do *x, y, or z*, what was going on in the room? Was a dog on the other side of the training building stampeding through a tunnel, and your puppy had never heard that sound before? Did the UPS man deliver a package during dinner when you were rushing around and then you had a fight with your teenager, and then threw the puppy in the car because you were late for class? Change in weather? Stars not in the right alignment? When you are aware of the Bite Threshold Model you will stop saying, "Well, that just happened out of the blue." Things do not just happen out of the blue. Everything affects everything else, and that is what this model means to me. Even missing a regularly scheduled walk could possibly affect your puppy's behavior later.

A client did not believe me the other day when I told her that her rescued hound puppy, a dog with some aggression problems, had escalated his behavior in part because of the stress of getting his shots at the vet, and then being left with a pet sitter. She could not connect the dots, but I was sure these were factors. Being aware of this helps us get a better perspective and also have more patience when training. We can't control the forces at work behind this model, but we can be aware of them and try to manage the environment as best we can when training so that we are not adding more of those threshold-pushing variables into the mix. And rather than saying, "he's just being a pill today," maybe we can have some empathy and say, "we can't know all the factors at play here but he isn't at his best right now. How should we address that so that he can give a better performance later?"

All of us sentient beings have a threshold, and once we've passed it, we aren't so nice to be around. The learning theory term is Bite Threshold Model but you can think of is as the Icky Behavior Threshold Model. The traditional meaning here is about all the variables that come together to push a dog past a behavioral point of no return, that causes him to react aggressively.

That is why this model is so great for us as trainers, because it reminds us to be aware of the variables that come together in order to predict how our training session, class or trial, on any given day, is going to go. It allows us to adjust what we ask for accordingly.

So for our purposes, once your puppy has passed his threshold, he has gone from that nice receptive learning state into a *suboptimal learning state*. In terms of behavior, maybe you can tell he is over threshold because he started zooming! Or maybe he started frustration-barking at you, or reacted badly to the new person who walked in the door, or shut down and didn't want to play anymore. Maybe he wandered off and sniffed the ground. Maybe he is stalky, creepy and crouchy, and started staring at the wading pool while you were asking for a sit and eye contact.

If any one of these situations occurred, you could adjust your criteria so that he could succeed. You could move him farther away from the wading pool, to a distance where he was able to access his "thinking brain." Or maybe just body blocking the wading pool would help, or sending him to mat or asking him to breathe might be enough to "reset" him. Or you could micro-shape him to come back to planet Earth. (And then I might use Premack here and send him to the pool after getting the level of attention I wanted.)

Now, in this example, it's pretty obvious what put the puppy over threshold; proximity of the wading pool (don't laugh; if he is related to Easy, there is a chance this could happen). However, the—we'll call it the plain-old threshold model for short—reminds us that something which happened earlier that day, or even before that, can affect our puppy's mind state and, therefore, his behavior.

My student's Border Collie did beautifully for three runs at his first trial and then lost his mind for the fourth run, giving me a good example of the threshold model. This Border Collie has worked hard on overcoming his anxiety about strange people, particularly judges who look at him in the ring. He was doing so well; he had three awesome runs. But by the fourth run, things seemed to be too much for him and he popped out of the poles when the judge ran behind them. Sometimes little stressors just pile up throughout a day. I'd guess that, although he was performing well, he was keeping a checklist of trial stressors and that judge was just the last straw.

My student could have left after the second or third run, and I think next time he will. His dog can build up to being there a whole day without crossing his threshold into his reactive state.

My students learn to look at behavior that is undesirable to us and take it as information that their puppy is "over threshold" or past the point of an optimal learning state; that way they can reset the puppy, adjust the situation or adjust what they are asking, and both team members can be successful.

Chapter 22

TRANSITIONING

CU uses transitions to create the best possible learning conditions for the puppy. Some puppies process new information better when they have a "warm up to learning" period; some need a "cool down from learning" period. These periods should be thought of as part of the training process itself, not separate from it. We will discuss how to use "passive attention" and "active attention" exercises to tailor a training session to match your puppy's learning profile.

When you finish a formal training session, you are changing from a highly structured activity to a much less structured one. For some puppies this is a complete nonissue; you can train or play and then stop cold and they will settle and go about their business. For other puppies this is a huge deal. These puppies get aroused by the training session and, if you leave them in this state of arousal without any structure, they will likely turn to evil as a way of dealing with their leftover arousal. Mouthy puppies will bite harder, vocal puppies will bark louder.

Puppies that need to build confidence will feel a little lost and unsure what to do with themselves when the structure is taken away. And, *all* puppies can use a transitional time to calmly process what they were just learning. So if you aren't sure if your puppy really needs to transition, do it. Keep this concept of transitioning between direct learning and down time in mind for puppy class, too.

The first time I thought of this, I was watching my Snap interacting with a friend of mine soon after I adopted him as an adult. My friend got him very aroused playing tug and then she walked off and left him to go do something else. He was still in a very aroused state and looked frantic, like she had plugged him into the light socket and had forgotten to unplug him when she was finished. When he became frantic like that, he could not think and would get very frazzled. He got like that often, which is one of the reasons he was very hard to train. As I watched him vibrate, I had the realization that he needed help transitioning back to a less-aroused state. I had never thought of it before in those terms.

Giving your dog a bone, perhaps to work on in their bed, crate, or mat so they have a specific place to go to as part of their "transition ritual," is a really easy way to do this. But you have lots of options; others include taking your puppy for a walk to sniff around or playing with her in the yard, if that's appropriate for your puppy's temperament. As always, tailor things to fit your puppy. When I was training Easy, I just let him go in the yard with my other dogs after a clicker session in the living room. This definitely signaled the end of work so that he didn't hang around staring at me.

All puppies can use transitional time to calmly process what they were just learning. Giving your puppy a bone on his mat, taking him for a walk to sniff, or letting him play with your other dogs are examples of an activity that could be a part of your puppy's transition ritual.

The concept of transitioning has another layer. Some puppies need help preparing to begin a training session, not just end it. Just as some shouldn't end "cold," there are plenty who shouldn't begin "cold" either. Puppies that aren't immediately engaged the second they see you getting ready to train (getting out your treats, your clicker, whatever) need to get into the spirit so that learning is enjoyable.

An excellent training warm-up is the attention part of the Give Me a Break game (Chapter 29). This game will put your puppy in the mood to pay attention, and your puppy will have fun doing it. This game is perfect for taking the pressure off a sensitive or easily stressed puppy, and for building concentration skills for the easily distracted puppy.

For puppies at the other end of the spectrum, (that is, puppies that go over the top at the idea of training and aren't in a good mental space to think clearly), doing bodywork, possibly on their mat, is a good way to start. (If your puppy doesn't like being touched, you have a whole other set of problems to address first.) Rewarding these puppies for sitting and taking a breath is another good way to start a session. So is slow loose-leash walking in a circular or figure eight pattern. You can punctuate this walking pattern with brief periods of sit/take a breath. That is a very basic Off-switch game. Off-switch games are discussed more in Chapter 28. The purpose of these exercises is to provide a structure that helps the puppy get to an arousal level where he is excited to train, but not so excited that he can't be thoughtful.

The whole point of transitioning is to create the best possible learning conditions for the puppy.

PASSIVE AND ACTIVE ATTENTION ACTIVITIES

In CU we talk about passive and active attention as part of the transitions concept. By passive attention I mean low-pressure, low-structure activities such as sniffing walks, walking in figure eights, and bodywork. These activities allow a team to begin the process of connecting, without the handler asking her dog to do a behavior he may not be ready for yet.

For dogs that walk into my CU classes with their heads on Mars, typically I have their handlers rub their ears or do some TTouch, while the dogs lay on their mats, until the dogs looked more grounded and more present. Some puppies don't particularly like being still; others don't take to bodywork right away. For these puppies I offer a compromise: I will do a few seconds of basic TTouches (in the beginning, they could be eating or chewing a bone while I do this) and then release them from their mat and move with them in a structured way, like a

figure-eight pattern or a circle, then back to the mat for several more seconds of staying still and being touched. The time spent moving around will get increasingly shorter as the time spent staying (reasonably) still will get longer. This is another use of Premack in CU.

Stretching exercises could be part of passive attention, too. By this I mean the handler is stretching the dog. In contrast, warm-up or cool-down exercises, where the dog is stretching his back by "sitting pretty," turning his neck to both sides, or weaving between his handler's legs, are great active attention activities.

When you feel ready to move from passive to active attention, you could start by asking for brief eye contact coupled with taking a breath, then returning to the more passive activity. Starting with a balance rather than just switching "cold" from one form of connection to the other isn't usually needed but can be helpful for puppies that shut down easily, or for handlers that aren't quite sure when it's the right time to switch to active mode.

Bodywork allows a team to begin the process of connecting without the handler asking the dog to do a behavior he may not be ready for yet.

Active attention in CU is any cued behavior that is fun and easy for the dog, such as tricks they like to do. The goal is to get the puppy in the mood for training and deepen the team connection. Toy play with self-control also falls in the active attention category, as does flat work. Some puppies are ready to start training sessions cold, others could use some active attention to help them get their brains ready to learn something new, and others need passive attention or Off-switch work to help them find their balance.

When you enter a training space with your puppy, the ritual of going to your station and then doing some bodywork on the mat is a nice way to start the learning experience. It also gives you an alternative to crating your puppy during class, if you want to take a break from training.

READING YOUR PUPPY

The concept of transitions helps handlers be more skilled at reading their puppies and knowing when to actively engage with them, and when to give them a break. *Starting a class experience by doing passive attention at your station should include your doing a check-in of your pup's behavior and body language.* This is a perfect opportunity to practice reading your puppy.

When deciding what type of interaction your puppy needs in order to reach his optimal state for a training session, watch his body language. His body will tell you everything you need to know about his state of mind. Here are some questions for you to think about:

- Are his eyes soft or hard? Can you see a lot of white in them, which would indicate stress? Is he blinking them more or less than normal? If he is blinking them a lot (without a reinforcement history for "sleepy eyes"), he could be giving you a social signal that indicates he wants to defuse a feeling of tension or conflict. This is sometimes called a "calming signal."

- Conversely, if he is super high in anticipation of work and he has that electrified look, he might seem like he isn't blinking at all. If he looks like this and can't settle to do passive attention or rest on his mat, you can do biofeedback training to teach him to offer a calm expression. I don't encourage clicking a dog like this for sleepy eyes, taking a breath, relaxing ears, or moving from a furious wag to a slow, swishy wag because most students I have would accidentally make their dogs even more excited. So, I have them quietly reward their dog for these behaviors. If a treat is too exciting, I have students just smile with soft, sleepy eyes to mark a behavior, taking deep breaths themselves.

- Are his ears swiveling around, picking up information about everything around him? Is the base of the ear relaxed? Even if he has prick ears, his ears look different when they're relaxed.

- Is his breathing fast and shallow? Is he air scenting in a particular direction? Puppies don't just get information with their eyes and ears: they get a lot of information from their nose. Often you can tell beforehand if a puppy is going to run away from his handler in a particular direction, because he was air scenting in that direction.

- Is he carrying his weight evenly? Does he appear to be connected to the ground or does he look like he could pop up at any moment? Is he carrying a disproportionate amount of weight in his rear, like he is ready to back up or run away if he feels threatened?

- Is he giving you any other social signals that indicate a state of stress or conflict, particularly after you ask him to do something? These include: looking away from you and licking his muzzle repeatedly, yawning, scratching imaginary itches, shaking as if he were wet when he is dry.

People ask, "How do I know if my puppy really just had an itch versus responding to a feeling of tension?" It's all about context. Social behaviors are not random; they are responses to the environment. For example, I have a new student whose Italian Greyhound starts scratching every time she takes his leash off in an agility class.

PREPARING TO READ YOUR PUPPY

There is a lot of good information available on how to read your puppy. What I don't see readily available is information about how you can prepare your own body and mind for connecting with your dog.

When you are reading your puppy, chances are you are "in your head" (that is, looking at and thinking about his behaviors). But what about the rest of your body? Dogs are great at being present in their entire body, and in order to successfully connect with them, we need to work at this, too. Dogs will respond differently to you if you are training them while maintaining a sense of being in your body. If you do yoga or Pilates, or if you ride horses, you may already be bringing the concept of working from your core strength into dog training. Most of my students don't do this, so here is a quick rundown of what I ask them to do (with a thank you to my yoga teacher Anna Trezzi):

- **Feet:** First, become very aware of your feet. Sit in a chair (or on the floor, if you're really flexible) and cross your legs. Grasp your right foot with your left hand, putting each finger between each toe. Guide your foot in clockwise circles with your hand and then change direction. This is a great ankle stretch. Then, give your right foot a quick massage and grasp it by your right hand, fingers between the toes. This time you are going to make a fist with your feet, squeezing your fingers for a count of six. Then spread your toes as wide as you can with your fingers for a count of six. Repeat. Then start over with the opposite side.

- **Legs:** After several bad back injuries over the years I have finally learned how to stand, walk, handle a lunging, reactive leashed dog, and tug while staying totally comfortable and balanced. "Standing mountain" pose is the stance I always start in when I am working with dogs. Stand with your middle toes facing forward in a straight line toward the wall, and make sure your heels are straight behind your toes. Engage your leg muscles by pretending you have a block (or you could actually use a block) between your calves. Squeeze the block with your calves so you can feel your calf muscles moving toward each other. Then imagine your inner thigh muscles are moving away from each other: calves toward, thighs away. Then, stand proud and feel that core place, just under your navel. That core is where you should be moving from; *your arms and legs should just be extensions of your core.* I can't make a big enough point of that. When I see people handling leashes, I just see their arms jerking about without any core connection, and the same goes for most agility handlers I see. The dogs aren't just following your arms! You need to be aware of your alignment.

- **Arms:** Take a deep breath as you raise your arms over your head. Feel your shoulder blades move down your back. Exhale as your arms return to your sides. Another good one is to just let your arms hang loosely like clothing as you twist from side to side. The third arm exercise is the hard one. Make a slow circle as big as you can with one arm, turning your head with your arm as it circles behind you. Then start making faster and faster circles until it feels that your arm is going to fly off. Then let that arm hang at your side and feel the difference between your arms. The arm you have been stretching will feel a lot longer than the other arm. Then do the other arm.

After working on these things in a seminar, I will invite people to come up and take hold of a leash that I am also holding. I will tell them to stand as they normally would when working with their dog and then I will suddenly yank the leash. They always lose their balance; some even take steps toward me. Then I remind them about their alignment: ankles, knees, hips, and shoulders all in a line. I remind them to engage their calf and thigh muscles and move from their core, letting their leash be an extension of their core. They work on bending the knee and elbow joints slightly and staying soft. If the leash pulls them, their arms are to move in the direction they get pulled while the elbows stay bent and they maintain their core balance. In that way, they are "un-yankable." So they stand like this and I yank the leash again, and nothing happens.

I went a step further with this in the CU camp I taught one summer at Glen Highland Farm. I told my students that since we were expecting our dogs to concentrate and pay attention to us, we needed to practice concentrating so that we could pay attention to them without thinking about other things. I put a stuffed dog in the middle of the room and told my campers to just be aware they were looking at the dog for five minutes. If they had a thought about what training we were doing next, what was for lunch, or what their dog was doing, or if they heard barking or something distracted them from knowing they were looking at the stuffed dog, they were to just note that they had a thought and then return to knowing they were looking at the stuffed dog.

The following day I had them do this exercise with their own dogs. The dogs that were typically reactive to other dogs lay quietly next to them while they meditated in this way: no barking! I also told them to think about the parts of their feet while they were walking: the heel touches the ground, then the ball of the foot, then the toes. I took them on a nature walk—no talking allowed—and kept reminding them to remember their feet, to move from their core, and let the leash be an extension of their core. I told them that if there was barking they should just note they heard it and return to their feet. There were 13 camp dogs and they all walked quietly down a long hiking trail, quite near each other. I even walked my dogs up to the camp dogs on the trail and let them sniff, while reminding their very anxious handlers to breathe. Everybody was so happy and relaxed at the end of the walk! Sometimes connecting with both yourself and your dog in this way gets you a lot further than a training session will.

This type of exercise isn't just good for owners of reactive dogs who are tense walking them. It is also good for anybody getting ready for a training session who feels stress from their day, stress in their body, stress about performing in class, tired, or disconnected in any way from their puppy. After doing these exercises not only will your body awareness increase, but you will realize it's easier to read your puppy because you will notice so much more with a quiet mind. And, you will start noticing how your club friends get so easily agitated and hyper about dog training, and you'll find yourself telling them to stop for a second and breathe!

SECTION IV

GAMES AND EXERCISES

Chapter 23

REORIENTING

© DIANE LEWIS PHOTOGRAPHY

Underlying reorienting behaviors is the leave-it concept. Reorienting behaviors are about the dog's disengaging from something and orienting to the handler. While a Whiplash Turn involves reorienting to you, it is a behavior that you must cue. Reorienting behaviors are cued by the environment, not by you. It happens at physical thresholds; exits and entrances, spaces where your dog is leaving a less-stimulating space and entering a more-stimulating space. Reorienting is a targeting behavior that helps the dog momentarily "turn off" the new level of stimulus and reconnect with you.

We want reorienting behavior at two main locations: entering a training space and exiting a crate in a training space. Other possible locations for this behavior are exiting your home through the front door, getting out of the car, and entering any stimulating environment, like the park.

Reorienting is a very straightforward thing to teach. When you teach it using a crate, make sure that your puppy first knows to stay in an open crate until he's released. Then, open the crate door, leash the puppy (he should continue to stay because you haven't said a release word), and stand to the side of the crate—preferably the side opposite where the door swings—but either side will work. Say your release word; watch the corner of the crate between the front of it and the side of it. The second you see your puppy's head turning at that corner click or mark it in some way. You want to use your marker to highlight to the puppy exactly what body movement is causing the reward to happen. Marking the puppy for turning his head toward you, away from something else, over and over again is an awesome way to build a reliable leave-it foundation.

This puppy already knows how to stay in an open crate. I stand to the side of the crate and give the puppy his release word. As soon as his head turns the corner toward me, I click.

When the puppy figures out that the game is to turn toward you coming out of the crate, you can raise your criteria. You can take a few steps back so you are at the back end of the crate or actually stand behind it, or you can take a few more steps to the side. You can change distance and angles so that upon hearing the release word, all your puppy is thinking about is finding you upon exiting the crate. Then you can put something stimulating near you, like other dogs in crates (building up to other dogs out of crates but standing still, then other dogs walking, then running, then doing agility, and so on) and release your puppy from his crate. Each time you raise criteria, hold the leash (obviously you have to get a long leash for this). You may have to "help" your puppy by saying his name when he comes out of the crate as a Whiplash Turn cue. But if you have to do this more than a couple of times, you need to go back and lower your criteria. When you are happy with your puppy's success, don't pick up his leash when you release him from the crate. The goal is to have a dog that comes to find you, even if he can't see you from his crate, as soon as he is released, off leash, and isn't attending to anything else on the way to you.

In other words, work on this until you can confidently open your crate door in class, knowing your puppy will patiently wait in there until he hears his release word, at which point he will come "find" (or target) you as you stand behind the crate, while your friend is tugging loudly with her puppy directly in front of the open crate door, right in the line of sight of your puppy as you give the release word.

I teach a similar ritual at the front door of the training facility. I have had some students spend the first quarter of their CU class out in the parking lot working on getting their dog to focus/relax enough just to be able to reorient at the front door.

With some dogs I just have their handlers ask them to do the Whiplash Turn away from the front door while it is still closed. If they can't do that because they are glued to the door, there is no way I am opening that door and letting them into the building. Some dogs have to be asked for a Whiplash Turn every few seconds while walking from their car to the door. They need to learn to reorient upon coming out of the car as if it were a giant crate. Remember, class doesn't start in class; it starts in the parking lot on the way into the classroom. Then, anytime the dog pulls toward the building or toward anything else (like another dog in the parking lot), I have the handler stop moving, which should be taught as an "on the flat" Whiplash Turn cue, before trying it in real life. Once the dog turns back to the handler, the handler can continue moving toward the front door. Asking the dog to take a quick breath and maybe blink his eyes would be a good thing here too!

When the dog can turn right back to handler when she stops moving at the closed front door, then we can open the front door. I will usually baby gate the entranceway so that the dog has a little room to step into and swing around to her handler, but can't actually get anywhere good if she tries to just fly in (and therefore is not at risk of freaking out a sensitive dog that happens to be near the front door).

When the dog can step into the building and automatically swing back around to her handler, then I will let my student move to the next step, which is to walk to a "CU station." The CU station includes the handler's crate, toys and treats, and a chair. If the dog pulls or gets distracted while walking to his station, the handler will again stand still and wait for him to reorient before continuing. The dog will go in his crate, and when it is his turn to come out, the handler will work on reorienting upon coming out of the crate. I then put the dog's mat a few feet from the crate so that after he "finds" his handler he can go right to his mat. Going to the mat placed a certain distance from the crate is a way to help keep the dog's focus from one target to another without the dog getting overwhelmed by the larger world around him. Not every dog needs this much structure or these many baby steps, but my beginning CU class dogs do!

Easy demonstrates a much harder version of the reorienting behavior: Off lead, he turns toward me upon moving through an open gate, while a "distraction" is placed near the opening.

When I open the door at the training center, I expect my dogs to reorient to me in that space so fast that they turn back to me in midair and land staring at me. I "push" them into the space, meaning I don't heel them in or try to be on top of them. I send them ahead, knowing that if I am not moving, they will automatically turn back toward me after they enter the space. Since the dogs learn during Whiplash Turn training to read sudden cessation of movement as a reorienting cue, all you are doing here is adding an extra environmental cue, such as the front door or a gate or a tent. I send the dog ahead of me for two reasons:

It gives the dog the space he needs to turn back around vs. both of us squishing through a door at once.

It gives the dog the opportunity to perform a big "environmental leave-it" by turning his back to the entire training space and making contact with his handler instead.

Easy is always excited to discover which of his favorite people and which dog friends are at the center. So, while I no longer have a need to maintain a structure to help him focus at the building, I have kept the reorienting at the front door ritual to help him from going out of his head when we first step through the doorway. After he turns to me, I walk right in with him as his reward. I may cue him to say "hi" to a friend, or I may take him right to his crate, depending on what's happening there. I like to use Premack whenever possible to reward Easy for connecting with me in the doorway. So, if there is an available friend to greet near the door I always take him over.

All this reorienting stuff is simply about structure: about putting structure onto a chaotic environment where it would be difficult for your dog or puppy to focus otherwise. I did the same type of thing with puppy Easy at trials that I did at the training center. I taught him that when we exited the tent, there was another point of orientation to me. When I unzip our tent and send him ahead, he flies through, whips around in midair, and lands looking at me. It is more dramatic at trials because he is higher just to be there. When he was younger, once he exited the tent (which I try, for convenience, to set up as close to our ring as possible) I had a mat to send him to. That way he could start "taking in" some of the trial environment information while he was on "mat rules." Using the mat near the practice jump would be another good way to work on trial integration, as long as the team using the jump was okay with it.

Training is always fluid, and the degree of structure your puppy or dog needs can always be adjusted to stay up-to-date with your needs. My goal is always to just have a partner that walks around me, enters spaces with me, and feels confident and comfortable navigating the world with me at his side. It is not about control. Structure is about providing targets and rituals to help a dog that feels unanchored find his anchor. *It is about breaking what seems like a "big" environment into smaller pieces.* I wrote in CU about how I target trained myself to follow Deb's red van on the highway so that I wouldn't panic. Since then I, unfortunately, got to learn another way to use targeting to structure my environment so that I would not panic: I had to create an airport protocol for myself.

Finding my way around an airport while I was getting ready to teach a CU seminar was a nightmare for me. Being as environmentally sensitive as I am, the airport was overwhelming, and it didn't help that I would be feeling really anxious about traveling, being away from home, and giving a seminar. I would be in a fog of anxiety at the airport, and checking my bag, getting my boarding pass, finding my terminal, *everything* I had to do felt really difficult and confusing. So I used signs at the airport as targets and I separated the airport into "the space between signs." That way I wasn't looking at the airport as a whole but as small pieces of space regularly broken up by my targets. I would go from one sign to the next and all I had to worry about in between was getting to the next sign; that set me up to succeed easily over and over. Finding signs for my terminal or the bathroom or something else high value was like finding a jackpot.

Now that I have several years of traveling and teaching under my belt, I am still stressed, but to a much lesser degree and I don't need that structure anymore. I can't remember the last time I used signs in this way. But I do use other targeting behaviors, like staying aware of my breathing and feeling each step I take with my whole foot on the ground. I have learned to use my body as the anchor, but I know that I can always reframe the environment into a series of targets if I need to for some reason. Next I should try to learn how to shop at a mall using this approach. Okay, maybe I'll let that one go!

Chapter 24

LEAVE IT

O ne of the most important things for any dog to know is when something is on "leave-it rules." Following is my version of the leave-it training process.

Before you start, your puppy should have a default behavior. That way, if he gets frustrated or confused during leave-it training, he will always have his default to fall back on. The default behavior itself is usually incorporated (by the puppy) into what "leave it" means. Often when you put an object on leave-it rules, the puppy with a strong default will respond by trying out his default (remember the story of Ru sitting when he wanted access to a flock of sheep?) Perhaps your puppy will respond to the information that something he wants is not available by reorienting to you, sitting and looking in your face. If that is his default, and you aren't giving information about what to do just what *not* to do ("Don't eat that"), he will fill in that information vacuum with his default behavior(s).

I teach the popular Doggie Zen game as the introduction to leave-it training. This game entails holding up a treat (or a toy) and waiting for the puppy to "break" from it and turn back toward you. If the puppy is really stuck on the thing, you will need to shape the reorienting behavior, starting by rewarding the puppy for even slightly breaking from the thing—even if he just flicks his eyeballs for a split second, whatever you can get. You will be able to build up to his looking in your face or making eye contact, but don't ask for too much at once or you will just frustrate the puppy and yourself—especially if he has a strong predatory instinct and/or "eye" and you are holding a toy (which is why I always establish this behavior with food first for prey-driven dogs, and then switch to toys).

If he is having trouble breaking from the treat or toy, put it behind your back and reward eye contact. Then, let him see just a little bit of the treat or toy from behind your back, so that he isn't seeing the whole enchilada. This usually makes it easier for him to look away from it. When he is looking at you for a couple of seconds at a time, rather than zinging his eyeballs back and forth, you can make things a little more difficult with the "dancing treat." Move the treat around a little to make it dance. You may have to go back to shaping at this point to help him break from it and orient to you.

In these two examples of Doggie Zen, one with a toy and one with a treat, the handler is waiting for the dog to "break" from the object and reorient to the handler.

When your puppy is reading the treat or toy as an environmental cue to look at *you* not it, even if it is dancing, the next step is to place the object under your shoe. If your puppy has a strong default behavior, he may just give you that behavior when the object disappears under your shoe. Or, like many puppies, he may try to get it out from under your shoe. Stand strong! He can't have it! Wait for him to figure this out on his own and try something different—such as taking a step away from your shoe, or lifting his head up if he was staring down at your shoe. If he gives you the head lift, then you can shape that into actually looking in your direction. The second he disengages from your shoe, mark it and reward him. I usually give a treat from my pocket but occasionally I will pick up the treat under my shoe and let the puppy have it. In the early stages of training I don't tend to release the puppy to take the treat from the floor himself, I want to be the one to hand it over.

Your puppy may try to get the treat out from under your shoe. Wait for him to try something different on his own, even if it's just looking up from your foot. Click and reward!

When you are putting the object under your shoe and your puppy is immediately giving you his default or his disengaging behavior, then start putting the object next to your shoe. If the puppy makes a move, all you have to do is step over the object. *Please be careful when you do this.* Occasionally a sensitive puppy will get freaked out by the sudden foot coming down over the treat. If you have a puppy that sensitive, tread lightly. This is supposed to be a fun learning experience and it's frustrating enough for the puppy to see something he wants and not be able to take it, without adding in scary thudding feet in a "death from above" type way. If the feet are just too much, put the treat on a chair and stand near the chair. If the puppy goes toward it, you can pick it up from the chair. (Or you can have a friend pick it up from the chair; same with toys on the ground when you are training this game at a more advanced level. You can call your puppy off a toy he is running toward and, if he doesn't immediately respond, your friend standing near the toy can step on it or pick it up.) Fortunately, most puppies will not care if you step on the treat.

When you have the treat next to your shoe and you don't have to step on it, feed your puppy treats from your hand while the leave-it treat is in plain sight. The puppy may glance toward the leave-it treat and look back up at you. Give him a treat if he does. He is figuring out that this is all about availability, and that your cues are going to tell him what resource is available for him in the moment.

With puppies already savvy to the Look at That game, I will even ask them, "where is the treat?" so that they indicate the treat on the ground for me and then look at me. This gets the message across even stronger that the treat is an environmental cue to attend to me in that particular context. Plus, it's fun to have a conversation with your puppy about a treat or a toy that they really want, and release them to it as a reward for "finding" it.

Start raising criteria by stepping a little bit farther from the treat, increasing the distance between the treat and your foot, in baby steps. Another way you can raise criteria is by dropping the treat straight down next to your shoe, rather than placing it carefully under your shoe. Dropping it will make it more exciting and harder to leave. Then, you can drop the treat a couple of inches from your shoe instead of next to it. Keep going until you can throw the treat right past your puppy's face, or place it next to his foot (or on his foot!)

But When Do I Say, "Leave It?"

When you feel confident about dropping the treat near your foot, introduce your cue. Start saying "leave it" as you drop the treat. Be very clear about your cue placement. Do not frustrate your puppy by being unclear as to whether or not he is supposed to be leaving something alone or taking it for himself. If you throw treats and toys to reward your puppy, you have to be able to tell him when those resources are not available, even if you are throwing them. This is why I introduce the verbal cue "leave it" pretty early in this exercise, (that is, to avoid frustrating a puppy that is used to picking something up from the floor). If the puppy hears the cue, the resource is red-lighted. If the puppy doesn't hear the cue, the resource is green-lighted. Always mark and reward as soon as your puppy gives his chosen avoidance of the treat behavior—backing up, looking away from it, default sit or down, or a combo.

I do like my dogs to break from the treat or toy and actually look at me when I tell them to "leave it," so ultimately that is what I will wait for, mark, and reward; but, in the beginning, any of these behaviors a puppy may offer as if to say, "I get it, I am going to pretend that thing is not there" is a behavior to be rewarded. I see a lot of people telling their dogs with a strong eye to "leave" their toy; the dog stops moving but does not break his stare and stays in a predatory connection with the toy until the person releases him to it. I really prefer to teach the dog to visually break from the toy and actively turn toward me, in order to get the full benefit of the leave-it cue. Otherwise, I feel like the dog has not completely left the object, he has just temporarily stopped moving, but he is still "working" the toy.

Start generalizing the leave-it behavior by putting the treat on kitchen chairs, coffee tables, tops of crates, and start giving the cue using other dogs or people or kitties instead of just a toy or treat. When your puppy is perfect with one treat on the floor, put down several. Be ready to play "Twister" with the treats and step on whatever you need to if he forgets about leave-it rules.

As my puppies grow up, they become comfortable ignoring any object I ask them to leave.

So far the puppy has been mostly stationary during this training—he is not in a stay so he can move around, but he's basically near you and not running around—a huge pet peeve of mine: I can't stand when people tell their puppy to stay during leave-it training. You will never have time in a real-life emergency leave-it situation to set your puppy up to sit, then stay, then leave-it, so why would you teach him like that? Teach him that "leave it" means an immediate breaking from the thing, even if he is in motion!

Now, we are going to ask him to run around and then leave something: that is much harder because he will be more excited. To start, invite him to move with you on the side, give the leave-it cue, *stop* moving, and place the treat near your shoe, ready to step on it if he makes a move. When he is doing great with this game, you can try inviting him to move with you, giving the cue, and then rolling the treat either behind you or to the side, whatever you think will be easier for him.

I often drop the treat or toy behind me so that my body is blocking it from the puppy in the beginning. If he is doing well, I will just step aside so that the resource is directly in front of him. If he takes a step toward it, I can step between him and the treat again (an alternative to stepping on the treat, if the treat is too far away from you). If your body block isn't enough of a reminder to your puppy that you are playing leave it, you clearly need to go back several steps. When he is successful with you throwing the treat behind you, start throwing it to your side while you are still standing in front of him. Then, stand at *his* side and throw the treat straight ahead. The object is to build up in small, achievable steps to being able to throw the object straight ahead of him while you are both running, knowing for sure that he will break from it and orient to you when given the cue.

I use Easy to demo leave it to my students and I will send him to get a Frisbee; as he is flying toward the Frisbee I will give the leave-it cue and he will immediately stop and turn his head toward me. When he does I will give him his "get it" cue. Using Premack as much as possible during leave-it training ensures a very strong leave-it response. Easy knows part of the game of playing Frisbee is occasionally being asked to leave it and then sent to get it again; there is no conflict between obeying me and getting his Frisbee. You can also send your puppy to play with another puppy and ask for a leave it (or a Whiplash Turn, or a recall—can you see how they are connected?), as soon as he breaks from the other puppy and orients to you, you can send him back to keep playing. Using Premack in this way, again, is the best way to get an industrial-strength leave-it response from your puppy.

I toss the Frisbee and send Easy to retrieve it. As he goes flying to the toy, I give my leave-it cue. He immediately stops and turns toward me.

Chapter 25

WHIPLASH TURN

This is a simple behavior of the dog quickly turning his head toward his handler at the sound of his name. I call it the Whiplash Turn, because I wanted to make sure people are aware that my aim here is to have the dog turn from whatever stimulus he is engaged with as fast as physically possible and whip right back to his handler. As mentioned earlier, the Whiplash Turn is another one of my leave-it behaviors.

In CU the Whiplash Turn is often used by itself as an attention or recall cue, but it also is the second half of the Look at That behavior chain, which is discussed in the next chapter. In Look at That, the Whiplash turn does not get its own cue; it is implied that once you ask your puppy to look at—or point something out—for you, he is to reorient to you right after.

I start this by throwing a treat on the floor. While the puppy is eating the treat, I move so that I'm standing directly behind him. (Obviously if you have a puppy that would be fearful of somebody standing behind him, you need to adjust for that.) As he finishes eating, I say his name as I stare intently at his neck. I always remind people when I teach this game that the click or marker word helps us highlight the movement of a specific body part, to make it as clear as possible to the animal what behavior is causing the reward to happen. So as soon as that puppy's neck starts moving his head and ears in my direction, I mark that. At that point, I can either give the puppy a treat from my hand, or throw the treat away from me, so I create another opportunity to ask for the Whiplash Turn.

The handler tosses a treat on the floor. While the puppy is eating the treat, she moves so that she is standing directly behind the pup. As he finishes eating, the handler calls his name and clicks the instant the puppy's head starts moving in her direction.

When the puppy is doing this quickly, you can add another person into the pattern. Let the other person show a treat to the puppy so that the puppy is engaged, then stand behind the puppy and call him. When you call, the person holding the treat can put the treat behind her back, so that the only available treat is coming from you. When your puppy is ready for higher criteria, the person can leave the treat out as you call your puppy. Do not call your puppy more than once; if he doesn't turn around quickly, just wait. Have the person put the treat behind her back again.

You can also roll a toy away from your puppy as you hold his collar. I tell people to hold the collar, get down low, and slowly roll the toy so that it looks very different from when you are just throwing a toy for your puppy to catch. I do this because people tend to make their Whiplash Turn training with toys look too much like regular retrieving and then the puppy is confused as to why he didn't get to chase the toy. I never want to see this happen, so make it look different! Roll the toy and, as you are holding your puppy's collar, strategically step behind his head so that you can stare at his neck and mark the second it turns toward you. When it does turn toward you, mark it and release him to the toy.

Always remember to watch your puppy's neck and mark at just the right moment. Many people are quite late with their timing and the message doesn't come through strongly enough. Think of it like this: we are trying to create a muscle memory, that the puppy becomes strongly conditioned to orient to you no matter what he is doing; that his name and the physical movement of swiveling his head in your direction become inextricably linked for all time. This can and *does* happen. For CU students, this is the foundation for having a dog that is reliable off leash, whether he is hiking in a wooded area filled with deer or running in the agility ring.

When you're ready to take your training on the road, this behavior can be practiced easily during daily walks. You do not always need a treat to reward the behavior; giving the puppy access to the environment is often the most appropriate reward for the Whiplash Turn. For example, your male puppy is just dying to mark a particular tree as you walk him down the street. This is a perfect opportunity to practice this behavior. Say his name and watch his neck. If he immediately turns toward you, mark that movement and take him right to the tree. Be clear with your response that you are taking him to pee on the tree because he oriented to you: "Yes! Go!" could work well, if your puppy knows "yes" as a conditioned marker and "go" means he can move ahead to interact with the stimulus of interest. That is what I would say to my puppy. It would have a clear, pre-conditioned meaning, and not be random words.

I know what you are thinking: what if the puppy does not immediately turn his head back toward you? No problem. When you start this game, if you are worried about running into this problem, do it on leash. After you call the puppy, if he doesn't turn immediately, continue staring at his neck as your hands "walk up the leash." Walking up the leash means that you move your hands up the leash toward the dog in order to shorten the length. Do not pull back on the leash, jerk it, or in any way try to physically pull the puppy's head toward you. Walk toward the puppy rather than using the leash to move the puppy closer to you.

Never, during the Whiplash Turn game, use the leash to make the puppy turn to you. Do not take his collar to turn his head to you either. Let the puppy figure it out. Let him learn that his behavior causes new opportunities to arise. Let him get addicted to paying attention to you because the body movements associated with attention behavior, such as turning his head in your direction, cause awesome things to happen.

This puppy has not immediately turned his head toward me so I walk my hands up the leash, shortening the leash.

Once you have walked up the leash, just stand there, holding the leash at about groin level, and wait. Remind yourself it's a young animal and be patient. Maybe he will be sniffing the grass, or whatever, as you stand there reminding yourself to be patient. That is fine. Just watch his neck and head and be ready to mark the movement you want. As soon as you get it, reward him and send him back to sniff the grass.

Once you have walked up the leash, just stand there and wait. As soon as the dog starts moving his head toward you, mark it!

If you find yourself in a situation where, for safety's sake, you must turn your puppy away from something he is fixated on, you can encourage him to turn his head toward you and arc away from the thing by positioning yourself near his haunch on the side you want him to turn into. When you step near the haunch, most puppies will turn their head to that side to see what you are doing back there. Rather than trying to move in front of your puppy or parallel to his head, which is what most handlers tend to do naturally, it will take a lot less time to turn him around if you move back toward his rear instead. Keep turning in an arc once he has moved his head, the rest of his body will follow.

This game, like most CU games, is about patterning; creating a pattern that engages the dog, and meets the needs of both dog and handler. Dog attends to handler, dog sniffs grass. It's a win-win situation and it doesn't take nearly as long as you would think for the dog to decide that paying attention has higher value than sniffing the grass. It's the magic of our favorite principle: Premack.

Chapter 26

LOOK AT THAT!

© DIANE LEWIS PHOTOGRAPHY

Now that your puppy will turn away from things, you can teach him to look at, or orient to, things on your cue. Start with a neutral object. I put an object, such as a book, behind my back. Sometimes I use a stuffed animal, but that's not very neutral for some dogs. I used a pen at a seminar once, because it was handy, and the Cocker Spaniel I was demonstrating with tried to take it from me; his handler said she had trained him to retrieve pens. Not neutral! Another time at a seminar I used one of my Power Bars and a handler said, "I don't think of that as neutral, because I'd like to eat it!" So, give some thought to your neutral object choice.

Dogs, such as my own, that have a strong history of Doggie Zen, will assume that if you hold out an object, you want them to look in your face rather than at the object. To avoid frustrating these dogs, I hold the object out quickly making a little "whoosh!" sound effect so that they orient to the movement out of interest before misreading the situation as a Doggie Zen situation. I mark them as they turn in the direction of the object. This is a good time to remind you to be clear *and* to be fair. When teaching something new, make sure it doesn't look like something old.

As long as you're clear with what you are reinforcing, it is not a problem to teach your puppy to look at you and to look at other stuff. I promise! I certainly teach my puppies both. When people at seminars worry about confusing their dog by teaching him to look at something on cue, I usually ask them if their dog knows how to sit. The answer is yes. I then ask if their dog knows how to lie down. The answer is yes. I ask if their dog has a problem because they sometimes tell him sit and sometimes down. The answer is no. I tell them this is the same thing as asking your dog to attend to you or to attend to something else—it's two separate behaviors, no reason to be superstitious about it. In addition, guess what? Dogs already know how to look at stuff on their own! We are just taking that behavior and integrating it into a rule structure that allows us to teach attention without conflict.

After I mark the puppy for orienting to the object, I feed him as I put the object behind my back. The puppy has no chance to keep looking at the object (and if he really wanted to, that would be my indication that the object wasn't neutral enough). What he is learning is that the behavior of orienting toward a visual target gets reinforced. He then gets the treat from my hand, so the concept of "orient to handler for the reward as part of this game" is getting built in at the very beginning.

After marking the puppy for orienting to the object, I feed the puppy as I put the object behind my back.

It doesn't take many repetitions before the puppy is happily glancing toward the object and looking back at you expectantly for his treat. At this point I continue holding the object as I mark and treat him. This gives him the opportunity to learn that, even if the object is still within visual range, the same rule structure of "look at it, look at Leslie" applies. This is when you really start seeing the little wheels turning as the puppy figures out he can cause you to give her a treat by "pointing out" the object for you. This is where you start seeing the super fast little head tilts in the direction of the object. Later on, of course, the objects will get less and less neutral.

Whenever your puppy returns to the super fast little head tilt in any object's direction, that is your sign that you can move on, if you wish, rather than continuing to play the game. It is the puppy's way of saying, "Yeah, yeah, we both know it's over there, hurry up and give me my treat!" The first time your puppy does this behavior with a stimulus that is truly distracting or scary to him, pointing it out to you and quickly turning back, you will feel really excited about the potential of this game.

Remember, with Look at That we aim to teach the puppy that stimuli that would otherwise be distracting, worrisome, and/or overly stimulating in his environment are things he can use to make the game start rather than things he needs to react to. This makes the Look at That game a very powerful tool.

When the puppy is quickly indicating the object and turning back to me, I place the object on a chair or on the floor, making sure the puppy can't just run up and try to touch the object. Throughout this entire process, the puppy doesn't get the chance to touch the object. This is the beginning of the very necessary understanding that during Look at That we do not interact with the object we are looking at, and it does not interact with us! This is why I say this game puts stimuli on "look, but don't touch" status. This is the intersection of Look at That and leave-it training.

With the object safely on a chair or on the floor (puppy is on leash unless he is glued to your side and you're not concerned he might go up to touch the object), just mark your puppy when he orients to it and wait for him to look back at you before giving the treat. He will quickly figure out that the same rules he has been practicing apply here, too. You can make a triangle formation between yourself, your puppy, and the object. This makes it easier for your puppy to be very obvious about turning toward the object and back toward you.

When do you put this behavior chain on cue? As with any clicker training, we introduce the cue after we are satisfied with the behavior. It is fine to add the cue any time during the process of keeping the toy out so that your puppy practices indicating it and looking toward you, or practicing the same pattern when the object is on the chair. Just make sure your puppy understands the pattern and isn't trying to physically interact with the object before you introduce your cue. And remember, there is one cue here for two behaviors. My personal one is, "Where is _____?" If I ask my dogs where something is, they find it for me and turn back. There is no need to ask your puppy to turn back to you during this game and if you are, that means you need to start over because your puppy does not understand the game. Or, you have put the puppy in a situation where it is too difficult for him to turn away from the stimulus.

When you're ready to move on, you can use a friendly or neutral person—again, remembering that during the game this person is not to interact with the puppy, but is present as a visual target the puppy can use to earn treats. When the puppy is pointing out the person, and quickly, expectantly turning back to you, you can add a friendly or neutral dog into the picture. When your puppy really understands and he can generalize this behavior chain onto anything he sees, you can start using strange people, dogs, and objects that your puppy would find distracting. You can also start using this game to teach your puppy to stay calm when he sees other dogs running agility, or when he sees you working with another one of your own dogs or a student's dog. These are typical situations that make a sport puppy go nuts. Look at That will neutralize these situations and turn them into just another game. If you find yourself needing to reward your puppy at a distance—say in her crate at your training club—I recommend getting a Manners Minder. The Manners Minder is a very convenient treat-dispensing device that uses a remote control, allowing you to treat at quite a distance.

Remember, if your puppy reacts—for example, gets overly aroused or vocalizes at the sight of a dog running—while you are playing Look at That, you need to lower your criteria. Don't keep asking a puppy that can't succeed at playing this game in a given situation to play the game incorrectly. Instead, change the situation. As an example, you could take the puppy to a location where he can't see the situation and do some impulse-control training or give him a break. Or, you could increase the distance so he can still see but is far enough away that he isn't reacting, and resume Look at That from there. You could also see if he can stay engaged with a stuffed Kong or marrow bone in the presence of the stimulus. Sometimes a puppy that can't think clearly around a certain stimulus can still lie on his mat, or in his crate, and chew on a bone or Kong. That is a good way for the puppy to start taking in information about the stimulus while he is engaged with something that keeps him down here on earth with us.

If your puppy is having difficulty thinking clearly around a particular stimulus, see if he can lie on his mat and chew on a bone.

Below is a snapshot of the steps involved:

- Whiplash turn (Chapter 25)

- Neutral object

- Neutral object stays out longer

- Neutral object on chair or floor

- Known dog/person

- Strange dog/person

Always keep in mind that this is a game about balance. We want to allow the dog to see the stimulus, and we want the dog to attend to us. I happened to see a handler using this game incorrectly near the practice jump at a trial. She was clicking the dog for watching another dog take the practice jump, and then offering food to her dog while he was still watching the other dog. Her dog was not turning back to her and was clearly over threshold.

If your puppy is not immediately turning back, as I said before, do not keep going. I approached that handler and suggested she step in between her dog and the other dog and ask him to take a breath (I showed her how), and reward both breathing and eye contact before stepping aside and letting him see the other dog again. Then I told her to continue alternating between the two until she felt her dog was ready to play the game "for real." If you don't take your dog out of the picture, you need to change the picture for your dog. By breaking up the game in this way, giving clear body language about what is available to look at, adding the breathing into it, and asking for a longer duration of handler focus, she was able to get her dog to start turning back to her after glancing at the other dog. If her dog had fought to look around her when she stepped in front and asked him to breathe, I would have asked her to give him a break and re-evaluate how to set him up for success next time.

VERBALLY CUED VS. OFFERED LOOK AT THAT GAME

Here is another way the Look at That game is about balance. An adept trainer will learn to read her puppy and the situation well enough to know when to *ask* the puppy to play the game, and when to let the puppy orient back and forth between a stimulus and handler on her own. "Offered" is a clicker word meaning the dog is giving you the behavior without your asking to see if he can make a reward happen. Dogs savvy to Look at That will offer initiating the game by glancing at distracting stuff and pointedly turning right back to you, saying, "Did you notice what I just did? Do I get paid for that?"

I have had students who were so happy with the offered version of the game that they did not put the time in to teach their dog a verbal cue—they were just happy that their dog turned to them as soon as he saw something that used to trigger a reaction. So I tell everybody now that, yes, it is important to teach a verbal cue also. It gives you more structure, and you may just find yourself in a situation where you need more structure! It also can serve as an early warning system, which is extremely convenient. Here is what I mean. If I am hiking with my dogs and they are running loose ahead of me, and I see a strange dog coming toward us in the distance, I say to my dogs, "Where is the dog?" They know "where is…" as a Look at That cue and they also know that the word dog means dog. So upon hearing this cue they know the following:

- There is a dog approaching.

- That dog can be used to play Look at That with me.

- That dog will not be available for interaction, because he is on Look at That (look, but don't touch) status unless I give a "go say hi" cue, which I probably will, unless the strange dog is foaming at the mouth.

My dogs do understand all that information when I say, "Where's that dog?" and yours can, too.

Being able to use the verbal cue as information that something is about to happen in the environment is incredibly helpful for puppies that might act from anxiety or excitement upon seeing a particular thing. It "plugs them into" the structure of the game so that they are already calm and playing with you when they see that thing. *This takes the element of surprise out of the situation.*

Another time you would choose to use a verbal cue rather than letting your puppy just orient back and forth at will, is if your puppy escalates his excitement whipping his head around. This game is meant to be used as a tool to calm your puppy! So, if he is using it to jazz himself up, ask for the Whiplash Turn while he is looking away from you. Click and treat him when he reorients to you. Then ask him to take a breath, reward that, and possibly eye contact as well, for several seconds. (You can figure that one breath = one second, so let's say, ask him to close his mouth or flare his nostrils three to five times.) Then you can cue him to "look at that." By giving the additional structure of the verbal cue and letting him know he has to stay focused on you until the next verbal cue, you will calm everything back down. If he can't stay focused on you for a few seconds and insists on whipping his head around, you need to take him farther from the stimulus and find a situation where he is able to take a breath and make eye contact, and start from there. With the type of puppy that excites himself with all his operant behaviors ("Yay! I'm sitting! OMG, sitting! I'm about to explode from excitement because I'm sitting!"), you can use a mat to help him settle and then work on Look at That while he is on mat rules.

Speaking of taking a breath, that behavior goes oh-so-well with the Look at That game. If you are playing it because your puppy is truly excited or nervous, then asking for a breath when he reorients to you before treating him will make a difference. Then the game is, see the thing, turn back to me, and breathe. This is a great one, for example, when your puppy goes to agility kindergarten and gets high when the other puppies are tugging or running across boards or whatever.

Growing up with this game, your puppy will learn to deal skillfully with all sorts of weird, exciting, distracting stuff that appears in the environment. Rather than asking for your puppy's attention away from something distracting, ("No Flash, you must look only at *me*, not the monkey that is riding a pony right behind you!") you will be able to allow the distraction itself to signal your puppy to pay attention to you. (Flash says, "Hmm, there is a monkey riding a pony behind me. I should point that out to mommy and see if she has a treat.")

By the time your puppy is an adolescent, when the hormones kick in and the distractions get more distracting, he will have a long successful history with using the environment to get you to pay up.

As you know, if you've played this game before, the reverse psychology component, courtesy of the Premack principle, is strong here. The more you tell your puppy he can look at stuff, the more he ends up just wanting to look at you.

Using the Environment to Teach Handler Focus 101

On a weekend in July, 2009 I was teaching at Camp Border Collie and Friends, an awesome doggie camp that takes place every summer at Glen Highland Farm, a Border Collie rescue sanctuary. Some of the campers were seasoned dog sport folks; others were just there to enjoy being on the beautiful farm with their best friends, and trying out the sports taught at camp—flyball, agility, herding—for the first time. A couple people had brought their puppies along with their adult dogs. I needed to find a Control Unleashed® topic that would work for everybody, with relevance for any dog. The Look at That Game seemed like the obvious place for me to start.

My friend Rose, who has known Easy literally since the day he was born, was at camp with her own dogs, including Easy's litter brother Snitch. Whenever Easy sees Rose he squeals and cries, and whenever Snitch sees me, he squeals and cries. As our boys come from a line known for being quite verbal, this greeting ritual quickly becomes deafening, and nobody within a 10-mile radius can focus on anything else but blocking out the noise.

I decided to take advantage of this to show people the power of the Look at That game. So Rose hid from Easy until it was time for me to teach, so that he would not know she was at camp and be totally surprised to see her at the workshop. Finally it was time to start the workshop, so I brought Easy out and explained that with Rose's help I was going to demonstrate how Look at That is part of the repertoire of behaviors I call leave-it behaviors.

So I brought Easy out of his crate telling him Rose was here by saying, "Rose is here. Are you ready? Reaaaaady? Ready to find Rose?" so he was becoming highly aroused. Then he spotted Rose and I let him go. He flew to her screaming. She got on the floor with him and he covered her with kisses as he cried and cried. Everybody was cracking up. Then I said, "Easy." And he stopped his public display of affection and ran to my side. I said, "Where is Rose?" The "where is…" is Easy's cue to start Look at That.) Easy quickly indicated where Rose was with his head and turned back to me. I said, "You can go see Rose." Easy indicated Rose to me again and then lay down, staring at me. My Look at That cue had put him in training mode and he was done with his greeting.

Everybody laughed in disbelief as Easy lay down and "refused" to go visit Rose. I wanted to drive the point home to them that Look at That is one of my "leave-it" behaviors. Once I ask my dogs to look at something for me, I am placing them in a structure that tells them they will be interacting with me and not the stimulus. The Look at That cue puts the stimulus under "you can look, but you can't touch" status; that is its connection to the concept of availability, which is behind all leave-it training.

Reliable, clear rule structures such as Look at That engage dogs in a pattern they can trust. Anxious dogs can trust they are not under threat, and distracted dogs can trust that they will get a reward that is of equal or higher value than the distraction through the act of playing the game. Perhaps even more importantly, Look at That, like most CU games, creates a pattern that engages the dog. Ultimately, repetition of the pattern becomes so ingrained that performing the pattern itself (such as seeing the stimulus and focusing on the handler) becomes the strongest thing for the dog, rather than the emotions about seeing the stimulus, or going to sniff grass (obviously, there is a strong patterning element in how the Give Me a Break game and all games associated with the Premack principle works). Dogs like patterns. People do, too! We can rely on them. They are predictable, and they always work.

One of the common questions I get about Look at That is, "My dog only wants to look at me, not the other thing. What do I do?" It's a funny question considering people who teach their dogs Look at That usually do so because they want more handler focus! It's really up to you if you want to pay your dog for taking the "shortcut" and just staring at you pointedly because there is a challenging stimulus nearby—and many dogs will do this once they become savvy to the game— or if you want to keep him orienting to the stimulus behavior on cue, then once you have given the cue, wait for *something* that shows he is pointing it out to you. At this point your puppy might offer an eyeball toward the other thing, or even twitch his ear in its direction (this is hilarious to see and often happens!) without bothering to turn his head all the way and really look at the thing. I will reward that happily, knowing the puppy is understanding what the game is about and how to use it for his benefit.

Look at That is not a traditional clicker-trained behavior chain because *the dog gets to keep deciding if he wants to change the behavioral response to the Look at That cue.* It may start out in the beginning that you say, "Ace, where is the whatever?" and Ace turns around to visually orient to it. Then one day Ace says, "I don't need to waste the energy to turn my head around. I will see if it works if I slightly move my eyeball in that direction." And another day he says, "Well, I'm really invested in keeping my eyeballs on Mom now, maybe I will see if just twitching my ear in that direction is enough." Different responses to the same cue, and it's all good. I'm way more interested in flexible social feedback than in teaching a specific cued behavior here.

Chapter 27

MAT WORK

CU mat work is an important part of my foundation training. If you know me at all, you know I am a self-described mat freak. Mats are just plain awesome, but if you need more specifics, here they are:

- Mats are the perfect way to introduce the concept of targeting which, if you're going to clicker train your puppy, is an essential part of his schooling.

- Mats give the puppy a specific place to be, which is convenient for all sorts of stuff, from door manners to table manners to teaching obstacle focus and distance work, to learning to stay calm while other dogs are running next to them and other CU Parallel games.

- You can associate a relaxed and happy emotional state with the mat so that, not only does your puppy have somewhere to be, he is helped into the perfect state for learning just by being there.

- You can use mats as part of your Off-switch game training.

- You can use mats as a "reset button."

- You can use mats to countercondition spaces or objects your puppy is worried about (the back seat of the car, the teeter totter, the grooming table, the lap of a tall dark stranger wearing a bowler hat, etc.)

- You can use mats to re-teach table and contact behavior to a dog that was traumatized by a judge looming over him on the table or eyeballing him on the contacts. The mat work steps help a "judge-soft" dog gain confidence about this stuff. This is a very common mat application I use with my students.

There are more reasons; as I've written before, I am coming up with new applications all the time.

Mat Stories

Joey: The Blind Besenji

One of my favorite mat applications was for Joey, the blind rescue Basenji. He would bite the pants (and occasionally, the legs) of people who walked up to him or near him. He would then hang on, looking like a crazed cartoon animal, and have to be removed from the offending appendage. I taught him that if pants approached his comfort zone, he could find his handler as part of a game. This went very well, but then we worried about his being in a room without his handler and not having that coping option available. So I taught him to find a mat when pants approached his comfort zone. We would scent the mat with lavender so he could find it easily, and then any new space he was taken to, he would be taken to the mat first and that would become his point of reference for the space. This strategy worked so well that vet techs were able to examine him amazingly bite-free while he lay calmly on his mat!

Rumor: The Jerky Teenager

When Ru was a teenager he became a jerk to other dogs. He would get very aroused and very sharp at the sight of them and I felt extremely frustrated. I spent a *lot* of time teaching him to relax, focus on his job, and not react when other dogs were around. In fact, because of this problem, Ru was my very first experimental subject for what was to become the Look at That game.

One of the things that helped us get through this annoying time was mat work. As soon as he started behaving reactively, I made sure Ru had a strong foundation of the Protocol for Relaxation and biofeedback training on his mat. Ru got to the point where he would find a mat from any distance, fly to it, lie down, take a breath, blink, and happily ignore everything around him as he lay there. I took the mat to a training facility and we successfully worked in the corner of different classes. Then I decided to take the mat to the hiking trail because Ru had started growling and flinging himself at dogs we passed on the trail. I left him in the car and I laid the mat down under a tree at the beginning of the trail. I wanted to test Ru's generalization skills and his emotional association with the mat by creating a situation where he suddenly unexpectedly "found" a mat in a novel context.

Ru and I started walking. When we came near the tree I told Ru there was a mat there. His face brightened in amazement, he scanned, saw the mat and flew to it. He slammed down on it, looked up at me, closed his mouth, and softened his eyes. I was cracking up because I could imagine him thinking, "Wow! Who knew they had mats here, too?" It wasn't a minute before the first dog walked down the hiking trail right past our tree. It was a big, lumbering Newfoundland, which was a very triggering phenotype for Ru. I don't remember saying anything, because as soon as Ru became aware of the dog he looked at me like, "Look, there's a dog there. Are we doing the Relaxation Protocol?" I did not get a reaction out of him that day as a variety of dogs walked past the mat.

Maggie: The Child Snapper

Maggie and I did a tremendous amount of work getting her comfortable enough around children that she could assist me in my pet obedience classes. As a puppy, she growled and snapped at any child that came near her. I micromanaged her, making sure there wouldn't be any trouble with her and my students' children. She got to the point that, throughout her career as my assistant, children could just walk up and pet her and she stayed perfectly relaxed and happy. It was a huge accomplishment for her.

Before she evolved to the point where I allowed children to touch her, a student once asked me if her son could play with Maggie. I explained that Maggie was afraid of children and that the little boy could not pet her, but that he was allowed to throw a ball for her. I gave the child her ball. Another student walked in and asked me a question. I started answering her and forgot to supervise the child/Maggie interaction. After a few minutes of talking I got a funny feeling and I turned around to look for Maggie. Maggie was lying on her mat staring at me. *The little boy sitting on the mat with his arms wrapped around her neck, his face level with hers.* I almost had a heart attack, but the expression on Maggie's face said, "I am so very uncomfortable with this, but I am on my mat and I trust that I will be safe and that you will make this child go away; I've just been waiting for you to notice and fix it!" Calmly I smiled and asked the child to go sit with his mother.

When she didn't have immediate access to me because I was distracted, Maggie used her mat as a safe space when faced with her worst child nightmare. I should never have let this happen to her, but it certainly was a lesson for me on how "mat trained" Maggie really was.

THE FOUR STEPS OF MAT WORK

After writing Control Unleashed®, I decided to break mat work down into steps that people could train progressively.

Step One: Mat Mechanics

This step is about all the training mechanics necessary to teach your puppy a cue that means orient to a mat, go to it and lie down until a verbal release:

Mutt Mats makes a travel mat that is very convenient for mat work.

- Get a new mat, doggie bed, blanket, or towel (I like the Mutt Mats myself; they are available from www.cleanrun.com) and examine it as if you have never seen anything so fascinating. If there is another person around, show it to that person and you can both marvel at the new mat. That way, when you put it down on the ground, most likely your puppy will be curious and go right up to it. The instant he shows interest, click and put a treat on the mat.

- Keep putting treats on the mat for as long as your puppy stays on it. At this point it doesn't matter if he is sitting, lying down, standing; as long as he is on the mat, he is making rewards happen. If he is only partially on it, it is your judgment call. I'd reward him for that at first to build his interest and confidence, but I'd start raising my criteria as soon as I could so that he understood that all of his body needs to be touching the mat. Remember, as long as your puppy is on the mat, he is not "wrong!"

As long as your puppy is on the mat, keep putting treats on the mat for him to eat. Initially we only care that he is on the mat.

- Next, incorporate your release cue. Release your puppy from the mat *calmly.* If he has become glued to the mat, you may need to encourage him to move by backing away, clapping; whatever it takes. Do not ask him to come very far off the mat; he should be standing next to the mat at first. Once he is off the mat, reward him for coming to you, and then just stand there and see if he shows interest in returning to the mat. As soon as he starts returning, click and put a treat on the mat. And the fun begins again! Every time you give your release cue, step a little farther from the mat so

After getting a treat from his handler, this puppy immediately offers to return to the mat.

that when he returns to you for his treat, he will have to go a little farther to get back on the mat and restart the game. That is how I teach the distance component.

- At some point, your puppy will offer behavior on the mat, such as a sit or down. I like an automatic down on the mat. Practice *lots* of fun, rewarding downs before introducing the mat, so that it's on your puppy's mind when learning mat work. Yes, you can cheat and tell him to lie down, but at some point the mat itself should be a cue for him to lie down. Again, I get the down behavior by building up a strong reward history with downs off the mat and then clicking and treating the instant the puppy offers a down on the mat.

The first puppy is offering a sit on the mat. While I may initially mark the sit, I continue shaping until a down on the mat is the default behavior.

- When your puppy understands he can run away from you and find his mat at a distance and lie down on it, you can start adding in a mat cue that will mean four things: orient to your mat, go to your mat, lie down on your mat, and wait on your mat until you hear your release cue. My cue is "go to your mat." If the puppy ever gets off the mat before being released, just send him back to the mat and then release him. He doesn't need a treat for going back to the mat if it is a re-send. Your puppy should be learning from the very beginning to stay on the mat until released because he should be getting intermittent treats on the mat until he hears the release word.

- If you have a clicker-happy puppy he may offer other behaviors on the mat such as waving, barking, putting his head between his paws, etc. Don't reward any of those behaviors. In CU mats are used to help a dog calm down. Dogs allowed to frantically offer behaviors on their mats cannot calm down. So, once the puppy understands that down is the most awesome thing to do on a mat, if he does something else, I give his release word, calling him off the mat. I don't give a treat for his coming off, but I do give him another chance and give his mat cue again so he can start over with his down. If you find yourself doing this more than a few times, put the mat aside and go back to rewarding downs until they're a default behavior. And examine your training style, your timing, and your rate of reinforcement. Your puppy should not feel like he has to throw everything he knows at you just because you have a treat in your pocket. That's another reason I love default behavior.

Step Two: Open Bar, Closed Bar

This is a dog training term I learned from Jean Donaldson. The application of it here is the first step of teaching the puppy that when people or dogs come near the mat while he's on it, it's a good thing. This is a big part of training the puppy to stay relaxed and focused around potentially exciting or even upsetting distractions.

Give your puppy his mat cue. Have a friend approach the mat. *Don't forget to adjust for your puppy's temperament.* If he worries about people walking up to him, have your friend walk to the side rather than head on. If he gets overly excited or distracted when people are two feet away, tell your friend to stand four feet away. You can even put a ring gate or other barrier between your friend and your puppy so the puppy has a visual assurance that the person isn't coming all the way over (until the puppy is ready!) In other words, always remember to start sub-threshold!

Don't wait for your puppy to do anything, just "open the bar" by feeding on the mat as the person approaches. As soon as the person turns to walk away, stop feeding. Your goal is for the puppy to associate somebody coming near him when

This Sheltie puppy learns to associate a stranger approaching his mat with treats from his handler.

he's on her mat with two things: treats and *you*. This is why mat training is part of leave-it training (isn't everything?) People coming up to the mat are not available for interaction. But you are available for interaction and treats when people come up to the mat. Therefore, people coming up to the mat are an *environmental* cue for the puppy to look to you for something nice.

For a puppy that loves people, this will help with training handler focus around distractions; for a puppy that worries about people, this will help teach him to feel confident and to relax when people approach while he is on "mat rules." Mat rules state that when the puppy is on a mat and somebody, person or animal, comes up to him, he is non-interactive and he gets a treat from his handler. Therefore, puppies that worry about social interaction with new people or dogs do not have to worry when they are approached once mat rules have been activated. The pressure to possibly interact is off and the game is on.

When will you stop doing this step? As soon as your puppy starts looking longingly at the person leaving the mat as if to say, "Hey… come back here! When you're here I get treats!" That is the point at which you are basically done with this step. However, you could raise criteria by having the person:

- Move closer to the puppy

- Look directly at the puppy, if the person hasn't already been doing this

- Talk while approaching the puppy ("Ohhhh, what a cute puppy. What is that, a Rottiepoo?")

Here I've raised the criteria and am walking up to the puppy's mat with my dog.

- Move strangely

- Having the person walk a dog up

- Drop something as he or she is walking

- Shake your hand

I do not normally bother with raising criteria like that myself for this step; once the association is made I move on. You can use these same criteria, however, for steps three and four as well and I *do* raise criteria during steps three and four.

Step Three: Informal Look at That Game from the Mat

Here is one way to start teaching the concept of the Look at That game.

Have the person start walking up to the mat, but instead of immediately opening the bar, wait for your puppy to orient to the person. Keep waiting; the instant the puppy looks back at you, open the bar. Have the person leave and close the bar.

Wait for your puppy to orient to the person walking up to the mat. As soon as he reorients to you, open the bar.

This step is to teach your puppy that if he notices something in the environment while he is on her mat, he can turn to you and get paid. Do not give any cues during this step, let the puppy figure it out.

If your puppy does not just briefly orient to the person, but is actively watching the person, have that person stand still rather than continue moving toward the mat until the puppy looks back at you. You can help your puppy by making a little kissy sound or saying his name to get his attention so that you can reward him. If you have to do that more than once or twice, however, you are obviously working *over threshold* and you need to change what you're doing.

The more common problem here is that the puppy won't orient to the other person at all, but will stay fixated on you, waiting for treats, because he understoods the step one training so well. If this happens, smile at your puppy and then look at your friend with curiosity, and hope that your puppy will follow your gaze. Eventually, your puppy isn't going to want to orient to anything but you when he's following mat rules. That means you taught him the mat rules correctly. This is where step four comes in.

Step Four: Actual Look at That Game from the Mat

You could teach the Look at That game from a mat, but if you do this, you have to be very careful to teach the puppy that he can also play this game from a stand, a sit, or down. He needs to learn the game is about where he puts his head and eyes *independent of what he's doing with the rest of her body.* Typically I start the game while the puppy is just standing there casually. However, it is easy to put a cue on the behavior of orienting to a stimulus during step three of mat work, so that is another appropriate way to start Look at That training. For puppies that insist on touching whatever they're supposed to be just looking at, or for nervous puppies that feel better when they're on mat rules, you could start on the mat. Also, for more advanced Look at That training, when you want your puppy to briefly glance at a running or tugging dog, but it's hard for them not to move toward that dog, use the mat during that part of training. Puppies on mat rules can control themselves much better and play "look at the dog flying over the A-frame" much easier when they're on mat rules. The mat can be faded in time.

This step looks suspiciously like step three, but the difference is you are going to give the "look at that" cue before the puppy orients to the person. Once you've given it, if the puppy is still staring at you, smile and look at the person yourself and wait it out. When your puppy gets proficient at playing Look at That he will start "refusing" to look and will stay focused on you, wanting to "cut out the middleman" by playing the second half of the game (orienting to you), the half that ends with getting the treat. In real life, if your puppy is doing that, you don't need to be playing the game with whatever stimulus you are using; your puppy is saying he's ready to work and he doesn't need to be seeing that thing. In real life, we just use this game for a stimulus that your puppy needs to visually process. This game can easily be modified to a "Where's that noise coming from?" game.

Once your puppy is fluent in her mat rules, she has earned the official CU title of Mat Brat. Life is much easier with a Mat Brat puppy,

This puppy is pointing out something in the environment to his handler.

especially in class and at trials. Once you have experienced life with a Mat Brat, you will never want to go back.

TALE OF A MAT BRAT

My student Jen's Cattle Dog, Cruzin, was the first Mat Brat to use her mat as a way of getting her over that last obstacle (pardon the agility pun) to being a successful trial dog. Since then I have used the same protocol on other dogs with the same results.

Cruzin had come so far in her CU training that she was ready to trial. She came to me because watching other dogs run turned on her prey drive; she would visually lock on and then want to chase them. It took close to a year for Cruzin to evolve from being a dog that could not watch Easy moving at a moderate pace in my backyard without getting "stuck" in a staring, crouching, straining at the leash, and ready to explode mode, to a dog that happily attended group classes, ignored the other dogs doing agility, and was reliable and totally handler-focused near them off leash, even if they were tugging or weaving. In fact, Cruzin got so good that once as she was practicing weaving with Easy as a distraction near the poles, Easy actually left me and started weaving, two poles behind Cruzin who had not finished weaving yet. So I learned two things: I learned there is a point at which Easy could go over his threshold while being my helper dog, and I learned that Cruzin was such a rock star that a dog she could not even watch walking on a leash in my yard the previous summer was *flying through weave poles right behind her*, and she did not even turn around. When she came out of the poles, she ran to her owner to tug.

So, Cruzin had made amazing progress but now that she was trialing in earnest, a new problem had emerged. She had great handler focus while waiting for her turn, but as soon as she stepped into the ring and saw the other dog finishing the last couple obstacles before her turn, she devolved back into that staring, crouching, straining rocket girl. She was still able to get her head back and run the course but, being a great student and handler, Jen wanted to change this situation before it potentially got worse.

My first thought was that we could use mats to fix this. I felt that Cruzin, being a seasoned Mat Brat, should be capable of handling the same stimulus gracefully while on her mat. Of course, Jen could not bring her mat inside the ring at a trial, but in the beginning of training we could use one to "reframe" the ring-entry experience into a high-criteria mat challenge. I changed the training area around to make it look more trial-like and created a line of ring gates Cruzin would have to walk through before entering the ring, a setup I had seen at some local shows.

I put her mat outside that line of ring gates and sent another student to take her dog through the last few obstacles of a course and run out of an exit point in the ring. I had Jen walk Cruzin a few feet from the mat, facing the other dog finishing his course, and asked her to send Cruzin to her mat. Cruzin did go to her mat, but her eyes were on the other dog running instead of her mat. I had Jen leave Cruzin in a sit and go stand on the other side of the mat. That way she could call Cruzin to her rather than walking next to Cruzin toward the mat. This helped Cruzin focus and once she was lying on her mat, Jen switched from front to side and played the Look at That game. By that point Cruzin was totally focused on Jen and we saw that if we got that initial response of reasonably calm focus when entering a ring while another dog was finishing up, the rest would be easy.

To raise criteria I had Jen once again send Cruzin to her mat face-on, walking at her side without body-blocking her from what was happening in the ring. As soon as she heard her mat cue, Cruzin fixated on her mat and dove on it never glancing toward the ring. I then began moving the mat closer to the start line. Upon hearing her cue, Cruzin was happily fixating on her mat, with no notice of the other dog, when I had placed it about halfway between the entrance point and the start line. Once Cruzin was on it, Jen would reward her and leave the ring so we could start over. I knew the best reward would be to let Cruzin run the course, so I finally put the mat at the start line. Jen gave the mat cue from outside of the ring as the other dog was finishing his course, and Cruzin took her right to the start line without once looking at the other dog. At that point I had Jen remove the leash and leave her in a stay. We had the other dog do a couple more obstacles and Jen, who was on the other side of the start line jump, tossed treats onto Cruzin's mat. She was completely focused and wanting to work, so after the other dog finished, Jen released Cruzin and ran a sequence. Both of them were delighted.

We worked on this for several weeks and then it was time for the next trial. Jen did mat work outside the ring and as they were waiting in line to enter the ring I had her do a mix of asking Cruzin to take a breath and play the Look at That game with the dog running in the ring. Jen gave her mat cue as that dog was leaving the ring and although Cruzin was not as hyper-focused on Jen as in class (her eyes were a little glazed over from the excitement) she went right to the start line and was about 90% in her head as opposed to, say, 10%. At the next trial she did even better. That is what my students call a "CU Q."

One of my agility teachers, Leslie Whitney, showed me how to put toys a few feet from the end of contacts to help keep the dog's head straight as he did his contact behavior. Once he did his contacts, she would release and send him to the toy. She started "on the flat" by sending the dog to touch a target lid on the ground instead of at the end of a contact, with the toy a couple feet from the lid. Easy loved this and I started using this same rule structure as a mat game. As well as being a great self-control lesson, this structure can also be used as a fun, active attention activity, once your puppy really understands what the game is about.

Back to Cruzin. During her mat training, she had learned to orient to and then run to a mat, even if her Frisbee was lying on the other side of it. In setting this up, I was trying to communicate that, even if something really exciting is on the other side of the mat, if she has been given her mat cue her job is to find the mat, get on it, and lie down. Doing this correctly, of course, resulted in a Premack reward. She would get released from her mat and sent to her Frisbee. I liken this to teaching dogs to enter the ring while the other dog is finishing the course because it's the same idea. The mat creates a "stop," a pause, and get-in-your-head space, as the dog is moving forward into a "stimulation situation."

Once your dog learns his mat rules, you could add a toy, or put the mat in front of a pond, another dog, whatever floats his boat. You could run with him toward the mat or, if he lost focus, you could call him to his mat while you were standing on the other side of it, blocking whatever the stimulus was, as Jen did in the example above, and go through the same steps. Of course this situation is easier to work on than Cruzin's situation, as you have the extra support of your leave-it cue as you put the toy down on the other side of the mat, then give his mat cue. As you play with this, you may discover that the toy needs to be a certain distance away before the dog can successfully do his mat behaviors. As with all training, you can keep adjusting so he gets it right. You can also enlist the help of a friend to step on the toy if he goes for it instead of his mat. But, if you find him doing this, he is just letting you know you need to make things a little easier for him.

Chapter 28

OFF-SWITCH GAME

This is such an essential skill for every puppy to practice, regardless of what his job is going to be as an adult. In the CU version of this exercise we use default behavior and biofeedback to help bring the puppy to a calmer state after play. Just asking for a "control Band-Aid" sit or down after tugging or another stimulating activity is not good enough here. We are going to ask the puppy to *calm himself* before resuming play.

As you well know, a dog can be in a start-line-type sit, where his butt is on the floor but he is highly aroused and ready to pop. I am not looking for this type of sit in this particular context, although you certainly can play an Off-switch game with that type of sit, using it as a fast control behavior. When you do, be aware that the sit is a control Band-Aid but you are not working on helping the puppy regulate his level of arousal much. In other words, cueing your tugging puppy to sit and drop his toy is not a guarantee he is going to "settle down" without extra help.

Before starting this game, your puppy will need to have a *strong* default behavior: sit, down, and eye contact are some standard default behaviors. A stacking stand could be another one, if you are going to show in conformation.

Your puppy will also need to have at least one activity that he finds stimulating in order to play this game. I am guessing that this is not going to be a problem! If your puppy doesn't want to play with toys, I will address that in the discussion of the Give Me a Break game in the next chapter. You do not need to play with a toy to start your Off-switch game training, although in my opinion it's really fun. Instead, you could just run around with your puppy, or even just pet him a lot if he is a very tactile-sensitive puppy that gets very excited by touch. *Any* stimulating activity will work to get the Off-switch game started. Conversely, you can use the game to teach your puppy to calm down after *any* activity that overstimulates him!

I'm going to use tugging as our example of a stimulating activity. Determine how many seconds of tugging will take your puppy from "excited, but still in thinking brain" to "BANZAI brain!" Then initiate a tug game and mentally count the seconds while watching your puppy's expression. Try to take him to the very edge of banzai brain and then stop moving and do your best imitation of a potted plant, which should, at this point, serve as the cue for the puppy's default behavior. Most puppies will drop the toy as they offer their default behavior.

Easy's default is a sit and, if he sits when I stop tugging but holds onto the toy, it's a given that he is over the banzai threshold and his eyes will have a faraway trance-like look (in contrast, Snap's Terrier eyes will have a hard look that says, "this toy must *DIE*.") When this happens I just stand still, holding the tug at groin level with my hands close together, and watch him come back to earth and drop the toy while remaining in his sit. So if your puppy keeps tugging after you behave like a potted plant, just stand there with the toy at groin level and wait. Watch his eyes, willing them with your mind to soften. To speed things up, as soon as he drops the toy, mark that behavior and offer the toy back. You could hold his collar during this process, though in the long run I want the puppy to be able to release the toy without that "help."

Premack is our best friend here, as usual. The message is always, if you drop the toy, you get the toy.

As you progress with this game, you can add biofeedback behaviors into it. It will look like this:

- You invite your puppy to tug

- You get him jacked up just at, but not over, the banzai threshold and then you stop and become a potted plant

- Puppy will give the default behavior and drop the toy

- Ask him to take a breath and you could also reward a blink, or relaxed ears, or a slower tail wag

- When your puppy has a settled expression, you say "Reeeady? Get it!" and start the game over again

You can also add a mat to this game. Instead of a default behavior, you can cue the puppy to go to his mat. You can do the biofeedback behaviors while the puppy is on the mat and then invite him off to tug again. Sometimes the mat helps the puppy calm down faster. It is also good practice for stimulating class environments, where your puppy does an exercise out on the floor, probably gets rewarded with tugging, and then returns to his mat by your chair (or to his crate). You can ask for the same biofeedback behaviors in that context and view your entire class as an Off-switch game.

I tell my students I want their puppy to learn this game at a physiological level. What I mean by this is that I want the puppy to learn how it *feels* to calm himself down after something has excited him. That is an awesome life skill for a puppy to have, and this is a fun way to teach it. Is he going to be dead calm a second after tugging? No, but I'm not trying to get him there. The goal is for the puppy to learn how to dial it down, quickly. We are not asking him to dial it down to zero. How low he actually learns to dial it down depends on your personal criteria and how much biofeedback you feel like doing.

What if your puppy won't drop his toy? Then you need to separate that piece out from this game and just work on drop/trade behavior. In the meantime you can still play Off-switch games, just do it without a toy. Run around with your puppy acting like a goofball instead. What if your puppy won't offer his default behavior when you stand still? If he won't default, it means he doesn't actually have a default behavior. Teach him one before you play another Off-switch game.

How does the Off-switch game help with teaching focus? If your puppy can't easily switch from banzai brain back to thinking brain, and he has trouble thinking clearly enough to do agility obstacles or anything else successfully when he is high… do I really have to finish this sentence?

Sky: The Mouth Without a Brain

Sky was a delightful, sweet young girl with a very low arousal threshold. Being from a line of working retrievers, the sight of toys sent her over the top. She'd been asked to leave a puppy agility class and work with me due to her excitability. She got so high on praise alone that if her handler said "good girl" in a happy voice, Sky jumped all over her handler and mouthed her. When I observed her in this state, I affectionately referred to her as the "mouth without a brain."

As I watched Sky interact with her handler, Erica, I quickly formulated a plan. Basically I wanted to turn all her learning interactions into off–switch games.

First, she needed the basics: she needed to settle and take a breath, and she needed a strong default behavior. I explained to Erica that just telling her to sit wasn't enough; I wanted it to be a default behavior so that when Sky was worked up, she had to think through that arousal. Defaults encourage puppies to be thoughtful because the puppy has to figure out what behavior to do for himself, rather than having a person always telling him what to do. It puts the responsibility for his behavior on him.

I brought Easy out to demonstrate first. I showed Erica how he closes his mouth and flares his nostrils at me, and how he does look calmer while doing that than if he just sat. I picked up a Frisbee and stood near the weave poles, and he flew to me and landed at my side in a sit. It was a nice example of a default behavior because he clearly wanted to be released to do the poles and get his Frisbee, and he was asking for it with his behavior.

I then showed her some leave-it steps, starting with holding the Frisbee away from my body, which was a cue for Easy to make eye contact with me instead of eyeing the Frisbee. I then showed her that I could throw the Frisbee to the side or behind me, while Easy maintained eye contact. I sent Easy to retrieve the toy, threw it as far as I could, then I asked him to leave it just before he caught it. Easy stopped on a dime, turned back toward us, and sat. I don't expect his default behavior in that context, I just want him to honor his leave-it behavior by stopping his chase and orienting in my direction. But it was perfect because his addition of a default behavior to his leave-it behavior was exactly what I wanted Erica to understand we could teach her puppy. I often tell people that my games are all connected by a few powerful concepts and this was a good illustration of it.

Holding the Frisbee away from my body is a cue for Easy to make eye contact with me instead of eyeing the Frisbee. I can even throw the Frisbee while he maintains eye contact.

Sky started learning a "take a breath" behavior. She already had the makings of a default sit. If I got treats out, she sat politely; however, if I got a toy out, she jumped all over me. So jumping was her default when she at a certain level of arousal. I saw that if Erica fumbled around in the canvas bag where Sky's toys were kept, Sky jumped all over her wanting to take whatever was in the bag. So I decided to make that the beginning of her leave-it lesson.

I put the canvas bag on a lawn chair and when Sky went for it, I picked the bag up and turned away from her. When she landed on the ground I put the bag back on the chair. My aim was to teach her that she had to keep all four paws on the ground for the bag to remain on the chair. As long as she remained standing I rummaged around the bag talking to her about how interesting everything was in there. If she got jumpy, I removed the bag. When Sky was standing calmly, watching as I rummaged through the bag, I held up her pink bunny. Sky read my mind and immediately sat when she saw the toy. Erica looked very surprised!

Because Sky sat right away I invited her to play with the bunny. She tugged like a maniac, just what I love to see. She already had a good drop-it instilled. I took the toy and held it out to my side, wanting her to look away from it in my direction to do some Doggie Zen as a start to her leave-it training, but she went after the toy. So I held the toy behind my back and turned away from her. Sky collected herself and sat. I took some treats out and rewarded her for taking a breath a bunch of times. She was not able to sit still for this if the toy was visible, but if I kept it behind my back she could sit still, remaining excited because she knew it was there. After she did her breathing I released her to get the bunny toy. The next time I got it back, I was able to raise criteria by holding the toy out in plain sight as I gave her treats for closing her mouth. I then went back to Doggie Zen, holding the toy out at arm's length, and Sky looked right at me so I threw it for her again.

The next time, I decided to just walk around holding the toy. Sky followed me excitedly, bouncing, but not jumping on me. And, when I stopped walking, she did a default sit! Her mommy was very proud of her. I told Erica that I would do this as a starter-level Off-switch game, just walking around with the toy and stopping, waiting for the default behavior. If she were my puppy, I would build up this particular game to the point where Sky could heel off lead, keeping her head up and making eye contact with me while I moved the toy around. Easy enjoyed that one when he was a puppy and it made heeling a lot more exciting when I reframed it as another fun leave-it game with Frisbees.

I returned to the more formal leave-it work and put the pink bunny under my shoe, explaining to Erica that we would click as soon as Sky lifted her head toward me, away from my shoe, which did not take her very long to figure out.

I then showed Erica how she could use what we'd been working on to teach Sky not to mouth her while they were running together. She wanted to do agility with her, but Sky would get worked up and grab Erica. We put "running with mom" into an Off-switch game structure, where they moved together a few steps, and Erica stopped until Sky gave the default behavior. Then Sky got rewarded for her default, and for taking breaths, and the movement started again. This, coupled with the leave-it training, would enable Erica to run, even with toys, without falling prey to the "mouth without a brain." Each time they played this game, Erica could run a little longer and stop moving a little less, until they were running all over the place without stopping until the end, with Sky remaining in excited, but thoughtful enough to not lose control mode.

When I had Erica start from the beginning, it took Sky a few minutes to be able to watch her rummage through the toy bag on the chair without jumping on the chair, but she got it and was calmly standing watching Erica as she picked up different toys from the bag. Then Erica held up a ball, waiting for the default sit. Sky lost control and jumped toward her. I told Erica to put the ball back in the bag, pick up the bag, and wait until Sky settled. Sky quickly remembered herself and was calmly walking around with Erica and watching her, defaulting to a sit and not trying to take the toy, and taking breaths for treats. Erica rewarded her by releasing her to the toy, of course. This private lesson took an hour and 20 minutes.

This was the perfect type of training to start Sky on while she was still a puppy, nearing adolescence. Who wants to start from scratch teaching impulse control to an adult high-drive working Labrador in her full glory?

Chapter 29

GIVE ME A BREAK GAME

The CU way of teaching your puppy to attend to you off lead for long periods of time is all about the Give Me a Break game. This game truly puts the ball in the dog's court, by empowering the dog to ask for *more* work, rather than the handler having to ask for it from a tired or distracted puppy! Dogs that usually can just repeat a behavior a few times and then are "done" do exceptionally well when they are trained using this game. I work with a lot of dogs that just lose steam quickly and the Give Me a Break game is a terrific way to help them build their stamina and concentration.

USING GIVE ME A BREAK FOR HANDLER ORIENTATION: THE ATTENTION VARIANT

You will be playing the first variant of the Give Me a Break game, attention, while you are walking around with your puppy. In order to play this game you will need:

- A release word.

- A cue that directs the puppy to "go see" or "go sniff" a specific stimulus in your training space that you can use as the Premack reward.

You may find that all you need is a release word and no further direction will be needed. The better your puppy gets at this game, however, the more you will have to point out the distractions.

TEACHING THE RELEASE

Some people just use their body language in a natural way to communicate to the dog to go on, but other people seem to get stuck with this. In this game you need to be able to release your puppy to go somewhere or do something. So for my students who need a formal way of telling their pup to go on, I have them hold the puppy, usually by the collar, while letting the puppy watch them roll a treat or toy down a line straight ahead of them. I may pull back a little on the collar, or hold the puppy flyball-style, saying, "ready?" to add excitement about moving forward. Then I will say the release word, let go, and the puppy will move ahead of me in a straight line to get the treat or toy. I do the same thing to teach the dog to move ahead of me down a straight line in agility. So, this is "two for the price of one" training.

Holding the puppy by his collar, roll a treat across the floor in a straight line from you. Say the release word and let go of the puppy's collar.

By doing it this way, when the handler releases her pup to take his break, she can say, "O.K. go!" (She could also say "go sniff" or "go see the dog," whatever). Working on the going-away part separately also helps people remember that they actually need *to do* the going-away part. People often just remember to reward the dog for coming back to them but then let the dog take off on his own, without remembering to release the dog.

Releasing the dog to take another break is the important thing here, because this game relies on the power of the Premack principle to make it work.

To start, move around within an enclosed space. When your pup comes up to you, praise or click and treat him. Then give your release word, which can be coupled with a go-away cue: "O.K., go play!" As you say this, turn away from the puppy and walk off, keeping one eye on the puppy so that as soon as he orients toward you, you can mark it. Treat him when he catches up, then say, "O.K. go away!" Turn your back and change directions.

Here I am walking around in an area closed in by a fence and ring gates. When the puppy comes up to me, click and treat him. I then release him to go sniff.

I intermittently throw treats on the ground for the puppy to find as I turn and walk in the other direction. I watch the puppy out of the corner of my eye to see if he looks for me after finishing the treats; this lets me know whether he is really getting the point.

Many people give their release cue in the same tone of voice as they praise the dog for coming, and they aren't clear with their body language that the dog is being told that training time is over and he is on break. For this reason, I will have the student walk next to me as if she is the dog and the first time we walk I'll say, "Oh good girl, that's great. O.K. go play," and I'll just keep walking in a straight line, which many people do when they start learning this game. This body language is incompatible with the verbal cue and helps the handler see that unclear information is never going to teach the dog what the game is about.

Then I will walk with the handler again, but this time when I say, "Oh good girl, that's great," I stop moving and look at the handler and say, "O.K." and make an "all done" motion with my hands for effect. I turn my back on the handler and walk off in a different direction. It needs to be clear to your puppy that you have dismissed him from interaction. Showing students like this always helps them understand the timing and finesse necessary.

Sometimes I tell students to feed three treats to the dog every time he comes back, because it gives them extra time to prepare to give their release word and turn around.

Usually the puppy catches on quickly and starts trotting after his handler after he's been released to take his break. Every time he does so, he is marked for orienting to the handler, rewarded when he catches up, and released to take another break. Sometimes students get hung up on "heel position," and I have to remind

them that this is attention training and the puppy is being rewarded for orienting to his handler instead of "taking a break." Let's not overcomplicate things here! The goal is for the puppy to "refuse" his break and just follow his person around the yard. Worry about the puppy's position in relation to your body later, please.

The puppy quickly follows me after I've released him to go take a break.

BUILDING FOCUS AND DRIVE FOR MORE COMPLEX TASKS: THE CHAIR VARIANT

In this variant of the game I often use a chair for the handler to go to and sit in after releasing her puppy. I like the chair for three reasons:

1. It gives the handler a specific place to go, which helps clarify the handler's body language.

2. It can be used as a restart button of sorts: once your puppy is fluent in this game, if he loses focus while working, you can simply go sit in the chair and he will return to you, rather than your walking around calling him when he's not being responsive (one of my pet peeves with students).

This puppy has oriented to me while I'm sitting in the chair.

3. It helps lock the puppy into a feedback pattern where he will start racing to the chair before you can even get over there saying, "Don't leave. We are not done working!"

You don't need the chair when using the first variant of the game, where you are walking around your club or your yard, because you want to reward the puppy for finding you wherever you've gone; however, in this second variant, you are focused on rewarding a behavior that is independent of your position (unless you're heeling).

When your puppy is fluent in the first variant of the game, in other words he is following you around the learning space, off leash, without gates, not taking your "go away!" seriously and insisting on attending to you, then you can start the second variant.

Put your chair out, typically inside a box of ring gates to start, and add in a behavior you have been working on such as sit or down, an agility obstacle, a rally sign, or whatever. Ask for the behavior several times, *at the opposite end of the box from the chair so that you have space to turn and walk back to the chair.* Reward each repetition of the behavior. Then release your puppy (you could do this with your verbal release cue, or you could throw a treat and tell him to get it, which I often like to do) and go sit in your chair. Wait for your puppy to orient to you in the chair.

When your puppy comes over to the chair, get up enthusiastically and run with him back to the other end of the box. Ask for some repetitions of the behavior, rewarding each one. How many repetitions? Always ask for less than the amount that will make it seem like drudgery to your puppy. One puppy could do a down five times, another one could do it once and that would be enough. Then, release your puppy and walk purposefully and briskly back to the chair.

This Border Collie puppy gets rewarded for heeling and, upon being released, heads right back to the chair to reinitiate the game.

WHAT ARE YOUR CRITERIA FOR GETTING UP FROM THE CHAIR?

Some puppies will walk or run right over to the chair to see you; while others, if they even notice your return to the chair, should be rewarded for just noticing. Adjust your reinforcement criteria here to help your puppy succeed. If your puppy is highly distractible and he even turns toward the chair, get up right away, go over to him, ask for the behavior again, reward it, release, and return to the chair. Over time you can raise criteria, waiting for your puppy to come closer to the chair before you get up and restart the game. If your puppy is readily running over to the chair, wait for him to come all the way to you before getting up and returning with him to the other end of the box.

Using the Attention Variant as a Warm-up to the Chair Variant

You may find that you need to play the attention variant as a warm-up to prepare your puppy to play the chair variant. Or, you may find that you never need the attention variant at home before using the chair variant or another training structure, but you need to use it at class, or at a show, or at the park.

Using the Chair Variant for Sequencing

If you are working on building drive and focus for short agility sequences, then after two or three repetitions of an obstacle, release the puppy to take a break and return to your chair. When the puppy goes over to the chair, get up immediately and in a *happy* manner run over to the obstacles. You can then ask for two different obstacles, rewarding after the second one, and release. Building from there you can end up doing entire courses with full focus and enthusiasm from a dog that would have gotten sniffy, wandered off, or felt burnt out, if you used the conventional way of asking him to keep going.

What If My Puppy Loses Focus Before I Release Him?

If, at any point, your puppy disengages from you before you give your release word, *just give the word anyway and walk away.* When he returns to you, keep playing but adjust your criteria to set him up for success (ask for fewer repetitions, an easier version of what he is working on, put the ring gates back up, etc). This game reminds us to always build break time into the training session, rather than working your puppy to the point where he needs to disengage from you because he needs a break. And the more breaks you offer your puppy, the fewer he will want and need as you progress, until you create a pest!

What If My Puppy Refuses to Lose Focus, Ever, and Will Not Leave Me Alone?

When this happens, you will have gotten the most out of the Give Me a Break game. Truly, this game creates monsters. If, and when, your puppy starts pestering you to train him because of this game, you will need a second release word or just a social cue (such as sitting down with a book, going online, turning the TV on, or handing your puppy a bone) that means, "No, *really*, this time I mean it." A lot of my students started using a different release word, at which point their original release word isn't really a release word anymore. I never did this and it took me a while to figure out what I was doing differently from my students. I never had this problem of telling my dogs a training session was over, and I never came up with anything other than "O.K." to communicate everything.

Two reasons for this are body and context: 1) My dogs are watching all of me, not just listening to a word, and I am always very clear with my body language, without even thinking about it. So if they pester me to keep going when I am really done, my manner and energy communicates that I am not available right now to play that game. 2) My dogs know how to read contexts (and so do yours!) If I release them and then I go lie on my hammock, or pick up a book, or go online, obviously I meant it. So this issue of "how can you release a dog that you have turned into a training maniac" just never came up for me. My dogs know what's going on, usually better than I do.

Chapter 30

PARALLEL GAMES

© DIANE LEWIS PHOTOGRAPHY

You can raise your box work criteria by incorporating Parallel games into your training. The Parallel game structure allows your puppy to learn how to focus on his task while another puppy or person is moving next to him doing their own task.

Once your puppy is ignoring a person standing neutrally outside his box, have him start slowly walking around the edges of the box, gradually moving faster. Do not tell the person to speak to your dog or say his name in an attempt to distract him. The Parallel Game person or dog should remain non-interactive; the message here is, "Yeah, so that dog is next to you going to his mat, that has nothing to do with you: it's just happening nearby."

When I do the exercise with another dog, I always add the dog lying calmly on his mat first. Then you can build up to having a dog standing up, being walked by a person, and eventually to the dogs running parallel and then running past each other. I got the Parallel Game idea from my very first sport, which was fly-ball. A lot of the dogs, when learning to race, would run at each other or at least turn and react as the other dog flew by, before they reoriented to the ball. Not only do these dogs have to learn to run next to each other, they also have to learn to pass each other basically head-on over a jump. Since I like to break things down and teach each piece, I naturally saw the opportunity in flyball training to take the racing parallel and passing behaviors and teach them separately from the other behaviors. Dogs that get a foundation of Parallel games are learning to be great flyball dogs, regardless of whether they will ever play flyball!

Here is the standard dog/dog Parallel Game sequence. I start by making a long row of ring gates in a "T" shape. The "T" is so that puppies that race to the end of the row don't then run into the other row to see the other dog; so your puppy should be starting on the opposite end of the top of the "T."

- The puppy sits with his handler positioned on the inside
of the lane (next to the line
of gates). The other dog and
handler are in their lane, with
the handler also next to the
line of gates. So the puppies
are on the outside of each lane.
The puppy may do better if
the other dog and handler

Ring gates set up in a "T."

are there first, or he may do better if he gets there first and watches the other dog and handler approach. You can apply a testing strategy here by asking the puppy to play the Look at That game. If he doesn't care about the other dog, then continue. If he does, change the picture. See if he can handle it better if the other dog is farther away, for example. Or maybe he can better handle seeing the other dog approach if he is on his mat. These games are like a recipe where you have to add pinches of this and that in, according to taste.

- The puppy watches the other dog and handler walk down their lane and back. The other handler is walking between her dog and the line of gates.

- The puppy walks with his handler parallel to the other dog and handler walking in their lane. Both handlers are between their dogs and the line of ring gates.

When starting this exercise, have the puppies on the outside so that the handlers are between the two dogs.

- The handlers step to the outside of their lanes so that the puppy and the other dog are now on the inside of their lanes, closer to each other.

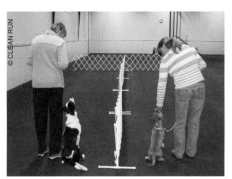

With success, you can move the puppies to the inside of the lanes.

- The puppy watches the other dog and handler walk down their lane and back, with the other dog on the inside of the lane.

- The puppy walks with his handler parallel to the other dog and handler walking in their lane.

- Both teams pick up the pace!

- Take a gate down: I usually start with the middle gate. This allows the puppy to start moving next to the other dog, but still separated by a gate.

When the puppy gets to the middle and he has his rhythm going, he will pass next to the other dog and then quickly be separated again by the next gate. When you take the gates down, it's important to have the handlers return to the inside of their lanes, with dogs on the outside.

When you begin taking gates down, start with the middle gate.

- Take the next gate down!

- And the next one!

- When you are ready to have the handlers on the outside of their lanes, with the dogs on the inside, start again with all the gates up.

- Take a gate down, take the next one down, and the next one!

- Put the gates back up, have the other dog and handler start at the opposite end from the puppy.

- Walk.

- Walk faster.

- Run.

- Handlers on the outside, dogs on the inside.

- Walk.

- Walk faster.

- Run.

- Take the middle gate down.

- Keep taking gates down.

Sometimes a puppy will veer toward the other dog as they run past each other, just like a green flyball dog. If that happens and you cannot easily get your puppy's attention back, stop where you are and play the Look at That game until you have "neutralized" the other dog for your puppy; that is, the puppy is just looking at the other dog in order to get a treat. You may also want to put a gate back up to make things temporarily easier.

The handlers begin by walking parallel, separated by gates. These handlers are on the inside of the gates, making it less distracting for the puppies then if they were next to each other. To make things more challenging, the middle gate is taken down so the puppies walk parallel without the separation of the gate. Then the handlers let the puppies walk on the inside of the gate so they are closer together. When ready, the puppies can practice moving parallel with the middle gate up. The ultimate goal is for the puppies to be able to walk, or even run, parallel without any gates. Be sure to start all these exercises on leash before graduating to off leash; if a puppy starts to veer toward the other puppy, call him back and put the gates up before starting again.

PARALLEL GAMES: THE NEXT STEP

The Dog in Your Face game is just the next step for Parallel games.

Here's a typical Dog in Your Face setup:

- Instead of standing parallel to the other dog and handler, you and your puppy will now be perpendicular to the line of gates. Take a position about six feet from the center of the gates. The other dog and handler will move a distance away and will walk slowly head on toward the center of the line of gates and you and your puppy. This way, the other dog is moving head on toward your puppy with the row of gates in between them. If your puppy is sensitive to this, have the other dog's handler walk him in a curve the first few times, gradually making the curve straighter until they are taking a head-on. As always they will start slowly and pick up speed with each turn.

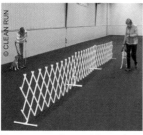

If your puppy is sensitive to being approached, have the other dog's handler walk him in a curve the first few times.

- Handlers start slowly walking dogs toward each other or the puppy in training is already waiting at the gate to watch the other dog being walked slowly toward him.

- When handlers approach a point a few inches from the gate (you can put a mark on the floor for handlers to target), they turn, putting themselves in front of the dogs and feed in front, before walking the dogs back to the starting point.

This Border Collie puppy is ready to practice having the other puppy walk head on toward the gates. The Border Collie puppy gets fed as the other puppy approaches; if he seems distracted by this activity, one way to handle it would be for both handlers to step in front of their puppies and reward them for refocusing and taking a nice deep breath.

- At the gate, you may choose to play Look at That and/or ask your puppy to take a breath; if your puppy is just watching you with interest asking, "What's next?" you can just keep going with the game.

- Handlers keep their dogs at their side upon hitting the mark and feed in position.

- Take the center gate down and go back to moving in front of the dogs to reward when the handlers hit the mark.

- Handlers keep their dogs at their side upon hitting the mark and feed in position.

- The next thing would be the pass. If your puppy is still watching you with interest and not caring at all about the other dog, then on your next go you can just keep walking instead of stopping where the gate would have been. You can talk to your puppy the whole time if you think it will help. Move briskly and confidently; don't stop to wonder if your puppy will try to interact with the other dog, just go.

Remember, at any point you can take a break here for the three natural behaviors, or just stop. Do not feel like you have to do the entire sequence at once if it seems like it will be too much. Use your tools of the Look at That game and asking your puppy to take a breath whenever you feel that your puppy is getting too distracted or excited by the proximity of the other dog. Only ask for something harder when your puppy is totally engaged with you.

Chapter 31

BOX WORK

What I called box work in CU is all about teaching off-lead attention in an increasingly distracting environment. We create a training structure during box work that allows the puppy or dog to easily and happily succeed at paying attention, and then we raise criteria. This is a very flexible, experimental process where we continually raise or lower what we are asking for and the puppy is always telling us exactly what he's ready to do or not do, and just how far we can push before it's too much.

In order to begin box work, you should have the following foundation:

- You must understand how to use the Give Me a Break game to get and sustain puppy's attention (see Chapter 29).

- The puppy must understanding that he can use distractions as a Look at That game with the handler (see Chapter 26).

First I set up the "box" with ring gates. This can be a tiny box or a large box. The smaller the box, the faster students get dizzy as they repeatedly move around in small circles with their puppy. The larger the box, the more space the puppy has to explore. If you welcome that, because you will incorporate "access to explore" into your reinforcement process, then it's no problem (and, good for you!). If you worry about your puppy leaving and not coming back for long periods of time, make the box smaller so that you feel like you've got a good handle on your environment.

The first thing to do in box work is reward attention. If your puppy is thinking, "Wow! This box is on grass and I looooooove grass!", then you are going to say, "Oh good, my puppy has just told me what his reward is going to be!" Then you will play Give Me a Break, calling your puppy and clicking him for lifting his head away from the grass, treating him, and giving him his release back to the grass.

This puppy is getting rewarded for offering a sit and attention while working off leash inside the box.

You could do the attention variant here and stand near your puppy or move around with your puppy, or you could put a chair in the box, dismiss him to sniff the grass, and go sit in your chair. When he comes toward the chair, get up and run with him back to the grass he was sniffing and release him to sniff it again.

You know you are done with Give Me a Break when your puppy is either ignoring the grass or engaging you to interact, or is actually *using* the grass to try to make you click him ("Look Mom, I'm touching this grass for you!") Junior the Jack Russell Terrier was the first dog that actually offered targeting grass as a behavior for *me* and it was quite an eye opener. Then I play my leash game within the box.

Without saying anything to the puppy, I let the leash drop and I treat the puppy when it drops. I want to classically condition a connection here; that I have good things for him when the leash drops. Initially, I stand still. I intermittently pick up the leash, then drop it and treat. If the puppy is saying, "This is great, drop the leash again lady!" I start moving. I walk with the puppy, on leash, occasionally letting the leash drop as we continue moving, and treat the puppy at my side, in motion.

If this is going well, I return to standing still and then unclip the leash, treating the puppy when I do so. Think of the sound of the leash unclipping like a click. It should signal to the puppy that you have something for him, rather than signaling to the puppy that he should head for the hills because he is *loose*!

Here I am treating the puppy as I unclip the leash. The sound of the leash unclipping becomes like a click.

I have always said in my CU classes that your puppy should be able differentiate between "working" and "not working," based on your cues, not based on whether a leash is on or off. Your goal is an attentive, happy, unleashed puppy keeping up with you as you move around the box. You can add agility flatwork into this, do some front crosses, etc.

If your puppy loses focus, a great option is to go sit in your Give Me a Break chair and wait him out. When he returns to you, run back into the middle of the box and start moving with him again (being very generous with the treats). Count three seconds of motion (adding on a couple seconds every time you do this), give him his release word, and go sit in the chair.

So, any time you need to turn your training into a Give Me a Break game to freshen up the enthusiasm and the attention span, do it. Then give your puppy a real break. If you have to keep returning to the Give Me a Break structure, your puppy may be saying he needs shorter sessions and more breaks to do his natural behaviors (see Chapter 7).

After you've gotten comfortable with the rhythm of the leash game, add touching your puppy's collar to it.

When the puppy is moving with you, keeping focused, and he thinks the leash coming off is great because it predicts training, you are ready for the next step. You have a choice here:

- **Take something away:** You could take down one of the gates and work on your puppy staying with you off leash in the face of this new escape route.

- **Add something:** You could add a low-level distraction such as a dog lying on a mat or a person standing still, outside the box (leaving all gates up).

If you choose to take down a gate, put the leash back on your puppy and make sure he can stay focused while moving with you around the box and past that escape route without caring that it's there. Then let the leash drag and treat him. Then unclip the leash. I often walk the puppies, leashed or not, right into the space of the escape route as if to say, look, we both know it's here, do you want to do something about it? The second the puppy turns back toward me, I click and treat.

I haven't actually had a puppy choose to run off versus turning back, but it could happen so make sure you have set up the environment so your puppy can succeed if you choose to "push him into the space" as I do. In other words, there should be a safe and relatively boring space outside your ring gates, such as a fenced yard or closed room. This way if your puppy does run off, you can calmly return to your chair without worrying about him (or, you could call your puppy, click the head turn, reward him, and send him back to sniff).

If all is well, keep removing gates. The point of box work is to have a puppy or dog that is focused, moving with you past any type of distraction, off lead, without any gates. We then can add agility obstacles into the box; what is a ring at a trial if not a big box-work exercise?

If you decide to add something first, have a person just standing casually without staring, outside of the gates. If the puppy needs to process that the person is there, play "look at the person" until the puppy says, "I'm bored with this, let's do something different!" at which point you can continue moving around, dropping or unclipping the leash, etc.

Once you have done your adding and subtracting separately—in other words, once the puppy is focused on you moving around without any gates, and focused on you within a box of gates when there is a distraction happening outside the box—you are ready to combine your strategies. So, when the puppy is ignoring the person or *using* that person as a Look at That target in order to initiate a game with you,

This puppy and his handler are doing their box work with a distraction outside the gates.

continue your flat work and create an escape route corner by making one of the gates shorter. If that goes well, fold up the gate on the opposite side of the person. If it doesn't go well, put the gates back as they were and go back to basics. Keep following this strategy of creating escape routes and folding up gates while the person stands there. Your goal is to have a happy working off-lead puppy with no environmental barriers.

What if the puppy walks over to the person or object? If the puppy is off lead and goes to see the person when the gate comes down, here are some options:

- Take a deep breath and go sit in your chair. Wait for the puppy to orient to you, click, get up without waiting for him to come all the way back, go up to her and give her a treat or put it on the ground near the person's shoe, give your release word, and return to your chair.

- Give the person a leash so that if the puppy goes up to him he can return the puppy to you, if you don't want to wait for the puppy to reorient to you on his own.

- Use the Premack principle; if the puppy really wants to go see the person, ask for the Whiplash Turn, as long as you think your puppy can do it successfully. Click the head turn, treat, and send the puppy back to see the person with a "go say hi" type of cue that means interaction with the person is now available. Use the Premack principle whenever possible to reinforce a Whiplash Turn—that is how you will really strengthen that superfast orienting to you. Then get your puppy, put the gates back up, and start over.

Remember to assess your puppy if he isn't staying within a rhythm of reorienting to you quickly. Does he need a "natural behavior" break? A potty break? Is he done?

Note: These options are meant to correct the situation, not the puppy! If your puppy loses focus, just think of how you can reset things for a better outcome. There is no need for punishment in box work training!

~~~~~~

TIM: THE RUNAWAY GOLDEN RETRIEVER

Tim is a Golden Retriever that I worked with in a private lesson while I was teaching for Hund I Fokus in Norway, at the first international CU seminar. Tim's mom wanted a private to address his habit of running away during competition obedience training (and trials). Tim was not running away from anxiety about work, nor was he sniffing from stress. Tim is a happy-go-lucky, intact male who loves a good romp about the field and loves to sniff and mark on, well, everything.

I knew that Give Me a Break was Tim's game. Here is how I set up his box work, in a very suboptimal environment.

We were doing lessons in a huge, gorgeous field. We did not have ring gates or any way to make a smaller space within the field. I hated to just have Tim's leash dragging through the wet grass, but we started off this way. After doing an attention variant warm-up, with Tim's mom, Wenche, putting treats in the grass when Tim oriented to her and then walking away and waiting for him to catch up, we chose competition-style heeling as the behavior to reward. I had her ask him to heel a few paces, then put a treat in the grass for him, and walk away from him to her… oh right, there was no chair! But there was a tree stump, so Wenche went and sat on it. Tim ate his treat, and ambled over to the chair, so Wenche got up quickly and asked Tim to heel a few more paces, put a treat in the grass (she could have handed it to him also, but sometimes I like to toss it or put it in the grass to give the handler the opportunity to get back to her chair before the dog is already engaging her) and returned to her stump.

Tim caught onto this pattern and was happily heeling around, eating and returning to the stump for more, so I raised criteria by telling Wenche she could heel in a pattern around several other tree stumps. When Wenche put her treat in the grass after heeling around the stumps, Tim ate it, then looked around, caught a scent, and ran filled with joy around the field. It was a safely fenced field, but it was so big it could have taken forever for Tim to return. I just had Wenche return to her stump, however, and we watched Tim enjoy running around, marking on things. When he finally looked toward Wenche, I had her click and walk to him with the treat, rather than waiting for him to return to the chair, which I will often do if I want to make things a little easier for the dog. She gave him the treat and picked up his leash. She gave him his release word to go sniff and let the leash be completely slack. He oriented to her quickly so she clicked, put a treat in the grass, dropped the leash and returned to the stump. He trotted over to the stump.

Wenche continued using heeling with the same structure and Tim was now running back to the stump looking for more, so I decided to add people. We did not have gates, so I just had my husband, Bill, and my brilliant host, Nina, stand the way people would stand for dogs to practice heeling in a figure eight pattern. They don't heel around people for figure eights in Norway, so this was new to Tim. Wenche asked him to heel around my husband, she clicked the heeling, put a treat on the ground and returned to her stump, hoping for the best. Tim looked up for her after eating, saw she was at the stump, and ran back to it. She got up and continued heeling around Bill and Nina. Not once did Tim try to engage Bill or Nina after Wenche released him; he kept going back to the stump. If he had I would have just asked them to stand neutrally.

Because Tim was being so good, I had Nina hold treats in her hand. Now Tim was heeling around two people, one of whom was holding treats! Tim sniffed Nina and I sent Wenche right back to the stump; as soon as he looked toward Wenche, she got up and went to his side, asked for more heeling and treated him (remember, the reward for the dog's orienting to you once you are back in your chair is that you get up and ask them to do the behavior again!). This time I had her put his treat right at Nina's feet, as if to say, "here is your distracting stranger if you want her, I'll make it easy for you and put your treat right next to her." Tim ate his treat and ran back to the stump without even looking at Nina. Wenche did several more repetitions, while Tim heeled past Nina's treats and got his own treats all around Nina's feet without so much as looking at her.

With some creativity you can do box work and Give Me a Break pretty much anywhere.

Chapter 32

Puppy Ping-Pong

This is another game about creating a rule structure that you can take with you and use in unfamiliar places or situations. For super-sensitive puppies it can be used as a warm-up to the Give Me a Break game, or it can be used on its own.

Use this game for:

- Puppies that need help refocusing on you in a distracting environment
- Puppies that are worried about a specific person, object, or dog (if the dog is totally appropriate and under control)
- Puppies that are being "sticky," staring, and stalking because another dog is running nearby

This game will help them switch back to thinking brain.

This is the easiest CU game and yet it can be a very powerful tool. Simply toss a treat on the ground where your puppy can see it. Watch your puppy carefully because, as always, timing is important. As soon as your puppy finishes eating the treat and lifts his head off the ground, throw another treat for him in the opposite direction. Repeat this pattern until your puppy is predicting the next treat and engaged with running back and forth, without being distracted. If your puppy is feeling any pressure at all from training or from the environment this is a great way to keep them connected to you while putting them in a pattern that is very user-friendly for them.

When your puppy gets it, you will raise criteria to waiting for your puppy to look up at you before you toss the next treat. So it will look like this:

- You toss a treat, puppy rushes to get it

- Instead of tossing the next treat in the other direction as puppy is expecting, you wait.

- Puppy looks at you as if to say, "You forgot to toss the next treat."

- As soon as puppy looks at you, toss the next treat.

This way you are adding yourself more directly into the ping-pong pattern. Once the puppy is staring at you happily and with interest after each treat toss, you can again raise your criteria. You could:

- Ask for eye contact rather than just orienting to you

- Ask for prolonged eye contact

- Ask the puppy to take a breath

- Ask for a sit or down, or any other simple behavior, such as a hand target

The treat-tossing piece will release the puppy from the pressure of the active-attention piece; therefore, for soft puppies, it will give them a double reinforcement; it's not just the treat but getting to leave the direct contact that is rewarding. This is also why this game works great for puppies that are worried about a particular thing.

Take the example of the Toy Fox Terrier puppy that was afraid of the air conditioning unit in her training facility. I established the ping-pong pattern with her and took it to the point where she would race to get her treat then come back to me and make eye contact, waiting for me to throw the next treat. As we were doing this, I was sneakily throwing treats closer to the air conditioner. She would notice the air conditioner but still eat her treat and then race back to me to restart the game (and note that leaving the air conditioner was part of the reinforcement for her). I kept her sub-threshold, meaning I watched her body language and did not throw the treat so close to the air conditioner that she was stressed beyond just noticing that it was there. This point could be different for every puppy.

Some people might ask a puppy that was worried about the air conditioner to go target it with his nose. For some puppies that could help them say, "Oh, I can use that game I know on this thing too, this thing must be O.K." But for others I think going right to that point without any warm-up is way too much pressure. The Look at That game is a better option: "Where is that scary air conditioner? Oh good job, you found it for me." That game doesn't pressure the puppy to interact with the thing beyond pointing it out visually—and it can be used as a warm-up for asking the dog to target. I think the ping-pong game puts the least amount of pressure on the dog, however. It is a good warm-up for either of the other two games in this context because of the whole "approach the thing, get to run away from the thing" pattern.

My next step with the toy Fox Terrier was to wait for her to look toward the air conditioner. When she looked up at me for her treat I smiled at her and moved slightly toward the air conditioner, looking at it. I waited and when she looked in the air conditioner's direction, I immediately tossed the next treat *away from the air conditioner*. She came back to me for the next treat and, again, I waited for her to look toward the air conditioner; as soon as she did I threw the treat away from it. This established her new ping-pong pattern, which wasn't about two treats, but about orienting to the air conditioner and then getting to run away from it and getting a treat in the opposite direction.

Since the air conditioner had become part of a game that the Fox Terrier felt comfortable with, she stopped worrying about it and only oriented to it in order to make the next treat happen. It was at that point that I allowed her owner to start the actual training exercise we had been planning on doing. I would not start training the puppy while she was concerned about something in the environment; that needed to be addressed first.

I did the same pattern with a Portuguese Water Dog (PWD) that was afraid of one of the handlers at a seminar I gave. He had trouble relaxing at the seminar because he was so concerned about this handler, a tall guy with a beard and glasses. Luckily that handler was a good sport and let me make him part of a PWD ping-pong game.

I established the same pattern with the PWD, throwing the treat first one direction than the other, and then waiting for him to look at me before throwing the next one. Then, as I continued this, I had the handler step closer to us. I had put ring gates up so that there was a visual barrier between this handler, and me and the PWD. When the PWD was ready, I started waiting for him to look toward the handler before throwing his treat in the opposite direction. He figured this out quickly and I removed the ring gate. When I did this, since that made it harder, I started throwing treats past the handler so that the PWD could move past him for his treat, look toward me and get his next treat, with the handler just part of the background. After several treat tosses I started waiting again for the puppy to orient to the handler before throwing the treat. When he looked to the handler, I threw the treat in the opposite direction, as I did with the air conditioner; the ping-pong pattern was now about orienting to the handler and then running for the treat, back and forth.

This PWD knew a lot of tricks and he had a "go say hello" cue where he would go to greet people. This is similar to Easy's cue. So after he was happily pointing out the handler and predicting his treat in the other direction, I gave him this cue and pointed at the handler. At that point he was able to respond to the cue without anxiety; he went and nosed at the handler then turned back to me predicting his treat. This ping-pong structure had created a situation for him where he felt comfortable enough to interact with the handler without his usual social anxiety. Anxiety is the dog's way of saying, "what's going to happen next, and is it going to be bad?" The PWD already knew what was going to happen next; as soon as he interacted with the tall bearded man he was going to run away from that man and get his treat.

A final example is Roxie the mixed breed. Roxie had been rescued by a student who had adopted several small mixed breeds from puppy mill busts. Roxie came to a seminar I gave, already with a lot of training and ready to work, but she was very concerned about the auditors who were sitting in a row of chairs on the other side of ring gates, all watching her. This was too much pressure for her and she just wilted.

I started tossing treats toward the other side of the ring; Roxie would run to get them and then take some tentative steps back toward me (and the auditors, sitting in a row behind me). I would mark her moving toward me and throw the next treat away from us. I shaped her to move all the way up to me, waiting for one tiny step closer each time before marking her behavior. When she was running all the way up to me confidently, I started stepping to the side so that the auditors weren't being visually blocked by me (as much as a row of people can be visually blocked by one person – I'm not *that* big!) This turned into a Look at That game, where she would orient toward the auditors, back to me, and then I would throw the next treat, again in the opposite direction. She would run back to me, offer looking toward the auditors and back to me, ready for the next treat to be thrown.

During this process I had moved closer to the gate so that eventually Roxie and I were standing very near the auditors on the other side. When she was *using* their presence as a tool to get me to continue the ping-pong game, I started walking with her up and down the gate line, basically making a Parallel game out of working next to the auditors. She was bouncy and walking around with me willingly, so at that point I returned her to her handler to work on the actual exercise they had come into the ring to do.

My student Jean used the ping-pong game recently to help her young Border Collie, Crave, keep his cool while watching another dog do the practice jump at a trial. Sometimes it's easier for motion-sensitive dogs to move while learning how to watch motion calmly; sometimes it's too much pressure to ask them to sit still and deal with it. If they are moving, however, they need to be moving within a rule structure that keeps them from going over the top, by creating a predictable little pattern they can settle into.

So ping pong was a wise alternative for Crave at the practice jump, until he got to the point where calmly glancing toward the jumping dog without reacting had been worked into his ping-pong game. At that point, if Jean chose, he could sit calmly and play Look at That instead. Another context in which the ping-pong game can be used is as a transition or warm-up into more challenging games.

Chapter 33

WATCH THE
DISTRACTED HANDLER

© DIANE LEWIS PHOTOGRAPHY

Easy made up this game and it has served us well.

I typically get a lot of handler focus from Easy while waiting for our turn in the ring, even when I'm not actively engaged with him. He will take weird stuff in the environment (Boy Scouts, people screaming and running around with MACH bars) and other dogs near us as cues to play the Look at That game with me. I do keep an eye on him around dogs that have a certain phenotype or body language that I know could trigger him; for example, he has serious reservations about Borzois.

As long as I'm tuned into him, he tends to live up to his name. I do not always keep my end of the attention contract, however. At trials, I get very distracted and excited; watching my friends' runs, talking to people, cheering on my students' dogs, wondering if the ice cream vendor is coming back. I noticed at some point that Easy would stare at me intensely outside the ring while I was watching runs, which is when I'm the most disconnected from him.

Once I noticed that, I also noticed that he had trained me to feed him intermittently while I was looking at something else. I had been reinforcing attention absent-mindedly. As part of my brain was thinking, "Easy is paying great attention while we are waiting our turn, give him a treat" another part of my brain was thinking, "Holy smoke, did you see those weaves?!"

So we have added the Watch the Distracted Mommy game into the repertoire. My NOT paying attention to Easy has become just another environmental cue for *him* to pay attention to *me*! It can't get more convenient than that.

This accidental game really paid off at one trial when there were a few dogs ahead of us waiting to go in the ring. I was talking to my friend and Easy was staring, staring, staring at me. I did not realize at the time that he was staring at me because his nemesis, evil cousin Merlin, was standing right behind us. So Easy's nemesis, evil cousin Merlin is actually not in the least bit evil, but he is Easy's cousin and, though I think we have gotten past it now, he was once Easy's nemesis. Easy bore a grudge because of a tiff that occurred in my backyard during what was supposed to be a puppy play date, before I knew better. Merlin forgot the incident about 30 seconds after it happened, but Easy was absolutely outraged every time he saw Merlin from that point on, for several years. Merlin and Easy were close in age and took a lot of the same agility classes. I never had to guess when Merlin arrived because Easy would get suddenly tall and puffy and, if I really wasn't paying attention, he would shoot to the end of his leash swearing like a sailor.

So I had to play the "Where is your nemesis, evil cousin Merlin?" game at our training club, a lot. We got the chance to play it when Merlin, who was absolutely oblivious to all of this, entered the building, and any time he walked by with his owner and my friend Elaine, also oblivious, to run a course. Did I mention that, in Easy's mind, Merlin was forbidden to run a course? Easy became incensed at the sight of Merlin doing agility. So I either played the game with Easy during Merlin's turn or just put a barrier up against his crate so he couldn't see. I did not give Easy one single chance to puff up or swear.

Easy became quite fluent in this game, letting me know whenever there was a Merlin sighting or whenever Merlin was possibly up to no good, and getting paid for it. Long gone were the days of his blowing up like a furious puffer fish whenever Merlin appeared in class. He would calmly point out where the Evil One was and turn back to me happily. But then Easy and Merlin started entering trials, and of course were in the same height class and kept being put near each other in the running order. So Easy had to find his nemesis for me in a new, even more challenging environment. I was careful the first several trials to make sure I knew where Merlin was in line, and play Look at That with Easy a couple of times so that he, too, knew exactly where Merlin was and could not pretend to be surprised by him later.

Easy let me know I no longer needed to worry about the Merlin situation during that trial, when he did not take his eyes off me the entire time we were waiting to go in the ring. I was involved in my conversation with my friend and totally missed the fact that Merlin was right behind us. Even though I didn't know he was there, and had not asked Easy to play the Look at That game, Merlin had become an environmental cue to focus on me. *And*, the very fact that I was waiting in line and not paying attention to Easy had also become a cue to focus on me!

At some point I turned around and saw that he was there. I said to my friend, "Wow, Merlin has been behind us this whole time and I don't think Easy's noticed it yet!" Easy then very pointedly tipped his head in Merlin's direction, his classic pointing out move, and then fixated his eyes on me again. He was saying, "Actually I *did* know he was there the entire time. Why do you think I have been staring at you? Thank goodness *somebody* knows what's going on around here, you distracted mommy!"

SECTION V

CONCLUSION

Chapter 34

MANAGING YOUR PUPPY IN CLASSES AND AT TRIALS

I am always seeking to create a structure for puppies and dogs that I can then transfer into different environments and situations so that wherever we are and whatever is happening, the message is always, "This is new but you don't have to react to it or get distracted by it because it's just another context for us to use the structure you already know."

To that end, when I used to teach puppy kindergarten classes, I would have everybody bring their mats and go to "stations" (the precursor to CU stations) around the room, sit with their puppies on the mat, and start some light massage while the puppy chews on a stuffed Kong or bone. I instituted this policy because I got tired of the chaotic way people used to enter my classroom, with puppies pulling and bopping around and playing with each other before class began, so that they were totally wired and not ready to work. There was a lot of puppy play-time in my class but it was basically presented in an Off-switch game structure.

We started with passive attention, moved to active attention, doing whatever obedience behavior the puppies were working on just for a little bit, then released them to play, then brought them back to either passive or active depending on what they needed, then released them to play.

Years later when I created CU classes, I had all my students set up stations before bringing their dogs into the classroom. Their stations consisted of a chair, a crate, a mat, and whatever toys and treats they brought. The CU dogs knew upon entering the classroom that they were going right to their station and doing their target behavior on a mat or crate. That way they were focused on a task as soon as they entered the space.

A station in CU class consists of a crate, a chair, a mat, and a stock of treats and toys.

The station concept can be used at trials, too. I live in an area where we have a lot of outdoor trials and people bring tents. I *love* this. I love having my students do passive attention or "mommy and me" time with their puppy in tents set up in the backyard so that being tented carries with it a strong emotional association of relaxing and bonding. I have the puppies learn to target their tent just like they would their crate or mat. You can move a mat several feet from the tent and send them back and forth; you can do the same thing with a crate.

The actual targeting behavior is up to you. If you're marking the puppy for running into the tent or running into the crate, that is pretty vague. What is your puppy doing when you click? Front paws in tent? All four paws in tent? For "extra credit" you could also teach a nose touch to the tent or the crate separate from entering the space. My friend sometimes sends her Border Collie to target obstacles with her nose or with her teeth (she grabs the outside of tunnels). She will alternate these cues with the cues to actually do the obstacle. It was part of her mission to make sure her dog really understood the concept of going away and finding specific targets (obstacles) for herself. The cue to bite a tunnel is used as reinforcement for doing an obstacle correctly, since her dog really loves that.

As your puppy is running back and forth between target locations, you can then set up another dog or person moving around in the environment. In other words, this is another structure for a Parallel game. The point would be to teach the puppy to ignore stuff that moves past and around them while they are going from one target location to another. This translates directly to trials.

I tend to have a chair outside the ring with treats packed in it somewhere, so that after a run Easy knows we are going back to our station. From the chair I might walk him around or I might go right back to the tent. If we needed structure, which, at this point we don't, at trials I would just take him to the tent from the chair so that he could predict this ritual and always know what order things happen in. Then I would take him for a walk. When he was little I would put his crate and mat outside the tent and send him back and forth near the ring while lots of stuff was going on. He practiced reorienting every time he left his crate and tent. It was a fun zigzag game for him that allowed him to process the environment peripherally without getting caught up in it. If he needed more direct processing we would stop and play the Look at That game with whatever needed attention.

These are very simple structures that you can have in class even if nobody else is doing it. Some puppies will require a lot of structure and a few won't need any and will be able to switch from work to play to rest mode appropriately, no matter what else is going on.

To Greet or Not to Greet, That Is the Question: Introducing Your Puppy to Strangers in a Class or Trial Environment
"Will you please feed my puppy? He's shy."

Often when I'm walking around trials somebody will come up to me with a cute little puppy and attempt to hand me food. They will tell me their puppy is shy with strangers, so they are socializing by having people feed him. Let me tell you my problem with this:

1. If this works, it tends to work *too well* and you have a dog that gets aroused when he sees people and possibly mugs them for food upon introduction.

2. If this doesn't work, you run the risk of making things worse.

Once somebody I knew with a young Border Collie approached my husband at a trial asking him to feed her. Well trained as he is, my husband remained very neutral and calm and fed the puppy. The puppy gained confidence and became almost playful with my husband, seeking attention and more treats. Delighted by this, my husband bent and pet the puppy. This terrified the puppy and he ducked, avoided my husband, and wanted to hide under a rock.

Even experienced people with the best of intentions can freak out a puppy. Why create a potential freak-out situation for your puppy involving strangers in a trial environment? I would rather teach the shy puppy that strangers at a trial are just white noise, just part of the background that will not bother them. I think it's too much pressure (for some, not all, puppies, I'm sure there are always exceptions) to bring them up to a stranger at a trial and demand that they have a direct interaction. Even if there is a treat involved, the interaction could still be too much pressure, or even scary. If your puppy is snatching treats from strangers and gulping them, he is not learning strangers are great because they feed him treats. He is being a normal dog by eating when food is available, but he is still stressed about the stranger so it's not really helping.

An extreme case of this was my client who adopted an adult Shepherd mix who was introduced to the concept of "house guests" during a dinner party. She was uncomfortable with people coming into the home so her well-meaning owner decided to line up the guests and bring her up to each of them one by one. I don't remember if treats were involved or not. By the end of that party, she was actively growling at everybody. It's a good example of too much pressure. I did a lot of relaxation training with her and taught her that she could look at, or even touch people, on cue and that she could take as many breaks from social pressure as she wanted in her crate.

Another problem with allowing strangers to touch or feed your puppy is that sometimes as the person's well-meaning hand reaches out to pet, the puppy reflexively ducks away. So the puppy is just practicing avoiding social interaction, not learning that strangers are nice.

So what would I do instead? There are a bunch of options:

- **Look at That Game:** I would, of course, start by playing the Look at That game with the goal of neutralizing that stranger and making him part of a structure the puppy already feels confident about. This game would also put the stranger on "look, but don't touch" status, so that the puppy could relax knowing that she could *use* the stranger to play the game without worrying that he was going to come up and interact with her.

- **Targeting:** You can build confidence to interact in puppies that are fluent in touching peoples' hands or other objects, by making the stranger into just another target. Look at That is a target game also, it just uses a visual target whereas what I'm talking about here uses a tactile target—an obviously more interactive form of contact with the stranger.

You could hand the stranger a target that the puppy already knows well, so that the puppy could confidently approach to touch his bear or whatever without worrying about the stranger. Or you could send him to touch the stranger's hand, if the stranger is willing to stand there with her hand out and not speak to or touch the puppy. Maggie was very afraid of kids as a youngster and would snap if they came too close. She made up her own behavior chain, where she went up to a kid (always one of my clients' kids that I had permission to practice with), put her paw on their shoe (one of her favorite freestyle tricks, so it made her feel comfortable), then returned to me and sat in front.

Maggie had the tools to create her own ritual to help her feel comfortable using kids as "target practice." She knew she could offer a target behavior such as touching them with a nose or paw and she also knew that once she performed a behavior away from me, she could return to me to collect payment. She liked finishing an exercise by sitting in front because she had learned competitive obedience behaviors. As time passed, Maggie raised criteria herself, allowing kids to bend down and even touch her before returning to me. She knew she could leave the situation and return to front whenever she wanted and it empowered her to become more and more social until she no longer needed the behavior chain she had created.

This type of experience, where my dog and I co-created a rule structure that helped her feel comfortable in the world, is exactly why I am a clicker trainer.

Once the puppy is very happy about using targeting to make good things happen, I might let the other person treat the puppy. It depends on the savvy of that person, and on what the puppy is ready for. Otherwise, I would just keep treating the puppy myself for being brave and interacting with the person. There are a lot of "mights" here because it would depend on the puppy and the situation, that is, everything that makes up the threshold model!

- **Use relief from the pressure of social interaction as the reward:** Note here that the Premack reward for Maggie wasn't so much the treat she got after she came to front as much as knowing she could leave the kids as soon as she put her paw on their shoe. Remember, sometimes relief from pressure is the most valuable reinforcement. Keeping this in mind, you may want to reward a shy puppy for being brave enough to approach a stranger holding their target, or even for playing Look at That with something or someone they are worried about, by walking them *away* from the person or thing. Your timing has to be good here to get the message across. I noticed myself in seminars walking dogs away from triggers as a reward for orienting to them calmly, and feeding them after we "escaped" the situation. So I was pleased when my colleague Grisha Stewart used elements of the Look at That game similarly in her BAT (behavior adjustment training) protocol, which teaches dogs that socially appropriate, relaxed behaviors will allow them to get what they need from the environment, so they don't have to go into fight-or-flight mode.

Rewarding by relief from social pressure is what I am working on with my horse, King, right now because when I got him he was reactive to being touched on the head and neck. I clicker trained him to put his head down, which is a relaxation cue for him. Then I taught him that he could get me to leave him alone if he put his head down when I petted his neck. Then I was able to increase the amount of time he kept his head down while I touched him before I moved away. Now I can groom him safely. I sometimes give him treats for head down and stay in position near him; other times I just walk away from him when he puts his head down. I watch him to see if he seems to prefer the treat or being left alone. The head down behavior replaced his aggressive behavior of snaking his head toward me with his ears back and sometimes snapping toward my arm. He was saying, "Go away, new mommy!" I taught him a nicer way to ask. In the process he has started becoming desensitized to my being around him, and will automatically put his head down when I start petting without looking so crabby.

- **Puppy Ping Pong:** Remember, this game builds on the theme of relief from social pressure—but it can be used even with a puppy who actually *wants* to get to the stranger, just as the Look at That game can. So whether your puppy is wary of a stranger or just overly excited by one and dying to see them, "plugging" the stranger into a predictable rule structure will let the puppy know what the rules are, which again will neutralize the stranger. You could opt to just toss treats back and forth past the stranger, rather than directly involving the stranger in a ping-pong game, and teach your puppy to indicate the stranger to you (much as we did with the scary air conditioner in Chapter 32) by orienting to him or her in order to get the next treat toss.

  If there is any other object drawing your puppy's attention, gauge whether you could use the Look at That game, Ping Pong, or targeting to reframe that object as something the puppy can use to get you to play the game. Also, be aware of what is most reinforcing for your puppy in these social situations and use it.

- **Give Me a Break:** Use the Give Me a Break game to build social confidence. Remember, this game is about building drive and enthusiasm to do a certain behavior; the behavior you focus on does not have to be a standard training behavior, it could also be a social behavior, such as approaching somebody in a friendly manner. This game empowers the puppy to choose to take on more pressure by asking for a continuation of the game, when you have released her to take a break. Here's how it works:

  Last night a good friend of mine brought her young Pomeranian to agility class for socialization. She told me that the Pom was ducking away from peoples' hands reaching toward her and did not want to be petted around the head. Having people give her treats had not helped—she would take the treat and jump back, practicing social avoidance. Watching this adorable, irresistible fluffy puppy looking grumpy, I formed a quick plan so that I could pet her without stress.

I started by petting under her chin because I saw she was much more open to that move than a top-of-the-head move. I offered her a treat, keeping a hold on it as she began gnawing. I did not release the treat into her mouth until I had pet her under her chin. She did great with this so I started adding in the Give Me a Break game structure. I petted her chin as she gnawed on the treat and after I let her take the treat I said, "Bye," stood up (I was kneeling down for the treat delivery and petting), and walked a few feet away from her. I ignored her and after about one second she looked up at me brightly and sat in front of me! She was saying, "Hey lady, why did you walk away, we were doing something over here!" so I bent down, let her nibble the treat, petted her chin and then released the treat, said, "Bye," and walked away again. She came right up to me, staring at me and offered a sit again.

My friend and I were very pleased. So I kept responding to her, and after a while I upped the ante so that I was petting the top of her head and leaving, and she was still engaging me to continue. I had never played the Give Me a Break game for puppy socialization skills before, but it worked great.

- **Biofeedback:** Never forget that you can always ask your puppy to take a breath during any of the games above! This will help him "stay in his head" and help him learn. For example, you can incorporate taking a breath into the Look at That game so it becomes a three-behavior game: Look at the "monster," reorient to me, and breathe.

- **Management:** You may decide simply to protect your puppy from possible uncomfortable situations instead of using them for training. Sometimes management is the most appropriate option, but we all know that sometimes you find yourself in an environment you can't manage. For example, at one trial where Boy Scouts were the ring crew, Easy had to play "where is the Boy Scout?" before entering the ring. A more dramatic example is the rally trial at which I was helping, which took place during a pet fair at the convention center. Nobody told my club that there would be elephant rides in the ring *next* to our trial. Yes, elephant rides!

What Is the Antidote to "20 Televisions Syndrome"?

I once had a client whose son was diagnosed with attention deficit disorder (ADD). She told me that her son's psychiatrist had described her son's experience of ADD like a person watching 20 television screens at once, each one on a different channel, without being able to turn off any of them.

Imagine having to take all that information in at once, how would you be able to really concentrate on what was important? How would you know how to prioritize what was important? I think a lot of puppies feel this way when being introduced to class and trial environments.

Using the Look at That game will teach your puppy how to focus on one channel at a time, always returning to Channel You. That is a great way to help your puppy break up an otherwise-overwhelming environment into smaller pieces. Another way is using targeting and setting up a station. Your puppy can peripherally process the world around him as he moves from one designated target to another (crate to mat, for example, or mat to cooler filled with treats, or tent to chair outside tent).

Asking your puppy to take a breath after he processes smaller bits of information about the environment is another big help. It is never a waste of time to remind your puppy to breathe! Doing passive attention, perhaps massaging your puppy as he lies on a mat, is another way to help him take in the world around him from his station. Or he could chew on a bone in his crate, you could call him out to go to his mat or play "Look at That and send him back to his crate to rest then call him out again. You can be creative in figuring out just how much stimulation and how much information your puppy needs in order to give his best performance.

You Get What You Teach: Be Careful What You Teach Your Puppy About Being Near the Ring

Speaking of 20 Televisions Syndrome, a beautiful blue merle Border Collie puppy, not more than 5 months old, caught my eye at a recent trial. Her eyes were everywhere at once. She wasn't concerned or afraid in the slightest; she was a confident pup, pulling to get to anything and everything in a sprightly, cheerful, "Here I am, world!" manner. She was pretty aroused; not vocalizing, but bouncing about. She never offered any focus to her handler that could have been captured by anyone other than a pro—she was all over the place.

We want a certain level of arousal in the ring, but we don't need it outside of the ring. Your puppy needs to learn to relax outside the ring and walk calmly around the trial site.

With a pup like this I'd want the CU puppy foundation games in place before bringing her into a trial environment, and then when we went to our first trial I'd start by bringing her to a station away from the action (this pup was a few feet outside the ring and in the middle of heavy foot traffic). From that point I might do some passive attention, some mat work, and then play the Look at That game with whatever was drawing her attention. I would not want to give her the chance to fall victim to 20 Televisions Syndrome. Remember, Look at That allows your puppy to process one channel at a time and continuously return to Channel You. You are the control or default channel.

If the puppy was able to stay on her mat looking relatively relaxed—not necessarily true relaxation but just not like somebody plugged her into the light socket, to start with—and focus on me for whatever duration it seemed like she needed before being cued to look at something else (somewhere between 5 and 10 seconds, I would guess), *then* I would walk her closer to the foot traffic.

My goal would be to keep that level of focus and calm in this new higher criteria situation. If there were room to put her mat down, I would do that because it would help "ground" her, and she could take in the new sights, sounds, and smells while lying on her mat, just as if we had raised criteria during a Parallel game. If I found myself questioning how much to push at any point, I would use the testing system discussed in Chapter 38.

This puppy's handler's strategy for working her pup near the ring was accidentally reinforcing all the wrong stuff. The handler was standing still and letting her puppy whoosh all around her, watching everything go by without any structure. Then she was intermittently goosing the puppy to get her attention and encouraging her to play rough, which the puppy would do briefly and then go back to excitedly scanning the room. The handler was attempting to reinforce attention by playing with her puppy near the ring, but all she was reinforcing was the idea that *being in that environment = high arousal*. Not necessarily good high arousal—the puppy wasn't thinking clearly and never did start offering attention or play with her handler for any duration. She would react to the goosing by orienting to her person briefly and following her person's hands as they moved all around in an exciting, chase-my-hand game, then go right back to the other stuff.

The entire time, she was in a state of frantic-type arousal and she did not appear connected with her person during their brief interactions. It looked like she was just reacting to her immediate environment which occasionally included moving hands in her face. I know that many people are told to keep their puppies aroused to make trials exciting and fun. But, you have to look at your puppy to know the when, where, and how of this. This particular Border Collie already thought trials were exciting and fun. She had no ability to settle enough to stay in her head or pay real attention to her person, and that is what she needed to work on. The goosing and playing had no real learning value in terms of using play with her person in training; the puppy was just responding to things in her environment that caught her eye for the moment, and her handler was occasionally one of them.

That isn't to say you shouldn't play with your puppy at trials. But the play should have a real quality of connection to it. Off-switch games with toys are great for this. Rev up, settle, and connect with your person. And the puppy first needs to be able to take in the trial environment from whatever distance is appropriate, using her foundation behaviors to help her process this new world without the stimulus overload she was experiencing.

For a puppy with a more laid-back personality, that stayed "even" while walking around a trial like the young Corgi with the huge ears I saw last weekend, I would not go through so many steps. The Corgi I saw was fine walking around without much structure and occasionally getting cuddled by passersby. I definitely would have made sure he had enough potty and water breaks and rest periods with something to chew on, in a crate away from the action. And I would have put a bit more structure into his day, using the trial setting as an opportunity to do some attention training—but I wouldn't want to overdo it, either. *The important thing is to read your puppy in each new environment to gauge how much or how little structure would be the most effective for him.* Your goal is to help the puppy stay in balance, alternating between focus and rest periods (and possibly social time with other people and dogs, when appropriate) and feel happy about where he is.

Using Give Me a Break to Get Focus In a Trial Environment

On the opposite end of the spectrum from that Border Collie puppy is the puppy that shuts down from stress and compensates with displacement behaviors like sniffing. My Jack Russell mix Snap comes to mind: being at class or at trials at first was so much stimulation for him that he was glued to the ground, being too overwhelmed to pay attention. I developed the Give Me a Break game just for Snap since he was so pressure-sensitive and shut down so easily. Using this game for him in challenging environments was just what he needed to develop his attention span and start thinking clearly.

You don't need my official Give Me a Break game equipment, the fencing and the chair, to play this game at a trial. If you can't control the environment so that your puppy can be loose safely, you can play the game on leash. Just give your Whiplash Turn cue while your puppy is sniffing around. If your puppy does not orient to you right away, fine. Walk up the leash without putting any pressure on it and wait. As soon as your puppy starts turning toward you, click and treat then give your release word and send your puppy back to the ground. Once puppies are familiar with this game they quickly start offering their focus to you and the ground is not so interesting anymore. Now here we are talking about puppies that shut down, but whether they were sniffing around as a stress displacement or because the ground smelled good, this game and the good old Premack Principle will help you get them back.

Chapter 35

AROUSAL IS NOT DRIVE

The agility culture tends to focus too much on arousal, equating it with the vague term "drive," which means different things to different people. I have a friend who just thinks "drive" means really fast, while I usually use the term to convey the dog has focused enthusiasm on his task.

Because of this vagueness, a lot of people just tug or whoop around, smacking the puppy and encouraging him to go hog-wild, thinking this will make him more excited to do agility. It could, but if it isn't presented in a balanced way, it could also make him a lot less thoughtful about his job and leave him sort of scatter-brained, unable to put all that energy into a job that requires concentration. That is why I love Off-switch games, and also using transition time for a puppy that is unbalanced by intense toy play and needs some help finding his equilibrium.

A lot of people are taught to put their dogs into a predatory state during agility training, to put them in prey drive. But prey drive looks different in different dogs.

In many Border Collies that are being predatory, prey drive manifests as a slow, creepy, stalky pace. In many hunting breeds, prey drive manifests as standing with their front paw lifted up slightly and adopting a pointing or a flushing-out stance. When we encourage prey drive in training, we are going to get these very deep instinctive behaviors and they do not always mean "fast." I know a lot of Border Collies that got excruciatingly slow and creepy on their contacts, on the pause table, and also creeping up to the flyball box in slow motion, because they made the correct association that those behaviors meant a game of tug or retrieving.

Prey drive manifests itself differently in different breeds. Border Collies, for example, can often be slow, creepy, and stalky when in prey drive.

Remember, toy play is about the most instinctive thing our domesticated predators can do: hunting and killing. That is great and I always use toy play in my training. But I have found with some puppies, mostly field line hunting breeds and Border Collies, that they can get sticky and they need to practice switching back and forth between that sticky state and thinking brain. This enables them to do their agility behaviors quickly, even though there is an opportunity to kill a Frisbee at the end of it.

I worked with several German Shorthaired Pointers that were part of a hunting club a few years ago. Their handlers brought them to me because they were having trouble listening long-distance in the field, even while wearing their shock collars, which I would have nothing to do with. The handlers were looking at it as an obedience problem, but I saw that the dogs were getting really sticky and just unable to process the information from their handlers correctly because they were just stuck in point mode.

I started teaching them Doggie Zen using a tennis ball that elicited that same sticky response in them; it was very hard for them to break from it. I worked up to being able to throw it and to do leave-its, helping the Pointers switch from being predatory to good old click-and-treat thinking brain. It is not saying that the predatory mind state is bad; it is a huge part of what makes a dog a dog. It is just a question of teaching the dog to switch around so that he can listen to us even in an environment that is bringing out his hunter nature. How many dogs, particularly Border Collies, but other breeds as well, have you seen unable to keep a start line stay because they lower their head, get stalky, and start creeping slowly toward that first obstacle before their handler releases them?

I worked with a sweet Border Collie that developed a phobia of going on the pause table because she had been physically corrected for not lying down on it, while standing on it. Her handler brought her to me with a story about how she used to automatically lie down on it, and then at some point decided to be disobedient and refuse to lie down. I

knew that didn't sound like the whole picture, and I asked about stickiness, thinking that she was having trouble lying on the table because she was getting locked into a crouch stance. I thought this because I'd seen this happen many times before and get misinterpreted by the handler.

The handler didn't understand what I meant by stickiness so I asked her if her dog could quickly lie down in the presence of a tennis ball, or if she would stalk and crouch. The handler got a ball and as soon as her dog saw it, she was a picture perfect example of exactly what I meant by sticky. Asking her to lie down while she was in that state did nothing for her. I explained that this was what was happening on the table as well. Using my tools for dealing with stickiness in Chapter 37, I got her lying down near her ball, then lying down with the ball moving on the ground back and forth past her, and then I started generalizing to the table.

The Big Picture Is Always There

Our line of communication gets broken when we lose sight of the big picture in our training. A lot of people, instructors and students alike, are still quick to jump on the "he's disobedient/disrespectful/dominant and you have to take charge and make him do it" train. Think about how counterproductive that attitude is in the context of Rumor's story and the table story above. If your dog isn't complying, *please* take a step back and look at the whole picture. You might be surprised at what he is really telling you. Try not to let your emotions, expectations, frustrations, and embarrassments ("everyone in class saw her refuse to get on that table!") create this narrow, dark filter that colors how you perceive your interactions with your dog. If you can let all your judgments, anxieties, and "supposed to" concepts go, you can take a step back and observe all the variables in play more objectively, like a scientist studying your situation. That is how you will gain insight into how you can adjust both your direct training and your environment to set up a fairer situation for both of you.

Training is a two-way conversation, and if your dog isn't doing something you ask, that is important feedback for you. It's when you forget that training is a two-way conversation and you just start telling your dog he has to do something without listening to him in return, that you get frustrated and feel things are out of balance. Do not expect your dog to put on his "listening ears" unless you put on yours, too!

Chapter 36

FINDING THE RIGHT TEACHER WHEN YOU'RE READY FOR AGILITY PUPPY CLASSES

Guess what? You already have the perfect performance sport puppy instructor. Chances are, he's staring at you right now wishing you'd put the book down and play, or sleeping on your shoe. Never forget that your puppy already knows the best way he should be introduced to training and to our sport and that his behavior will constantly give you feedback to help you refine your training, if you keep your eyes open.

But, you also need to find a human instructor and often that is a difficult thing to do. I have had many experiences where I felt I couldn't stand up to an instructor, even though I would have handled something in a different manner for my dog, and you may have, too. There is this mysterious balance between respecting a teacher's experience and station, and standing up for our puppies when we think it's warranted. As a perpetual student, I find it extremely important to get along well with my teachers. I have become very selective as to who I will trust enough to bring my dogs to. I don't *want* to ever be put in a position again where I feel I will "cause a problem" if I voice my feelings or opinion, especially with a puppy that is just starting out.

I'd rather have a less competitive teacher who takes the time to listen, gets to know me, and sees teaching as it should be; a co-creative process of communication and connection between teacher and student, just as it should be between you and your puppy. Teaching is about building relationships. You need to be able to trust your teacher, just as your puppy needs to be able to trust you. Remember, teaching you is its own skill set. Training dogs to do well in a sport is a different skill set. A good agility teacher is proficient in both.

This brings me back to integrative training. The best teachers are those who have the concept of integrative training, though they may not see it in those terms. No single teacher can have all the skill sets necessary to help you with every piece of the puzzle. I certainly don't. I am not an expert at reading movement, finding sore spots, doing bodywork… I am good at the mental/emotional stuff. I always let people know the importance of the physical component, however; I start them on simple TTouch movements and observe their dog's body and movement with them to get them inspired to learn more and I give them resources to help them on their path to a well-integrated training program.

I hate remembering this story, but I'm going to share it with you. This is a story about my Tervuren, Rumor. When he was a puppy I had ambitions for him to be this awesome competition dog: My first OTCH/MACH/ADCH/you-name-it dog. I was so excited to finally get him, and I taught him a lot of stuff early on. I should say here, though, I have found that each time I get a puppy I find myself doing *less* with that puppy than the previous puppy. I no longer feel the pressure to raise my puppies as if there is a timeline or a prize at the end; that they must be ready to compete the nanosecond they are eligible.

Ru and I were having an excellent time learning stuff together. He was the first puppy I shaped from the start and he knew lots of cute clicker tricks. He thought he was so very clever, and so did I. He was also enjoying doing baby stuff at our agility club, running through tunnels, etc. The problems did not start until he was old enough to start jumping in earnest. By this point, he had been jumping sequences at 16 inches with no problem and doing the sequences happily.

I then began taking private lessons with Ru. The instructor put the bar up to 22 inches and, for the first time, he refused a jump. She asked him to sit, and he did. Then she asked him to jump again, and he didn't want to. This went on a couple more times and then he ran into an open crate. My jaw was on the floor. I had never seen such avoidance behavior in him.

It did not cross my mind there was a physical problem behind this. The instructor was chalking it up to his being spoiled, being a Tervuren, and not thinking there's a consequence for not listening because I let him get away with too much, etc. She wanted to let him know it wasn't optional when she asked him to do something. And I was stuck in an ego storyline. I wanted her to think I was doing a great job with him. I wanted her to be impressed, and I was mortified that he was doing this. I had fears that it was suddenly going to become hard to train him; that the people at my club would talk about it and judge me, etc. I was so stuck in my ego and my anxiety that the message he was really giving completely passed me by.

This went on during our lessons for a couple of months. He started running away from me while we were sequencing and going to the front door of the building. I would call him back and we would keep going. What I actually wanted to do, when he came back to me, was take him out for a walk because I felt that it was an unfair punishment to make him do agility after he came to me, when what he wanted to do was leave the building.

By then I had another private instructor, and she wasn't comfortable with me doing anything but making him keep working when he returned. It really troubled me to do it this way, but I did.

He started being really difficult about dogwalks and A-frames. He didn't want to walk across them. I spent a crazy amount of time rewarding him for playing on boards. I put dogwalk boards on the living room floor and fed his meals on top of them. I wasted time being so reactive and was so hyper-focused on what he wasn't doing that I was not hearing what he was saying. He was telling me that he was in pain.

I finally trained him to do the dogwalk and A-frame and he became all puffed up, super pleased with himself for being so brilliant and he started offering doing those obstacles when I was standing around talking to the instructor. He started looking like the dog I knew when we were alone; the happy, confident dog that my teachers never got to see and thought didn't exist. The instructor got angry because I rewarded him for doing them on his own while I was talking. She did not want me to even look at him because it would be too rewarding. Frankly I didn't feel like leashing to stop him from doing the obstacles because his offering showed me that he was feeling really confident about them. I understood her desire for stimulus control, but I felt that the fact he was doing those obstacles happily overrode the fact that eventually he would have to learn that he should just do them when cued. I still think I was absolutely right in theory, but my instructor was right in the most practical sense, because Rumor offered going up a teeter, thinking, I imagine, that it was a dogwalk. He wasn't expecting the tip and he fell off, totally traumatized.

I had to start over from square one with the dogwalk and A-frame. In the meantime, he was still running to the door during lessons. He did not run to the door when it was just me training him, and he was happy to work at home. But I was under so much pressure in the lessons, wanting him to perform and make me look good, and he was being asked to do more by the instructor than I would have asked him to do.

While he was playing with the neighbor's golden, his best friend since puppyhood, he tripped over his own hind legs and fell. I was alarmed by this and observed him closely over the next few days. He fell a couple more times. I felt like I had eaten a hot flaming ball of lead. And I wasn't being paranoid: my worst nightmare at the time was about to come true.

Ru was diagnosed with a rare lumbosacral disease that would get worse over time. He was 18 months old at the time of diagnosis. I do not know if his agility training caused him to be symptomatic faster or not. The orthopedist explained that any hyperextension of the low back would cause pain. And, as she was explaining that in her own words, what I heard was, "Hyperextension means that if he jumps over 16 inches high, it hurts him. No wonder he was running away when the jumps were being raised. Why didn't we listen?"

Ru, now eight years old, has had a lifetime of chiropractic, acupuncture, massage, and Chinese and Western medicine. He is a terrific companion and a very intuitive boy that serves as a therapy dog for my neighbor who suffers from Alzheimer's. I will never know how much of his discomfort in agility lessons was emotional vs. physical. I suspect the A-frame and dogwalk were scary because he didn't have good balance and didn't know where his back end was, so it didn't feel safe. And, of course, falling off the teeter taught him that, in fact, boards were not safe. I did not learn until much later how to look at him and see that he was a dog that did not know where his back end was. My teachers, who were generally effective and skilled competitors, did not either.

After his retirement from being a would-be agility dog, I had a friend who kept insisting that if I hadn't babied Ru and had insisted he get on a teeter, he would get on a teeter. The teeter was the only obstacle I hadn't gotten a reliable performance on before I retired him, and it remained something of a "white whale" for me, always wondering if I could have trained him to do it.

One day he was hanging out in the training building with me, and there was a collapsed teeter on the floor. The movement it would make if a dog got on it was the tiniest movement possible. My friend was sure that if I let her, she could get him to do the teeter and prove to me that I babied him too much. Apparently I was out of my mind that day, because I let her try. Ru loved this particular friend and wanted to do stuff with her and eat her treats, so I let her try. She tried to be nice, but firm, and put Ru on the teeter, letting him know she wasn't going to hurt him but that she wasn't going to let him get away with not complying, either. She was so sure of herself, but she wasn't watching Ru's body. I saw the panic mounting but it was too late. He flipped out, got away from her, and ran. It was in that moment I finally found the inner strength I needed to be able to say *no* to well-meaning people and teachers who thought they knew better than I did.

I've gotten pretty good at reading my dog and honoring him at a physical as well as mental and emotional level, making sure his needs are being met. Dogs are not one-dimensional and their training should not be one-dimensional. The body and mind are not separate, and if you "train" one, you are affecting the other. What the body tells you is going to help you know better how to train the mind, if you are really looking.

Chapter 37

YOUR PUPPY DESERVES
A CUSTOM FIT

© DIANE LEWIS PHOTOGRAPHY

The most successful trainers are those who are creative and flexible, able to adjust to each dog they are working with in the moment. Trainers can be so good at doing this that people watching them do not even see it happening. Slight changes in body language and pressure can make a big difference.

Some trainers make these adaptations subconsciously because communicating with animals comes more naturally to them. Others have to learn through observation and experience. In the agility culture, we like to copy our best handlers, and train our dogs the way they trained their latest star. It makes total sense, of course, but we should also keep in mind that our best handlers know how to adjust for each dog, even if it's an adjustment so teeny that nobody notices it. And if that handler had your dog, she may teach something slightly differently than she taught it to her dog. Because of inevitable variations in physical and mental ability with each dog, she may teach her next dog in a way slightly differently than her last dog.

I raised Easy differently from the other puppies I have raised because from the age of four weeks he gave me signs as to what his personality would be like. Two incidents stand out most clearly in my mind: the first occurred when the puppies were exploring outside the whelping box, and Easy ventured into an open crate to sniff around. I wanted to pet him, and I put my hand into the crate toward him. He hopped backward, barking. It was the first bark I'd heard from him, and I'm guessing his first bark ever. I thought to myself, "This is what a fear response in him will look like later." He will vocalize as he moves backwards from the stimulus, which is exactly what he does if he's scared.

The second incident was when my breeder gave the puppies their first tiny rings of raw marrow bone. All of the puppies except for Easy started playing tug-of-war with each other and running around carrying the bones. Easy got an intense look on his face and crept over into a corner, holding his bone and keeping an eye on the others. At some point, one of the others ran by his bone and he "grrred" at them. I saw what was ahead of us, but fortunately I was experienced with resource guarding. It was interesting to see these behaviors emerging from a guinea-pig-sized puppy.

In the litter, Easy was very people-focused and did not play with the other puppies much. He did his own thing while the others were rolling around with each other. This never changed and he became hyper-focused on me when I was around, watching my every move. He was a "just add water" puppy in some ways. He never needed attention training; he never played the Give Me a Break game or did any box work. He learned things so fast that I wasn't done teaching one thing and he was already onto the next thing. He spent the day staring lovingly into my eyes and asking what fun thing we were going to do together next, and he spent the night sleeping with his head rested on my shoulder. But, he did give me plenty of things to work through as a youngster.

For starters, because his level of sociability to other dogs was low and his tendency to resource guard was high, he had dog-to-dog issues from the get-go. My then-assistant Kienan brought over her pit bull puppy Scorch that was roughly the same age as Easy. Scorch had a very laid-back, "Hey, buddy, want a beer?"

type temperament that did not change as he matured. But his earthy charm was lost on puppy Easy, who was absolutely offended that another puppy dared to have fun in his presence, and had no problem telling Scorch that he should not even exist in the same universe.

Not long after that my friend Diane brought over her puppy, Easy's littermate Spirit, for a reunion. Easy was thrilled as usual to see Diane and barely noticed that Spirit was in the yard until Spirit had the gall to splash in a tiny mud puddle. Easy flew over to her, growling and snapping, and let her know that this was *his* mud puddle and how dare she have the nerve to play in it?

It was at this time that puppy kindergarten was starting, and Spirit and brother Snitch were taking it together. I decided not to put Easy in class, as I didn't want him to get another opportunity to practice telling puppies exactly what he thought of them. I knew he would be able to learn to attend to me, off leash, while other dogs were moving around, which, to me, is a big aspect of puppy kindergarten. The other big aspect, from my perspective, is the socialization time. I did not believe for one second that Easy would suddenly love his fellow puppies, if he had the chance to socialize with them in puppy kindergarten. So while some of my friends were telling me it was a mistake and I wasn't exposing him to other puppies enough, I did not take him and I have never regretted or second guessed that decision.

I did come up with a plan that I felt would teach Easy what I needed him to know, which was that sometimes "dogs happen" and he could stay calm and work with me, without reacting to the other dog. I enlisted a few friends with adult Border Collies who cared more about playing Frisbee than playing with other dogs. These friends would come to my backyard and just throw the Frisbee for their dogs, while Easy sat next to me, on leash and just hung out. Easy learned that there could be strange dogs in the yard and that it was not a big deal. When he was comfortable, I let him loose and played with him while my friend played with her dog. He learned he did not have to guard his toy because the other dog was focused on his own toy and wasn't going to bother him.

One day, my friend Lynn's Border Collie, Quiz, took a break from retrieving and lay down under a plastic lawn chair, dropping his Frisbee a few feet away. Easy crept toward the Frisbee and then lay down on the other side of it, a mirror image of Quiz. I watched them like this, frozen in this Border Collie tableau with the toy exactly equidistant to both of them, and in that moment I stopped worrying about what he could be like as an adult. I am glad that from the beginning I accepted him for who he was rather than trying to "make" him like other puppies. It would not have been fair to the other puppies, and it would not have been fair to him to put him in that situation.

I had two separate rule structures for seeing dogs on the street and seeing dogs in the backyard during this time. I hand picked dogs to come over, and gradually Easy went from learning he didn't have to be offended by them, to playing with me near them, to actually interacting with them. At some point during this process he discovered that he, in fact, did like playing with strange dogs; primarily female Border Collies and Shelties, to which I had lots of convenient access.

Seeing dogs on the street, however, was another matter altogether. Easy felt discomfort at seeing strange dogs while we were out walking, or hiking in the nearby state park, so right from the beginning I taught him the Look at That game, and he learned that dogs on walks were environmental signals to orient to me for a treat. He learned that he could use these dogs to get me to play his game, and he stopped being concerned about seeing the dogs.

The Look at That game was extremely important to us when Easy was little. Not only did the sight of strange dogs cause discomfort, but he also worried about people who weren't "following the rules." Easy's rules for people were, they had to walk past him without looking directly at him, and they couldn't suddenly do anything that wasn't written down in his rulebook of "what people are supposed to do."

We hiked every day, and people would see his cute little white face with the intense blue eyes and stare at him. Some would call out to him, or walk directly toward us. Staring at him and/or walking toward him was just too much pressure on Easy, and he would bark reactively, charge and then back up, a testament to his anxiety and conflicted social feelings. So he learned two all-important things very early on:

- That I would not let strange people touch him or bother him when we were hiking, so he did not have to worry about them

- The sight of people staring at him or otherwise breaking the Rules meant that he could point out the infraction to me and get paid for it.

It seemed like with each week, the people we passed in the state park found new and exciting ways to break the rules. Easy would get used to people jogging, and remain totally cool and collected when people suddenly ran past us, and then he would see a jogger stop and stretch on the trail. Joggers were supposed to run past us, not stop and stretch! So he would react to that. Then I would spend several days explaining to him that he could use stretching people as a way to get me to play Look at That with him, and he would be totally cool and collected about stretching people, and then somebody would look at him while carrying a fishing pole. We'd already established that people carrying fishing poles were merely Look at That objects and so were people that looked at him, but we hadn't put these two rule infractions together yet.

He got used to that, and then one day he saw somebody sitting on a bench at a crossroads. People were apparently not supposed to be sitting on benches, they were supposed to be jogging, stretching, and staring at him while carrying fishing poles, but absolutely no sitting. So then I would have to explain that this, too, was just another opportunity to play Look at That.

Did I mention that Easy is an over-noticer? Many dogs are, especially if they are herding breeds, and mine is no exception. Look at That is a terrific game for over-noticers because it takes what they notice and plugs each thing into a rule structure that feels familiar and reliable. Without a structure like this, over-noticers can turn into announcers ("Mom! I saw something! Mom!"), or into full-fledged reactive dogs. This way, you have the tools to be able to say, "Yes, you are seeing a new thing, but this same old game works in this context, too." Being able to give this message to a puppy like Easy is paramount, if you don't want to end up with a reactive adult. Often people ignore or don't notice their puppy's behavior; others notice it and respond badly to it ("No! It's unacceptable to bark at the guy with the fishing pole!") This escalates their puppy's level of anxiety about seeing novel stimuli on outings.

At the same time Easy was learning how to interact with dogs in the yard and how to cope with seeing dogs and other stuff out in the world, he was learning he did not have to resource guard everything in the house, including myself, from my other dogs. I clicker trained him to back up and sit while I petted my other dogs, because without that kind of structure he would "split" by coming in between me and whatever dog I was petting and announce that I was only supposed to be petting him and what did we think we were doing. (I could also have taught him to find his mat when my other dogs came to say hello, but I took the resource guarding as a shaping challenge.) He had to learn to take turns, and he had to learn that the other dogs in the household got to keep their own toys and bones. I had to set up these lessons, and stay on top of things, because my three adult dogs never corrected Easy for taking their stuff or for pushing the boundaries. When he swaggered up to them, my dogs would make eye contact with me and ignore him. They had been trained to look to me for direction rather than reacting to the environment, and they apparently over-generalized their training! So I spent a lot of time managing resources.

Even with their lack of telling him where to get off, Easy was learning great social skills from my other dogs that had been interacting with him from the second he got home. This, too, was paramount to him learning terrific play skills and honing his social signaling in the process. This enabled him to grow into the dog he is today, who can adjust his body language to get along with different personality types, and who can communicate discomfort or disapproval by making the slightest nose wrinkle, versus behaving in a reactive or aggressive manner to get the same message across. I hear about people who don't let their puppies play with their adult dogs and it's just so not my style. Having the others helping me teach Easy how to be a socially acceptable dog was a Godsend.

My hope was for Easy to grow into a dog that could comfortably work and play near other dogs without reacting. But Easy surpassed my expectations by turning into a very social dog that likes playing (but only with the dogs who have read his rulebook, of course! That should go without saying.) I am always telling students who have Border Collies that don't care much for other dogs, it's so common for Border Collies to not like other dogs, especially females, that we even have a name for it—BCBS (Border Collie Bitch Syndrome). And we didn't get these dogs for them to have a fabulous time playing with other dogs, did we? We got them because we like the breed and it suits our competition needs well.

Yet, people keep bringing me snarky Border Collies and wanting me to wave the magic wand and make them love other dogs. People are either upset because their dog doesn't like other dogs enough, or because he likes them "too much" and needs attention training. It always shocks me when I get a student with a very social Border Collie that actually loves other dogs, and they complain that he likes dogs too much. Then I have to tell them, all my students with dog-reactive Border Collies would be so jealous, do they realize that? We can spend so much of our time wishing that our dogs were different, rather than appreciating who they are and just working with what we've got. It's ridiculous how much time we waste. Our dogs are with us for a limited time, and some leave us way too soon.

The other challenge Easy gave me when I was raising him was his stickiness. Stickiness does pose a huge training obstacle and it's one that I see affect my students' dogs over and over—and often people don't realize what is really going on.

"Sticky" is what people call Border Collies or other working breeds that get stuck in a hard-wired motor pattern and, well, get stuck there. Easy started getting stuck at the back door, which opens into the backyard. I teach my dogs to look away from the back door when I open it, as part of their leave-it training. Then they go out individually as I say their names. I do this because otherwise it gets chaotic and they can bump into each other as they rush through the door like a herd of buffalo. So when Easy was a puppy, I clicked him for turning away from the door when I opened it. This was no big deal and Easy was very reliable with it, until one day he suddenly couldn't do it any longer. He crept toward the back door painfully slowly, and then stared at it with the infamous Border Collie Eye, one front paw slightly raised, locked into the classic ancestral pose from planet BC. This clearly was not a puppy being disobedient, but a puppy that had associated being in the backyard with the toys and agility obstacles he knew were there.

The association made, thinking about going out the back door made him think about what he would get to do once he was out there, and this put him into prey drive. Remember, people tend to focus on the chase aspect of prey drive, but Border Collies were not bred chase sheep, but to control their movements using eye and subtle application of pressure.

Stickiness can affect performance. It's not something we should ever get mad at these dogs for, though I have seen lots of people get really mad about it. They can't help it; the part of their brain that says, "Get really low and then start creeping" has been activated and that message is so strong they can't hear you through it. We can train them to switch back into the "click and treat" part of their brain. So this is not a question of telling them not to go into sticky mode, which isn't going to do you any good, but rather a question of teaching them they can switch back and forth between mind states.

Back to puppy Easy at the door: I had to start over again teaching him to look away from the door, using my two favorite tools for working through stickiness.

LESLIE'S TWO FAVORITE TOOLS FOR WORKING THROUGH STICKINESS

- **Premack Principle:** The most rewarding thing to give your dog after he comes out of that sticky state and pays attention to what you're saying is by cueing him to return to the stimulus that elicited the sticky state in the first place. This is how sheepherding works: "You lie down when I ask, even if you felt like chasing the sheep instead, and then I'll give you access to the sheep."

- **Shaping:** Rewarding increments of behavior helps the stuck dog hear you through the haze of stickiness, and helps them break from the motor patterns faster.

I opened the door a crack and then I would wait for the teeniest hint of his head turning away from it. I clicked that and then verbally released him to go outside. Every time we went outside, I waited for a little bit more body movement away from the door and toward me, until I got the full head turn back. At that point, I added in a sit because it was a good way to help him "work through" being stuck—he had to use his body in a different way from what his instinct dictated. He could not be all stalky and creepy looking, if he was going to sit.

This process took a few weeks. During it, he presented me with a new, stranger challenge. He got into click-and-treat mode again by the back door, looking away from the door and sitting down readily, but suddenly he started getting stalky and creepy in the living room. I figured out that whenever he wanted to go outside, he went into stalk mode. It was a little unnerving to be sitting reading a book and see this animal acting as if there was a flock of sheep behind the couch. Then he started getting sticky in his crate. This one took me a while to figure out. He was always trained to sit and wait in his crate for me to call him out. He was crated when I went out for errands, and when I came back, I would let him out, and the first thing I'd do is let the dogs into the yard. He started getting all sticky in the crate and wasn't able to sit down when the crate door was open and I realized that he had made the association that when I come home and open the crate, he gets to go in the yard. So I had to re-teach the crate behavior like I re-taught the back door behavior.

He has some very sticky dogs in his family tree, and I had worked with a cousin of his that was really bad. This dog would come over and go into stalk mode as soon as she got in the yard, anticipating that a ball might be thrown. She didn't listen to her handler at all and was always just creeping about, unable to pay attention or respond to cues, hoping for the next ball. Ironically, her agility teacher had focused on tugging to teach this dog attention skills, not realizing that the tugging also elicited this sticky state from her. It was a good example of a formula that would fit other dogs, but not the one to whom it was applied. I had the handler walk around my yard with the dog on leash, occasionally asking for a Whiplash Turn, and then releasing the dog to stalk around looking for balls (which I had taken out of the yard temporarily) after she turned her head around. After a couple private lessons the dog was able to orient to her handler with her leash off, and then we were able to start teaching her some leave-it behaviors using toys so she could practice getting unstuck and being rewarded, of course, with the Premack Principle. I was determined to not let Easy get to that point, so my focus during much of his puppyhood was on un-sticking him.

The hardest place to un-stick Easy was, and still is, near any body of water. Swimming is his favorite thing and I take him almost every day to one of the creeks or ponds in the state park near us. We also have access to a lake a bit farther away. Most of Easy's early lessons on impulse control, leave-its and recall behaviors happened at the water's edge. When Easy is near water, he gets impossibly stalky and creepy. I would bring my clicker (he would not eat near water, and I would not bother to try to get him to) and shape him to turn his head away from the water, and then let him swim. I did not call him when he was in the water, but every time he did look in my direction I marked it and said, "Go swim!" and he would keep swimming. In this way I constantly used the Premack Principle while he was in the water.

At some point I would call him out, relying on the fact that he is a mama's boy and does not want to get left behind. He would creep out of the water and nine times out of ten, I immediately sent him back with a, "Yes! Go swim!"

I eventually realized that using his release word, "O.K." got him out of the water faster than his recall cue, for the reason I mentioned previously. An "O.K." caused him to rocket out of the water, hoping for a release to go back in, which he usually got.

It took months and was a huge pain in the neck to get him sitting and looking at me around water. It is hard to understand how hard it is for these sticky dogs to get unstuck unless you've seen a really bad case of stickiness for yourself.

A student of mine recently was told not to let her BC puppy swim because she was acting the way Easy did and the instructor was concerned it would somehow affect her future agility performance negatively. Ironically, teaching Easy to access his click-and-treat brain around water was probably the best training move I made with him. If he can listen to me when he's near water, he can listen to me anywhere, no matter what's going on. It was also the hardest thing I've had to teach him, and took the longest. But with some puppies, it is absolutely necessary. If not, you will end up with one of those dogs that gets stuck in a stalk position on the table, or takes five minutes creeping down to his contact zone.

Aside from the resource guarding, reactivity to some people and some dogs that were not following the rulebook, and the stickiness, Easy was a dream to raise and train. But those things that needed extra attention were tricky things that normal people tend to have a really hard time with. They were also things that the other people with his littermates were not focused on, so while they spent more time on agility foundations, I was playing the Look at That game. It's hard, especially when your friends have your pup's littermates and they are all being raised together, not to compare or push the puppy to keep up with or get ahead of the other puppies. Yet each puppy has his own time for things and his own needs.

There were several times when the littermates were adolescents that I took breaks from agility training and just hiked instead because I felt I was going too fast and needed to remind myself that he didn't need to know everything at once and, if a littermate learned something, it didn't mean he immediately needed to learn it to keep up. I got a great opportunity to work with my compulsiveness and competitiveness here, and I took it. Easy ended up advancing very quickly in agility and we found ourselves in Excellent after seven days of trialing, with placements for each Q, at the age of two, and I wouldn't have wanted to trial him earlier than that anyway. So it ended up not mattering at all that we took our time, and I'm glad we did.

Chapter 38

WRAPPING UP

TESTING SYSTEM

I thought of this after I wrote CU and introduced it in my seminars. It is my way of giving handlers extra help in knowing when they should raise or lower criteria when working with a puppy near a distraction that you are not sure they can handle yet. It shows when to push a little and when to step back.

The testing system is a series of five progressive questions for the handler to ask the dog. If the answer to all the questions is yes, then you can make things harder. If the answer to *any* of the questions is no, then you need to make an adjustment—for example, maybe there is something in the environment that could change (puppy can't play "look at that dog rushing directly toward you" but he can play "look at that dog running parallel to you"). Here are the questions:

1. Can you lie on your mat and orient to me while the "thing" is known to be "out there?" If your puppy can't even do that, there is no point asking

for anything harder until you've adjusted something. With all of these questions, if the answer is "yes," you can move to the next question. If it is "no," you need to change something. *Do not ask your puppy to do a complex behavior near the thing if he can't even stay on his mat and look at you near the thing.* People do this all the time and it is such a waste of everyone's energy, and a great way to set up your puppy to be "wrong." That is why we have this testing system, so that you can gauge better when to ask your puppy to work in the presence of something distracting, exciting, or worrisome.

2. Can you play "look at that thing" from your mat? (Great time to do some biofeedback here too!)

3. Can you sit in front of me and make eye contact while the thing is some distance behind my back? The puppy will say "yes" by sitting in front and making eye contact. He will say "no" by straining to look through or around your legs at the thing, or not being able to sit at all, or another variation.

4. Can you play "look at that thing" from heel position? If the answer is yes, he is ready to work in that environment, at a station.

5. Can you walk past the thing without caring that it's there? You can start walking with your puppy. If he can walk with you past the thing, either staying oriented to you or quickly glancing at the thing and back to you, then he is telling you he is ready to work while moving in that environment.

You can mix it up by having the thing move around too—at some point the testing system is simply a high-stakes Parallel game.

And, Finally!

In this book I have recorded the building blocks for nonreactive mindful attention, for internal control, and for focus that I teach my puppies. With the right foundation supporting you and your puppy as a team, you have a lifetime of smiles to look forward to.

I hope you feel encouraged and inspired, and I wish you all the best in your journey with your puppy. Train happy, run happy, and the rest will fall into place.

RECOMMENDED RESOURCES

BEHAVIORAL PROTOCOLS

Control Unleashed®: Creating a Focused and Confident Dog by Leslie McDevitt, MLA, CDBC, CPDT (2007) Clean Run Productions, LLC

Control Unleashed®: Foundation Seminar DVD by Leslie McDevitt, MLA, CDBC, CPDT (2009) Clean Run Productions, LLC

Control Unleashed®: Game Demonstrations DVD by Leslie McDevitt, MLA, CDBC, CPDT (2010) Clean Run Productions, LLC

Manual of Clinical Behavioral Medicine for Dogs and Cats by Karen Overall, Ph.D. (2007) Elsevier

Humane Behavioral Care for Dogs: Problem Prevention and Treatment DVD by Karen Overall, Ph.D. (2007) Elsevier (sold separately or with the manual above)

READING CANINE BODY LANGUAGE

On Talking Terms with Dogs: Calming Signals, 2nd Ed., by Turid Rugaas (2006) Dogwise Publishing

The Language of Dogs DVD by Sarah Kalnajs (2006) Blue Dog Training and Behavior

For the Love of a Dog—Understanding Emotion in You and Your Best Friend by Dr. Patricia B. McConnell (2006) Ballantine Books

The Bite-O-Meter and Yowser! A Guide to Defensive Handling Techniques DVDs by Sue Sternberg, Great Dog Productions

AGILITY FOUNDATION TRAINING

Agility Right from the Start: The Ultimate Training Guide to America's Fastest-growing Dog Sport by Eva Bertilsson and Emelie Johnson Vegh (2010) Sunshine Books, Inc.

Foundation Jumping DVD by Susan Salo (2008) Clean Run Productions, LLC

One Jump, Two Jump DVD by Sandy Rogers (2009) Clean Run Productions, LLC

Foundation Fundamentals DVD by Mary Ellen Barry (2010) Clean Run Productions, LLC

Foundation Agility Training DVD by Moe Strenfel, (2008) Clean Run Productions, LLC

Developing Handling Skills for Awesome Agility Teams by Linda Mecklenburg (2011) Clean Run Productions, LLC

Clean Run magazine, www.cleanrun.com

PLAYING WITH YOUR DOG

Tug More, Learn More (book & DVD) by Kay Laurence (2010) Learning About Dogs Limited

Play With Your Dog by Pat Miller, CPDT, CDBC (2008) Dogwise Publishing

Play Together, Stay Together: Happy and Healthy Play Between People and Dogs by Karen B. London, Ph.D. and Patricia B. McConnell, Ph.D., (2008) McConnell Publishing Ltd.

BODYWORK

Getting in Ttouch with Your Dog: A Gentle Approach To Influencing Behavior, Health, and Performance by Linda Tellington-Jones (2001) Trafalgar Square Publishing

Canine Massage in Plain English: Taking the Mystery out of Massaging Your Dog by Natalie Winter, CMT, JP, (2009) Clean Run Productions, LLC

CLICKER TRAINING

Know Way, Know How: The Science and Art of Clicker Training DVD by Kathy Sdao (2006) Tawzer Dog Videos

The How of Bow Wow: Building, Proofing, and Polishing Behaviors DVD by Virginia Broitman and Sherri Lippman (2003) Take a Bow…Wow!

Please check out the articles and other resources on Karen Pryor's website, www.clickertraining.com.

TRAINING AND LEARNING THEORY

The Power of Positive Dog Training by Pat Miller (2001) Howell Book House

The Culture Clash by Jean Donaldson (2005) James and Kenneth Publishers

Excel-erated Learning by Pamela J. Reid, Ph.D. (1996) James and Kenneth Publishers

Cujo Meets Pavlov: Classical Conditioning for Onleash Aggression DVD by Kathy Sdao (2004) Tawzer Dog Videos

ABOUT THE AUTHOR

Leslie McDevitt, MLA, CDBC, CPDT-KA is a dog behavior consultant and the author of the internationally acclaimed book, Control Unleashed®: Creating a Focused and Confident Dog, which has been published in several languages. Leslie's work with anxious and reactive dogs, coupled with her experience in dog sports training, gives her a unique perspective on stress prevention and management for working dogs. Leslie is known as a compassionate and intuitive teacher of both humans and dogs. She lives outside Philadelphia with four dogs, two cats, one horse, and one very understanding husband.

© LYNNE BRUBAKER PHOTOGRAPHY, INC.

EVERYTHING FOR
THE PERFORMANCE PUPPY

www.cleanrun.com